THE VENTURE CAFÉ

THE VENTURE CAFÉ

Secrets, Strategies, and Stories
from America's
High-Tech Entrepreneurs

TERESA ESSER

WARNER BOOKS

An AOL Time Warner Company

Warner Books, Inc., 1271 Avenue of the Americas, New York, NY 10020

Visit our Web site at www.twbookmark.com.

W An AOL Time Warner Company

Printed in the United States of America

First Printing: March 2002
10 9 8 7 6 5 4 3 2 1

Library of Congress Cataloging-in-Publication Data

Esser, Teresa.
    The venture café : secrets, strategies, and stories from America's high-tech
entrepreneurs / Teresa Esser.
        p. cm.
    Includes bibliographical references and index.
    ISBN 0-446-52783-1
    1. High technology industries—United States—Management—Case studies. 2.
Entrepreneurship—United States—Case studies. I. Title.

HD62.37. E77 2001
620'.0068—dc21   2001046533

Book design by H. Roberts Design

For my family:
Gloria, Ambrose, Diane, Mike, and Fred Esser

Author's Note

This publication is designed to provide general information regarding the subject matter covered. Laws and practices often vary from state to state and at the federal level and are subject to change, and because each factual situation is different, specific advice should be tailored to the particular circumstances. The reader is advised to consult with legal and financial advisers regarding specific situations. The author and publisher specifically disclaim any liability that is incurred from the use or application of the contents of this book.

Contents

Introduction

This is a story about a kid from North Dakota who went to MIT on financial aid and dropped out, four years into a five-year master's program, to turn a class project into a new high-tech company. The kid was not a straight-A student. In fact, he got a B on the class project. But he was excited about the device he had built and had the sense that he might be able to do something with it, maybe, if he talked to the right people.

As it turned out, the kid was right. Three years after Pehr Anderson dropped out of MIT to start NBX Corporation the little Ethernet telephone prototype had grown into a ninety-person business that was eventually acquired by 3Com Corporation for approximately $90 million.

I wrote this book because I am intimately acquainted with the story of NBX Corporation and because I believe that people can benefit from reading about some of the things that Pehr, his cofounders, and entrepreneurs like them go through when struggling to build their companies. I was engaged to Pehr Anderson during the time that he, Chris Gadda, and Alex Laats were starting NBX, and I am married to him now. My position as Pehr's fiancée gave me a unique vantage point from which to view the entrepreneurial process.

At the time that Pehr decided to drop out of school and start NBX Corporation, my student loans were beginning to come due, and our joint finances were rather strained. When I first heard that Pehr wanted to drop out of school and start a company, I became extremely frustrated, since I was doing my best just to make rent payments on our extremely modest apartment. I didn't believe in playing the lottery, and I certainly didn't believe that the strange little device that Pehr and Chris had wired together was ever going to turn into a multimillion-dollar success story.

When Pehr tried to tell me about the amazing future of NBX Corporation, I would go into the other room, spread the month's bills out on my desk, and try to figure out whether we would be able to pay them. Pehr would follow me to my desk and try to distract me from this reality by telling stories about the other Ethernet telephone company—which was not as good as his, of course—that had already been sold for $150 million!

That sort of talk made me uncomfortable, because it seemed to me that Pehr had moved way beyond simple pie-in-the sky dreaming and into the land of pure insanity. When he started talking like this, I would shut my eyes and plug my ears and wait for him to go away.

Fortunately, when Pehr got into one of these moods, there was a place where he could go.

About once a month Pehr would get an E-mail from a man named Joost Bonsen, asking him to come to a bar on the MIT campus known as the Muddy Charles Pub for some beer, pizza, and informal conversation. Bonsen's networking events were good for Pehr because they gave him a chance to wave his arms and float his ideas in a relatively safe environment. The other people that Bonsen invited to this event were entrepreneurs, too, and they knew that the boastful talk was an important part of the entrepreneurial process. And some of them—a fair number of them, actually—suspected that Pehr's company might wind up being as successful as it eventually proved to be.

The Muddy Charles Pub isn't a pretentious place. Its charter doesn't allow advertising of any kind (or even hanging a sign out front to let people know where it is), and the people who come to the pub like it that way. They like sitting in the heavy oak chairs, buying forty-cent bags of

Cheez Doodles, and entertaining one another by sticking plastic finger puppets (shaped like Kenny from the *South Park* television show) into the jaw of a Victor mousetrap.

During the day, people come to the pub to eat dollar slices of pizza, drink eight-five-cent cups of Budweiser, and watch the sailboats float past on the Charles River. Evenings aren't much different: People go there to play cribbage, do group-oriented homework assignments, or tell gossip about the people who work there. The pub's manager, Joe Contrada, tells me that the woman checking IDs in the entryway had to get a replacement last week so she could take one of her experiments up in the zero-gravity airplane. And it looks like they're going to have to get another bartender soon, because the woman who brought me my ginger ale has just gotten her Ph.D. in aerospace engineering, and she is about to join the faculty.

On most evenings, the pub is the kind of place where janitors and engineering professors can sit elbow to elbow and shoot the breeze. But one evening each month, when Bonsen sends out his invitations, the pub is transformed into a place where folks who are trying to decide whether to quit their jobs and start new high-tech companies can ask entrepreneurs what it's like on the front lines.

Bonsen holds his networking events at the Muddy Charles Pub because the beers are cheap, the atmosphere is conducive to enthusiastic conversations, and the bar has been a second home for entrepreneurs ever since it began in the late 1970s. "This is not a new thing for us," Joe Contrada tells me. "It's always been a great place for people to hang out and talk about baseball, their love lives, or how they are going to make their next million. And it's all very parallel. You always do your best stuff when you're comfortable and not under pressure to do something that has a very tiny vested interest. You have a little bit more brainstorming, a little bit more 'What if?' kind of stuff."

Because Bonsen's goal is to make entrepreneurs feel comfortable about what they are doing, he goes out of his way to ensure that the people he invites are truly interested in sharing their stories. All too often, Bonsen tells me, a person who does not understand the rules of entrepreneurial etiquette will try to profit from the experience of others without saying what they themselves are hoping to accomplish.

"Somebody says, 'I have this great idea,'" Bonsen says. "Well, what is it? 'I can't tell you.' Well, all right. Hmm. When faced with this, I usually try to be charitable and say, 'Well, okay. No problem, no problem. What's the general area that you are trying to address?' And then they look at me kind of blank. 'Well, what do you mean?' For example, is it industrial or agricultural? And they say, 'Well, I can't tell you; that would give it away.'

"You know, please.

"Sometimes I'm harsh, and I'll tell them, 'Don't waste my time.' Other times, I'm much kinder and I say, 'Listen, I'd be happy to think about this further. Send me a one-page summary of what you're up to.' And the fact is, that's a useful thing for anybody to do. But it's especially good advice for somebody who I think has been smoking a little too much of the Jamaican stuff or has a natural supply, intracranial. Under these conditions I say, 'Well, put it on one page—not very much, just the essentials—and send me an E-mail.' Ninety-nine percent of the time they don't send me anything."

Another criteria Bonsen uses to decide whether or not to add a new person to his mailing list is whether or not the idea seems as if it would be theoretically possible, given the current state of science. "I see people who say, 'I've got this great new idea: I'm going to build antigravity boots,'" Bonsen says. "And I think, 'Well, okay, are you bringing anything to the table here?' And they say, 'No, I'm an artist, but I have this vision.' And I say, 'Come on, what the hell are you bringing to the table? Vision? That's not vision; that's delusion!'

"Maybe eventually, in the future, after plenty of research and a few scientific breakthroughs, somebody will figure out how to do this. But I am highly dubious that some artist with a vision or some business weenie with a business plan will have cracked the nut of antigravity and be ready, for a mere two million dollars first round, to solve this problem and ship antigravity boots. Bullshit! It's just not going to happen."

When Bonsen asks the alleged antigravity-boot manufacturers to send him a one-page summary describing their plans, "They write up one paragraph that says, 'I propose to bring the world this earthshaking technology that will literally lift humanity. I'm a visionary. I can see humanity elevated already.'

"Aah, yes," Bonsen says. "You are indeed a visionary. Yes. You have visions."

Bonsen's elaborate screening processes are important because they allow him to introduce new entrepreneurs to the specific technologists, venture capitalists, and corporate lawyers with whom they're likely to share common interests. But even more importantly, they allow Bonsen to keep tabs on the progress of various individuals and to encourage technologists to make their own connections.

Bonsen knows that, in general, the scientists and engineers who hang out at the Muddy Charles Pub aren't all that great at networking. In fact, many of the folks on his mailing list need to be coaxed out of the lab and eased down to the pub in the first place. But Bonsen also knows that if he gives the technologists a short list of people that they absolutely must meet and provides them with specific reasons why they should overcome their shyness and attempt to strike up conversations, some rather important connections will eventually be forged. Therefore, to ensure that his events will be much more productive than a regular cocktail party, where the barriers between people who are not introduced to one another yield a situation "where all you do is talk about bullshit," the self-described "venture catalyst" positions himself in the pub's narrow doorway and provides instructions to every person who comes by.

"What I'm trying to do at my events," Bonsen says, "is orchestrate serendipity—boost the odds that some great connections actually occur so that the people leave better off than they were before. If I can help people concentrate on things that are more important and have greater odds of success, I can maximize human progress—at least in my own small way."

To help speed up the pace of human interaction, Bonsen might say, "Listen. So-and-so is in that circle, and so-and-so will introduce you to everybody else in that circle. If I were you, I would go up to him and say, 'Joost suggested that I talk to you about what I'm doing.'"

When Pehr Anderson was wandering around the MIT campus, trying to figure out what to do with his idea for a new kind of telephone, three separate people told him to look up Alex Laats inside MIT's Technology Licensing Office (TLO). Like many of the would-be entrepreneurs who hang out at the Muddy, Pehr was too shy to go up to Laats and introduce himself after only one or two suggestions. But the *third* time somebody told him to talk to Laats, he took the advice. It's a good thing that he did: Laats had already developed a significant trust relationship with a venture capitalist named Charles Harris, who has a habit of providing seed financing to new high-risk companies. And Harris had already developed a relationship with an executive headhunter named Chuck Ramsey, who has made a career out of pairing bright young technologists with top-notch CEOs.

By overcoming his shyness and forcing himself to share his Ethernet telephone idea, Anderson was able to create the trust relationships that were necessary for the formation of a successful company.

When Pehr started talking with people about his Ethernet telephone idea, he had a few things going for him. He was a highly skilled engineer, and he knew that he had stumbled upon a great idea. But he was also lucky: He made the right connections, and he developed trust relationships with the right people. Unfortunately, many other technologists are not as lucky as Pehr was.

Part of the reason why Bonsen makes such a big deal about keeping the paranoid schizophrenics and the antigravity-boot visionaries off his mailing list is because he understands what can happen when you trust the wrong people.

This is what happens: Your company breaks down from the inside, everybody's feelings get hurt, and people who used to be very excited about forging ahead in new areas of technology get jobs in the basements of big, impersonal labs and never, ever, talk about what happened.

"It's difficult for technical people to know whom to trust," a research scientist told me under the cover of anonymity during lunch at a seafood restaurant. After the scientist made this statement, he stood up, looked around the restaurant, and then went on with his story. "If you don't have the experience to know what is good or not, it's very easy to get screwed."

The research scientist wanted me to know, and to put in my book, that it is very hard for a highly trained technologist with no business experience to figure out whether a person who says he has certain business connections actually has them and whether a given business deal is actually fair. "This stuff isn't obvious," the scientist emphasized. "A lot of this stuff isn't written down, and the process is still a bit mystifying to me. I know you have to talk to people, but people aren't always forthcoming with information."

Part of the reason why I decided to put this book together was to provide scientists and engineers with the kind of business information that isn't always forthcoming in casual conversations. But another reason I wrote it was to illustrate how these barriers can be overcome through examples from NBX and other companies.

My goal was to find out what works, and what doesn't work, from the people who know: venture capitalists, entrepreneurs, chief executive officers, technologists, and spouses of the above. I was interested in studying the relationships that provide the foundation upon which new companies are built. I was interested in learning why some relationships worked well and why others fell apart. Finally, I was interested in finding out how people decided whom to trust and how they came to the realization that their trust had been misplaced.

To answer these questions, I interviewed more than 150 entrepreneurs, venture capitalists, corporate lawyers, and high-tech employees over a period of two and a half years.

I tried to get a diverse group of men and women from various ethnic and socioeconomic backgrounds. I interviewed people in small cafés and fancy restaurants, in corner offices within tall Boston skyscrapers and in dimly lit start-up warehouses.

I interviewed a software guru in Bellevue, Washington; a medical-records entrepreneur just outside New York City; and a research scientist in Palo Alto, California. But I mainly concentrated on people in the Boston area.

I interviewed a nineteen-year-old college student who had been in the country for less than two years and an eighty-two-year-old banker who could trace his ancestors back to the *Mayflower*. In the process of conducting these interviews, I learned all sorts of different things. The nineteen-year-old told me that when he is making the transition from student to entrepreneur, he puts on a special cap. The eighty-two-year-old told me that if a person has served as the captain of a nuclear submarine, it means he is level-headed.

Some of the stories made me laugh out loud; others defied all attempts at categorization. But all the stories took me inside people's minds and taught me things that I would never have been able to figure out on my own.

To supplement the information I was getting in my informal chats at the Muddy Charles Pub and my formal interviews in cafés, offices, and living rooms, I started going to early-morning networking breakfasts, late-night networking dinners, Saturday seminars, and everything else I could think of. I signed up for events at the MIT Enterprise Forum, I helped co-ordinate events at the MIT Founder Forum, and presented some of my research at Richard Shyduroff's Entrepreneur's Club.

As my research progressed, I got a job inside the Sloan School of Management, creating a written record of Ken Morse's "E-Lab" Entre-preneurship Class. And so I spent a semester writing down every single word that was uttered by professors, guest speakers, and students as each attempted to convey what he knew about high-tech entrepreneurship.

I went to these seminars not only to find out what the speakers had to say but also what the people in the audience were trying to learn.

The thing I discovered after sitting through countless hours of question-and-answer sessions was that entrepreneurs and would-be entrepreneurs really just wanted to hear other entrepreneurs tell their stories. No press-release mumbo jumbo, no holier-than-thou crap. Just the facts.

People wanted to hear someone say that when you get out of a situation that you truly detest it *really does* feel as if the weight of the world has been lifted off your shoulders and you *really do* start to walk taller. They wanted to hear, in as much detail as possible, what it felt like to go through a bankruptcy and how exactly a person could bounce back—fis-cally as well as emotionally. Finally, they wanted to know what specific things entrepreneurs would do differently if they had the chance to do it over again.

Some of the people I interviewed for this book were much better off for having quit their jobs and tried their hands at high-tech entrepre-neurship, while others were worse off for having had the experience. But all of them were glad that they had the opportunity to take matters into their own hands.

One woman told me that six weeks after she resigned from her job, "my colitis went away, and I've never had it back. It was just the stress of the job and all of that.

"Don't tell me that I've never had stress, now, running my own firm. But there is something about being in control of your own destiny and being able to make choices. I've had ups and downs in my business, but I just knew that I was the one who was to be depended on."

I'm not going to tell you that quitting your job and trying your hand at entrepreneurship is a surefire cure for colitis, and I'm certainly not going to tell you that following the advice laid out in this book will help you to become a multimillionaire. But I will say that if you've made up your mind to start your own company, there are some things you can do to avoid making mistakes that have already been made.

Some of the stories contained in this book will frighten you, others will teach you valuable lessons, and still others will make you laugh. But all of them will help you draw your own conclusions about what is "normal" within the crazy, mixed-up world of high-tech entrepreneurship.

Chapter One

THE ENTREPRENEURIAL MIND

A year ago my husband and I took a train ride through Germany's Rhine River valley. As I looked out the window at the gorgeous scenery, I noticed a curious event going on in the seat across from me. A four-year-old girl had dropped her ticket between the slats of the train's heating unit, and this carelessness had caused her mother to become extremely frustrated. The four-year-old was not at all sorry about dropping her ticket, but the mother was fighting back tears. She pressed her hand against her forehead and tried to avoid looking at her daughter.

A cyclist in a nearby seat noticed the woman's duress and removed a tool kit from his backpack. After a short conference with the woman, he began to disassemble the heating unit. While the cyclist labored over the air grate, the four-year-old pouted. "It's not my fault," she seemed to say. "I didn't do anything wrong." She made her hands into fists and kicked the side of the train.

Although the cyclist tried every screwdriver in his tool kit, he wasn't able to extract the fallen ticket. After fifteen minutes of tinkering, he reassembled the heating unit and went back to his seat.

The situation was eventually resolved when the ticket taker came around to collect our fares. He took one look at the angry four-year-old and let the family ride.

As I watched the scene play itself out, I began to feel sorry for the girl's mother. It must have been devastating to watch one's four-year-old drop an expensive ticket down an air vent. To have the child stage a tantrum about it must have been simply unbearable. Next time, I thought, the woman would have to do a better job of teaching her four-year-old to hold on to her ticket. Or perhaps she would learn that it's a bad idea to put train tickets into the hands of four-year-olds.

After the group had left the train, I asked my husband, Pehr Anderson, whether he had noticed the ticket incident.

"Of course," he snapped. "I could hardly ignore it."

I told him that I felt bad for the woman, since the lost ticket must have represented a significant financial hardship. I was glad that the ticket taker had allowed the family to ride, anyway.

"Eurail shouldn't be issuing paper-based tickets," Pehr retorted. "The airlines have switched to electronic ticketing. I don't know why the trains are still using paper."

I was surprised by Pehr's reaction, since it reminded me so much of the expression I had seen on the four-year-old's face. Pehr shared the four-year-old's view that the lost ticket was not the girl's fault. The system was broken, and it needed to be changed. The little girl had done the world a favor by pointing this out.

"Do you have any idea how impossible it would be to convince every train station in Europe to switch over to an electronic ticketing system?" I asked Pehr. "You'd have to negotiate with representatives from all sorts of different countries, and none of them would speak English as a first language."

"Paper-based tickets are obsolete," Pehr grumbled. "There's no reason to make people carry around paper tickets."

I thought about how difficult it would be to convince Eurail to change its ticketing system and how easy it would be to simply purchase another ticket. In my mind, there was no question about the better option. If riding Eurail meant keeping track of a paper ticket, then I would figure out a way to keep track of a paper ticket.

But then, I'm not an entrepreneur.

Instead of trying to change the world to meet my needs, I'm perfectly willing to alter my behavior to meet the world on its terms. When I encounter unpleasant situations, I try to resolve them quickly and then go on to other matters.

When the ticket problem was resolved, I opened my travel book and read about different places we could go for dinner. "There's a really famous cathedral in Cologne," I told Pehr. "Maybe we should look at it."

But Pehr was not interested in thinking about an ancient cathedral. Instead of being happy that the ticket situation had resolved itself, Pehr spent the remainder of the train ride scribbling notes onto his Palm Pilot. The ticket incident had provided him with an amazing entrepreneurial opportunity, and he was determined to figure out how much it was worth.

Pehr had no interest in worrying about something as boring as eating, since that was not the sort of problem that could be permanently solved. "We eat, and we get hungry again," he said. "If we fix the ticket problem, no one else will ever have to worry about losing a paper ticket."

Instead of helping evaluate the different restaurants in my guidebook, Pehr suggested that we grab a bag of doughnuts and jump back on the train. The little girl did not have the resources she needed to bring electronic tickets to Eurail, but Pehr might.

Or he might not.

I wasn't kidding when I told Pehr that it would be just about impossible to convince Eurail to adopt an electronic ticketing system. Pehr isn't European, and he doesn't even live in Europe. It would be better to leave the ticket opportunity for someone else.

But that didn't matter to Pehr. Pehr didn't care whether or not he would actually be able to transform the way Eurail handled its ticketing. What he cared about was that he had found a problem that needed to be fixed. It didn't matter whether Pehr would solve the problem or move on to something closer to his area of expertise. What mattered was that the problem existed.

When I told Pehr that I couldn't understand why he was spending so much time worrying about something that had nothing to do with him, he scowled. "You're no fun," he complained. If he had been back in Cambridge, hanging out at the Muddy Charles Pub, he would have received lots of praise and encouragement for his amazing ability to notice that Eurail was broken. But Pehr wasn't at the Muddy Charles Pub. He was stuck in a foreign city with a person who was not an entrepreneur, and his idea was not being encouraged. Frustrated, he scribbled the last fragments of his idea onto his Palm Pilot.

As Pehr wrote, I found a place for us to have dinner.

Throwing Teddy Out of the Pram

Entrepreneurs are like that. Instead of worrying about visiting historical landmarks and figuring out what to have for dinner, entrepreneurs try to figure out how they can change the world. A normal person would be satisfied with sampling the local cuisine and posing for a photograph in front of the ancient cathedral, but the people who start new high-tech businesses are different from normal people. It's not enough for them to touch a building or sample a recipe that has stood the test of time. Entrepreneurs aren't satisfied until they have made a lasting impact on their surroundings.

Unfortunately, this overwhelming desire to change the world can be extremely frustrating when it manifests itself on a daily basis.

A year after Pehr and I returned from Europe, I went out for a cappuccino with a man named David Gill. Gill is the head of the innovation and growth unit at London's HSBC bank, and he's seen hundreds of entrepreneurs struggle through the early phases of starting a new high-tech company. "The ideal entrepreneur is not the kind of person that you'd want as a personal friend," Gill tells me. "The phrase we use in England is 'throwing Teddy out of the pram.' If they don't get their way, they get very upset. Without realizing it, they tend to be manipulative.

"Entrepreneurs have to be completely driven by vision, such that they only see what they want to see. Sometimes businesses go off the rails because they have a CEO who can't see some of the warning signs, but that's why there needs to be a team of at least two. You need the 'Genghis Khan' CEO and the 'safe pair of hands' CFO.

"The CFO is the guy who looks after the numbers and tends to the casualties. He's the person who smooths things over after the great general chair comes through. And often you couldn't reverse the roles. The guy who is a superlative number two is probably never going to be a Genghis Khan."

I try to picture following Genghis Khan around on the fields of battle and counting the number of people he'd killed. I imagine it would be rather exhausting. Following Genghis Khan around would mean putting up with extremely unpleasant living conditions and pulling all sorts of wacky stunts. It would probably be something like traveling with Pehr around Europe and trying to convince him to trade doughnuts for a decent dinner.

Far from the Maddening Crowd

Making the decision to quit one's day job and become a Genghis Khan of entrepreneurship can make a person extremely lonely. "It's like suddenly going off to college when all of your friends stay in high school," entrepreneur Carol Gebert tells me. "Suddenly it seems that there are only about three people in the entire world you can talk to. You can't share the entrepreneurial experience with people around you because they don't understand."

Gebert and I were sitting in her kitchen in Cambridge, talking about her experience starting an "e-business infrastructure provider for the pharmaceutical industry" called Central Dogma. As Gebert described her plans for bringing the benefits of large-company vertical integration to the myriad of emerging biotech start-ups, I noticed a gleam in her eye that seemed vaguely familiar. The gleam spoke of stubbornness and intelligence, of mischief and curiosity. It was the same gleam I had seen in the eyes of Pehr and the unruly four-year-old.

"Do you really want to know what it's like to start a new high-tech company?" Gebert's eyes seemed to ask. I leaned forward to hear what she had to say. As I listened, I began to feel as though I were being challenged to a game of chicken.

"Before you can become an entrepreneur," Gebert instructs, "you've got to look deep inside yourself and overcome certain existential issues. Your ability to withstand adversity is directly related to your ability to understand those existential issues.

"It takes a lot of ego to start a new high-tech company. It takes so much self-confidence that sometimes you even start to wonder whether it's delusion. The very first thing you have to decide is whether or not you believe in yourself. Are you following a vision, or are you being deluded? Can you decide, deep down, that you're going to go for it? Or are you just dabbling? Because if you're dabbling, what's the point? It's just a hobby for you. You're not on the road to becoming an entrepreneur."

Gebert first started down the road toward becoming an entrepreneur when she was a postdoctoral researcher in Boston University's molecular biology department. Her first experience with the entrepreneurial process involved getting together with a friend, talking about starting a company, and filling notepad after notepad with amazing ideas. But after six weeks of "dabbling," Gebert realized that she wanted to progress to the next level. And that meant quitting her day job and working on the company full-time. As long as Gebert and her partner were fully employed as biotechnology researchers, their business idea was going to remain a hobby. And that wasn't good enough for Gebert.

Gebert was serious about starting a company, and she hoped her friend would demonstrate an equal level of commitment. But Gebert's friend wasn't willing to give up his safe job at the lab and take a risk on a high-tech start-up. He was proud of the work he had done to earn his position and saw no reason to walk away from what he had. More importantly, he didn't enjoy the entrepreneurial process as much as Gebert did.

"Every time there was a little bit of adversity, my friend would get downhearted," Gebert remembers. "He would say, 'This is not clear. It's only going to work if it's really simple and clear.'" Gebert's friend didn't understand that starting a company involves discovering new and better ways to get around some extremely difficult problems. "Every time you come up against adversity, you've got to find some way around it," Gebert says. "If it's easy, then it's likely that someone else has already come up with that idea."

Gebert tried to convince her friend that the little difficulties and frustrations were all part of the fun of starting a new enterprise, but her friend didn't share Gebert's passion for risk taking. Besides, Gebert's friend wasn't interested in changing the world. If he had been on the train with

Pehr and me, he would have been more than happy to check out the cathedral and help me look for a decent place to eat dinner.

When Gebert realized that her coworker wasn't going to join her, she had to reevaluate her own level of commitment. It had taken years of hard work to earn the position of postdoc at Boston University. Founding a new high-tech start-up would take even more hard work, and there was no guarantee that the enterprise would be successful. Was Gebert actually willing to walk away from everything she had worked for to start from scratch for the second time?

As Gebert pondered these issues, she tried to consider her predicament in a much larger historical context. There might be only three people that Gebert could talk to about her experience, but history books are filled with people who took gigantic risks and came out on top.

"When William the Conqueror crossed from Normandy into England, the first thing he did was burn all the ships," Gebert says. "His troops had to either fight to the death or win. I think the same thing happens in business. If you're really going to go all the way, then you must close your exits. You must create a situation where you can't go back."

Given the ease with which high-tech professionals can acquire new jobs, I have a hard time imagining how Gebert could reproduce the commitment level of burning one's ships. But for some people, the potential embarrassment of having to admit defeat is a powerful motivator. "When you resign from your job and tell everyone around you that you're going to do this, you start to really commit yourself," Gebert explains. "I hate admitting I'm wrong, so for me it was more of a psychological decision."

Whenever Gebert starts to feel downhearted about her business, she imagines being harassed by a jealous friend. "I thought you were going to start a business," the friend taunts. "Eeh! You've given up! You've gotten a job!"

"I don't think so," Gebert retorts.

Branded for Life: Start-ups and Navel Piercings

Making the decision to commit oneself fully to a new and uncertain enterprise can catapult a person into an entirely new psychological zone. And once a person has decided to take such a leap in her professional life, she may find it necessary to make similar adaptations in other parts of her life as well.

"When you reach that point, you start to listen to those little pieces of advice that everybody has been telling you all these years," Gebert reflects. "Is your marriage really so good? Is your health really so good? You've got to look inside yourself and figure out whether there is anything else you're deluding yourself about. Some people take up jogging or lose weight or face childhood trauma issues, or whatever. I've heard of people changing their style of clothing or getting a tattoo."

Gebert's decision to go for it professionally prompted her to make her own unique statement. "I pierced my navel," she says proudly. "The reason I pierced my navel was because I had been asking myself why I would want to give up a fairly safe track that was not going to lead to ten million dollars but was going to lead to a decent lifestyle. When I examined that question, I came down to the fact that I would never forgive myself if I didn't try.

"For me, the definition of hell is to be old and to say to yourself, 'Geez, I could have been great, and I should have been great, and I would have been great except that I couldn't take the risk.' I couldn't live my life like that. I pierced my navel to remind myself, for the rest of my life, that there is no reason other than the fact that I am compelled to try. And compulsion itself is a good enough reason to do something."

What Happens When the Lights Go Out?

While Carol Gebert was deciding to start Central Dogma, Owen Johnson and John Immel were launching Internet consulting companies in different parts of Cambridge. Johnson and Immel started their companies as undergraduates at MIT and Harvard, respectively. Both enjoyed a rapid increase in the demand for their consulting services, and both were obliged to move out of their university-sponsored housing shortly after they received their diplomas. When the time came to establish new corporate headquarters, both entrepreneurs chose to move their growing businesses into apartment-based offices in the greater Boston area.

Johnson and Immel were extremely pleased that the demand for their consulting services continued to grow and grow, and both entrepreneurs worked extremely hard to manage their growing businesses. Both became so engrossed with meeting their customers' needs that they forgot about how much they were straining the electrical systems of their ancient apartments.

On separate days during the hottest parts of the summer, both Owen Johnson and John Immel blew fuses.

Johnson's fuse blew in the middle of a standard workday. "The house didn't have a breaker box; it had an old-style fuse box, so we had to hunt down fuses at a local hardware store," Johnson remembers. "We found one old and dusty box of fuses that looked like it would work, and we were lucky that it did."

Realizing that the company's ever-increasing fleet of computers had exceeded the capabilities of the old house's electrical system, Johnson and his coworkers rearranged their office layout so that the computers would draw from different electrical circuits. But this solution was only temporary: After the power outages occurred several more times, Johnson resolved the situation by installing a proper breaker box and hoping for the best.

"Luckily, power wasn't an issue that winter," Johnson recalls.

The lights went out on John Immel while he was interviewing a prospective hire. He had just turned on the air conditioner when the house went dark. Immel was a bit surprised to have the lights go out during the middle of an interview, but he tried to appear nonchalant. "I guess we'll have to go downstairs to find the fuse box," he said.

Before coming to interview with Immel's company, the candidate had never set foot in a high-tech start-up. He had spent his entire professional life inside a major corporation, well shielded from the peculiarities of start-up life. Since he had no experience with young companies, he had no way to evaluate whether it was normal for an apartment-based Internet consulting company to experience a power outage during the hottest part of the summer. All the interview candidate knew was that he was dripping with sweat, he could barely see, and John Immel had just invited him to go down to the basement to hunt for a fuse box.

The candidate was surprised, but he was also curious. So he followed Immel down the stairs.

As he approached the darkened basement, he started to feel skeptical about the job he was walking into. When Immel stumbled around the dusty basement in search of the fuse box, the candidate had a chance to evaluate some of his own existential issues. *So this is what people mean when they say that start-ups are wacky,* the candidate thought. He hadn't expected the job to involve stumbling around a darkened basement, but that's exactly what happened.

As Immel searched, the candidate tried to gauge whether he wanted to deal with the rigors of start-up life.

In the end, he decided he didn't.

I did not spend four years in college, two years in grad school, and four years inside a major corporation so I could wander around a basement in search of a fuse box, the candidate thought. He was annoyed, and he was hot, and he was frustrated. He didn't see the light at the end of the tunnel in the same way that Johnson and Immel did. There was no gleam in the candidate's eye. When he looked around the darkened basement, he saw nothing but darkness.

If he had been on the train with me and Pehr, he would have borrowed my travel guide, taken out his cell phone, and called ahead to make reservations.

At a high-tech start-up there is no such thing as making reservations. The kind of person who is comfortable with the experience of entrepreneurship lives his life from minute to minute. A person who needs the security of a well-constructed itinerary would be better off inside a well-established corporation.

When the interview candidate stared into the blackness of Immel's basement, he became much more comfortable with his present job. The big company might not give him any stock options, but at least they provided electricity.

When the lights were back on, the candidate thanked Immel for his time.

And then he left.

And that was fine with John Immel.

At a high-tech start-up, it's extremely important for every single employee to feel comfortable dealing with things like blown fuse boxes. And it's far better to discover this during one's job interview than after one has made a serious commitment to the new organization.

Making Educated Guesses

The personality traits that make a person feel comfortable taking a risk on a high-tech start-up are very similar to those that make one comfortable with other forms of gambling, including blackjack. And at MIT, the blackjack players have organized themselves into an underground community that is very similar to the community of entrepreneurs that exists at the Muddy Charles Pub.

MIT's Blackjack Team, or card-counting club, attracts new members by stapling photocopied flyers onto bulletin boards around the institute. While the club has no official affiliation with the institute, no one on the MIT campus bats an eyelash when ten or fifteen students and alumni commandeer an empty classroom and play a few games of cards. "It's definitely not superorganized," a current card counter tells me. "It's more of a fly-by-the-seat-of-your-pants kind of thing. There is no faculty involvement whatsoever."

Because of the necessity of keeping one's card-counting skills hidden from the dealers at casinos, who prefer to play with those people who are more likely to lose, members of the MIT card-counting club tend to keep a rather low profile, often drifting in and out of the club over time. "It's not really a club," my contact emphasizes. "It's more of a team—a money-making venture. I think for most of the students it's a way to have fun and get a little cash for school. You have to be either a dropout or an alumnus to make it a serious endeavor."

Serious card counters understand that if they want to get good, they must spend a considerable amount of time playing blackjack, practicing hand signals, and developing trust relationships with fellow team members. The trust relationships are extremely important in the business of card counting because the most difficult thing about playing organized blackjack is making sure that dealers never figure out what is actually going on. Once a casino has identified a person as a card counter, the person's name and likeness are immediately circulated on something called the Griffin list, which, I am told, has the power to keep people out of casinos for the rest of their lives.

Casinos have good reason to be wary of card counters, because if blackjack players reach a certain level of proficiency, they can actually tip the odds in their favor.

If a person goes out onto the casino floor without any understanding of the rules of blackjack, he is likely to lose an average of $2 or $3 each time he lays down a $100 bet. A person who uses a technique called "basic strategy" to decide whether or not to request a new card is likely to lose an average of 33 cents every time he lays down a $100 bet.

The game of blackjack becomes interesting, and even profitable, when a blackjack player realizes that the probability of being dealt a winning hand changes depending on which cards have already been dealt. If a skilled blackjack player can train himself to keep track of those cards that have already been dealt, he can use this information to determine whether or not he is likely to be dealt a winning combination in his next hand.

If a blackjack player determines that all of the tens, jacks, queens, kings, and aces in a given deck have already been dealt, he can choose to wager a very small amount of money or avoid betting entirely. If, on the other hand, a blackjack player observes that a great many ones, twos, threes, fours, fives, and sixes have already left the deck, he may choose to increase the amount of money he puts on the table to take advantage of the fact that the cards remaining are likely to be tens, jacks, queens, kings, and aces.

It takes a great deal of study and a great deal of hands-on training to get good enough at counting cards to tip the odds in one's favor. The city of Las Vegas is itself a sizzling, smoking, flashing-neon-light reminder that the vast majority of would-be card counters fail miserably. But there are some people who enjoy math for its own sake and who enjoy the applied mathematics of casino gambling in particular. These are the people who spend weeks, months, and even years studying blackjack and casino gambling in an effort to determine, in any given card game, whether or not the next hand is likely to be a winner.

Skilled card counters know that if they can avoid becoming distracted by the free drinks and scantily clad women long enough to count cards, calculate the odds of winning, and make informed decisions about how much to wager, they can tip the odds in their favor. Instead of losing $3 each time they put down $100, a skilled card counter can actually win money.

How much a card counter wins depends on the amount of money that is being put to work and the numbers of bets that the card counter is willing to make. My contact tells me that in recent years the MIT blackjack team was gambling with approximately $1.5 million, built up from an initial investment of some $200,000. At one point the club had so much cash to put to work and so few card counters that they were forced to "push the max," playing up to a maximum bet of $15,000. "You'd do maybe one hand of a grand to two hands of $10,000," my contact remembers. "We had more money than the casinos would let us play with."

As long as the casinos are convinced that the card counters are no more than ignorant hicks taking a break from betting on hog futures to play a few hands of blackjack, they will do whatever it takes to keep the card counters around. My contact tells me stories of free food, free booze, and complimentary hotel rooms offered in the vain hope that the high rollers' luck will eventually change.

A skilled card counter must work very hard to convince jaded blackjack dealers that it was nothing more scientific than their lucky rabbit's foot that caused them to win so much money and that they really are putting their life's savings at risk when they decide to play another $10,000 hand. For if a card counter should slip up and reveal that he is being *paid* to make bets with a bankroll of his own and other people's money, his card-counting career will come to an abrupt end.

This is what happened to Semyon Dukach: He became so good at counting cards and won so much money that the casinos eventually caught on to his technique. Once Dukach's likeness was circulated on the notorious Griffin list—a report compiled by Las Vegas detective agency Griffin Investigations Inc.—he had no choice but to hang up his aces and look for a new game.

Dukach could still teach new kids how to count cards, and he was welcome to invest his own money in the club's communal kitty. But now that he was "burned out," the adrenaline rushes were reserved for the younger kids.

With card counting no longer an option, Dukach put some of his winnings into a high-tech company called Fast Engines, whose mission was to reduce the amount of time it takes to reach Web sites on the Internet. And the more time Dukach spent on his high-tech start-up, the more he began to like it. "You can't just make money," Dukach tells me. "You have to feel like you're doing something good for the world. I am very proud of creating this thing called Fast Engines."

The good work that Semyon did involved bringing together a group of really great people. "I had that in blackjack as well—a sense of teamwork with the people that we went to the casinos with and the people that I trained and organized. But there was nothing that we really created together. It was kind of like a quick thrill. We went, we played, we made money. It was fun, but we weren't creating real value. Whereas here, as a group, we can be proud of the product. We can be proud of the customers using the product, making their lives easier, making their Web sites faster. I mean, we have this thing that's really fast, and that generates pride as well."

Dukach has reason to be proud of the work he did at Fast Engines: in March 2000, the company was acquired by Adero, Inc. for an amount that the company's investors could feel very good about.

It's Only Dangerous If You Don't Know What You're Doing

One bright afternoon, sometime before Fast Engines was acquired by Adero, Pehr and I ran into Semyon and his family at a Cambridge café. After Pehr and Semyon had compared notes about their various entrepreneurial ideas, Semyon asked us if we wanted to go hang gliding with him the next day. I told Semyon that I thought the sport sounded too dangerous but if Pehr wanted to go, I'd be happy to watch.

Semyon tried to allay my fears by explaining his philosophy of risk management, which went something like this: Very few people die in hang gliding *crashes*. Problems occur when people forget to strap themselves into their safety harnesses. Thus, if a person trusts himself to perform a few simple safety checks, hang gliding can be viewed as a relatively safe activity.

Semyon Dukach is the kind of person who can be relied upon to perform a few simple safety checks each and every time he decides to go hang gliding. And for this reason, the sport of hang gliding appears nearly 100 percent safe, within Semyon's frame of reference.

Semyon's speech about the extremely rational, and completely safe, sport of hang gliding was enough to convince Pehr to join him on the mountain. But when I think about hang gliding, I imagine people who are much less rational, and much less methodical, than Semyon Dukach. The hang gliders in my imagination get so excited about the prospect of soaring like birds that they rush toward the edge of a cliff without buckling their safety harnesses. And in so doing, they mess up the sport's otherwise immaculate safety record.

As skeptical as I was about hang gliding, I was also a bit curious. So when Pehr and Semyon drove up to New Hampshire, I went with them.

On the way to the cliff, Semyon explained what Pehr had to look forward to. First he would go to the hangar and learn to identify the different parts of the apparatus. Then he would haul his glider onto the grassy hill and practice pushing it back and forth. Next, he would spend a few hours learning the basics: how to start, how to gather momentum, and how to stop without crashing. Finally, he would haul his glider to the top, strap himself into his safety harnesses, and race toward the edge of the cliff.

People who are good at hang gliding can travel as many as 190 miles before returning to the earth's surface. On the first day, however, a student is unlikely to leave the ground.

Pehr had an unexpected bonus during his first day of hang gliding: As he was rolling the apparatus back and forth across the side of the cliff, he caught a sudden updraft and soared about three meters. Unfortunately, Pehr's flight occurred well before the instructor had given his lesson on how to land, and Pehr's landing was a complete disaster. He bumped, he tripped, and he fell into the grass. Pehr did not sustain any serious injuries during his unpleasant landing, but he was held up as an example to his fellow students. "Let that be a lesson," the instructor thundered. "You don't leave the ground until I give the signal."

It was hard for the students to pay attention to the instructor's advice when the sky around them was filled with so many colorful gliders. Off in the distance Pehr could see Semyon Dukach, circling and dipping like a lark in springtime. He looked as if he were having the time of his life.

As Semyon soared and Pehr learned about the fundamentals, I sat in the hangar and read a book about shipwrecks. Reading about shipwrecks made me feel secure because I already knew what was going to happen.

With Pehr and Semyon, I had no idea.

Chapter Two

MAKING THE DECISION TO GO FOR IT

B efore a hang glider can feel comfortable hurling himself off the edge of a cliff, he needs to make absolutely certain that he is securely strapped into a safety harness strong enough to support his weight. Likewise, before an entrepreneur makes the decision to walk away from his job, drop out of his degree program, or walk off the edge of any financial cliff, he must make sure he will be supported by an adequate financial safety net.

By safety net I mean a network of people who promise to support the entrepreneur in the event that he needs their assistance. A well-crafted safety net includes venture capitalists who say they are likely to invest, skilled workers who say they are likely to come on board as employees, and potential customers who say they are likely to buy the product or service.

A few months after the hang-gliding excursion, I am sitting in a café in Kendall Square, asking Vanu Bose how he made the decision to start the software radio company known as Vanu, Inc. I am trying to get Bose to agree that before a person can feel comfortable making the decision to leave his job and start a new business, he needs to make sure that his safety net is strong enough to support his weight. But Bose does not think you can say "entrepreneurship" and "safety" in the same sentence.

"During the first few years of a high-tech start-up, there's no such thing as a safety net," Bose tells me. "You don't want to create a veneer that everything is okay, because if you've hired smart people, they'll see through it. You have to acknowledge the problems, explain what you're going to do, and challenge people to have a positive outlook. But if you think about it too much, you'll never do it.

"I know a lot of people who think that they will start businesses but never do. They are kind of standing on the edge of the cliff looking down. They think there might be something really good down there, or it might just be jagged rocks and they'll get wrecked. And so they line up on the cliff with a whole bunch of their buddies, and they're all sort of going, 'Well, I'll jump if you jump.' Nobody wants to jump, because it is a highly risky thing and there is a very high probability that you will fail."

I remind Bose that although he might talk about the importance of not overanalyzing the situation and simply going ahead and taking the leap, he actually did spend a great deal of time preparing himself to become an entrepreneur. He watched his father, Amar, start the stereo-equipment company that bears the family name. And in the process of eating a normal family dinner, he learned a great deal about entrepreneurship. For example, if Bose ever asked his father about a business decision, "it was never just an answer; it was always this complete lesson on all of the things he had considered doing," Bose reflects. "My dad would explain why he made this decision, what would have happened if he had made another decision, and what were the risks. I didn't think of it as a learning experience at the time, but clearly a lot of my philosophy comes from that."

The technical training that Bose undertook before deciding to start Vanu, Inc. involved a Ph.D. dissertation in exactly the same field in which he is working to grow his company. And in the process of being a good Ph.D. candidate—sharing his research in the form of white papers—Bose developed quite a reputation. "Software radio isn't a big area," Bose says, "and we were the de facto experts. Because of the papers we had written, both Raytheon and Boeing called us up and said, 'Hey, we want to learn about software radio.'"

Within a few months of starting his company, Bose was able to sign a contract with Boeing, which gave him an opportunity to have in-depth discussions with potential customers. And Bose's reputation has given him a leg up in other areas as well. "I have never called a venture capitalist; they have all called us," he admits. "We're in a very fortunate position."

If an entrepreneur has spent his entire life learning about the process of starting a new high-tech company and if he is recognized as the de facto expert in his particular field, it might be okay to wake up one morning and make the decision to jump off the entrepreneurial cliff. But even with a prefabricated safety net of the kind that Bose apparently stumbled into, he still found it necessary to add a few links to his network of business contacts.

After deciding to start Vanu, Inc., Bose spent some time at the Muddy Charles Pub, talking to entrepreneurs who had themselves started companies from scratch. And Bose says that this "preformation of the company phase" was extremely important. "You don't have it all," Bose says. "Nobody has it all. But it really comes down to having faith in yourself."

Internet entrepreneur Rosaline Gulati agrees. "Part of your safety net is your ability to believe in yourself," she says. "You have to believe that if things fail, you'll be able to get up and do it again. Then it doesn't matter if your business fails—you'll move on."

Don't Jump Until You're Ready

Even when a hang glider knows his sport, has the cliff picked out, and has the enthusiasm to go ahead with the jump, he may choose to delay his jump until the right gust of wind comes along. Likewise, even with the perfect idea, an entrepreneur should hold on to his financial support system until certain critical factors are in place.

The founders of Akamai Technologies spent eight months putting together a business plan, bringing in their first trial customers, and building the first part of their network before quitting their jobs and filing their official incorporation papers. And this preformation stage played a crucial role in the company's eventual success. "There was a lot of work that went into building that company before it had a name and was a corporation," remembers Akamai cofounder Jonathan Seelig.

Before the company was incorporated, Seelig spent a great deal of time inside the office of MIT professor of applied mathematics Tom Leighton, hanging out with other entrepreneurial-minded folks and trying to figure out what the company was going to do. "We'd all show up with our backpacks from class, make a pot of coffee, and work through ideas about how this was going to develop as a business," Seelig remembers. "And then we'd go away, and each person would try to pull together their pieces."

The ongoing conversations in Professor Leighton's office allowed a wide variety of people to add their two cents' worth. But as the conversations turned from abstract discussions of how Akamai was going to change the world to specific explorations of how the folks in the room were going to help the company meet its objectives, the group became smaller and smaller.

Having worked in the telephony industry previously, Seelig understood that if Professor Leighton's mathematical algorithms could reduce the so-called worldwide wait by routing and replicating content over a large network of distributed servers, he was likely to make a great deal of money. And because Seelig had already developed a network of business contacts in thirty different countries, he was able to bring something to Akamai that some of the more casual brainstormers were not. "Just knowing who you're trying to get in touch with, without needing to dig up a bunch of stuff, was a tremendously relevant asset," Seelig remembers. "Also, having done business in a lot of different places around the world is a pretty big asset, because a lot of people are not used to getting on airplanes, flying twelve hours, and trying to do a deal in a very different cultural and business environment."

To further differentiate himself from the folks who simply stopped by Leighton's office to shoot the breeze and drink a cup of coffee, Seelig began to take trips for Akamai. "Not the same kind of destinations that I have now," he emphasizes, "but I was getting on planes and going to meet people."

Apparently, Seelig's knowledge of the international telephony industry, coupled with his willingness to take trips, was enough to convince the folks in Tom Leighton's office that he was serious about becoming an entrepreneur. And when the time came to officially start the company and decide who among the wide circle of casual coffee drinkers was going to be counted as an official cofounder, Seelig's name was on the roster.

"A lot of people came in and out of those discussions over time," Seelig remembers, "and in the end we wound up with a core team of people who could really believe in this and say, 'Here's the idea of how we're going to execute this and make it a big business.' That ended up being Tom and [applied mathematics graduate student] Danny [Lewin] and I, who were sort of that core nucleus that said, 'Okay, time to make this a company and really go with it.'"

Don't Burn Your Bridges Before You're Ready

When Gary Culliss was thinking about creating an Internet search engine that could harness the power of human intelligence, he was extremely cautious about weighing his various options. To ensure that he would be able to take advantage of the degree he was earning at Harvard Law School, Culliss went through the school's standard interview process, pitching his legal skills to a variety of different law firms. Simultaneously, Culliss began to hang out in places like the Muddy Charles Pub, talking to MBA candidates and establishing a variety of trust relationships.

Although Culliss found it relatively easy to convince people to talk about his idea, it was hard to get anyone to commit to joining his team during those early days. Still, he tried to remain optimistic. "I didn't blame them," Culliss says. "I just said, 'You know, these guys just aren't persuaded yet.' At the end of each meeting, I told them, 'You don't have to commit now. Let me just put your name on our E-mail list and I'll keep you apprised of how things go.'"

Culliss's own job interviews went well, and during the spring of 1998 he received an offer from a prestigious law firm. Careful to avoid burning his bridges, Culliss told the firm that he would accept the offer upon graduation.

His future job prospects assured, Culliss then went about the process of obtaining venture capital. Amazingly, Culliss didn't have long to wait: Halfway through his first official meeting with the venture-capital

(VC) firm Draper Fisher Jurvetson, Culliss recalls hearing Tim Draper yell, "Would you take a million for a third?"

Culliss was thrilled by Draper's enthusiastic desire to back his idea and flattered by the speed with which they produced an official term sheet. But he decided to hold on to his job offer until the VC's money had been deposited in his bank account. "I didn't want to burn that bridge," Culliss explains. "I didn't want the firm to think that I was doing something foolish or silly. When you raise $1.4 million, it's clear that you're doing something serious. They understood that and said they would welcome me back to the legal profession through their firm at any time."

Choose Business Partners You Can Get Along With

By now, just about everyone knows that new high-tech companies are formed when a group of people with technology expertise team up with a group of people with business expertise. But all too often entrepreneurs assume that once they have found a potential business partner with a complementary résumé, the interpersonal aspects of the business relationship will take care of themselves. For example, some businesspeople assume that if their new technological partner can demonstrate his competence in a given technological area, it is all right if he cannot communicate. And some technologists assume that as long as their business partner can prove that he has been successful with his previous businesses, it's all right if he is an arrogant jerk.

Unfortunately, many entrepreneurs learn the hard way that it is actually not okay to start businesses with uncommunicative technologists and nasty business guys, since the pressures of entrepreneurship are likely to exaggerate the flaws in every personality. "I very much stress the importance of finding people that you enjoy working with," an entrepreneur tells me. If you don't get along with your cofounders, the entrepreneur says, "it just creates a dangerous working environment. I say dangerous because you never know what's happening on the outside of your business, but you should at least be able to depend on the inside."

If you are considering starting a company with an extremely smart or extremely well connected person that you think you can probably get along with, do not start the company. Wait until you can find an extremely smart or extremely well connected person that you *know* you can get along with.

The Importance of External Validation

An experienced hang glider won't jump off a cliff without first making certain that he has the right equipment—and a good place to land. Likewise, an experienced entrepreneur will postpone making the decision to jump off the entrepreneurial cliff until he has received a certain amount of validation for his idea. But while a hang glider's support system is tangible and obvious, an entrepreneur's can be much harder to pin down.

When Geeta Sankappanavar was putting together a business plan for a medical administrative-services outsourcing company, she shared a draft with a former mentor from McKinsey Consulting who had recently left to join a venture-capital firm. "He looked at it," Sankappanavar remembers, "and he said, 'You know what, I'm sold.' I didn't expect that to happen. I expected him to give us advice and introduce us to people. But instead he said, 'Okay, I'm interested.' All of a sudden we had been validated, and that was so tremendous."

The validation that Sankappanavar received was rescinded shortly thereafter when her mentor's VC firm underwent a merger and began to invest exclusively in business-to-consumer Internet companies. As a consequence, several of Sankappanavar's would-be business partners expressed a new desire to hold on to their high-paying jobs. But Sankappanavar herself was resolute. "For some reason, I became wedded to the idea," she reflects. "I had no income, but I said, 'You know what? I'm quitting my job to do this.'"

After Sankappanavar began working on the company full-time, "it mushroomed." Although the company still lacked seed funding, Sankappanavar discovered that her decision to work on the company full-time had a significant impact on the thought processes of her more conservative peers. "We started interviewing and hiring people," Sankappanavar remembers, "and then these guys all ended up quitting their jobs way, way ahead of schedule."

But Sankappanavar soon learned that quitting her job and convincing her partners to quit theirs was only the beginning of the decision-making process. After only a few months of full-time entrepreneurship, Sankappanavar was presented with an amazing opportunity: a job offer from a well-financed start-up that included some $2 million in equity and a salary of about $90,000 per year. Two months ago she would have jumped at the chance. This time, however, she found herself turning the start-up down. "It's a very, very difficult decision to stay with," Sankap-panavar says, "because every day you are continuously making the decision to keep on doing this."

Like quitting smoking, walking away from a job at a large corporation is the kind of decision that must be made anew every single day. New entrepreneurs are constantly being bombarded with the big-company equivalent of cigarette ads: images of glamorous and successful people who seem to have become successful by aligning themselves with household names. For this reason, it is helpful to establish a new support group of people who will meet on a regular basis and reinforce the desire to kick the big-company habit. This is one of the reasons why so many entrepreneurs gather at the Muddy Charles Pub: Spending some time in the presence of other people who have also made the decision to start new high-tech companies reinforces a person's own desire to remain entrepreneurial.

Something to Think About

It is clearly a bad idea to invest in a new high-tech company when one cannot be certain that the entrepreneur's judgment can be trusted. But it appears that it is even worse to invest in a young company when one cannot be certain whether the head of that company will eventually decide to get pregnant. Therefore, to reduce the risk of not knowing whether a female entrepreneur will decide to become pregnant while she is supposed to be saving all of her energy for running the young company, some VCs will ask women, point-blank, what their reproductive plans are.

"When I was running my company," says entrepreneur-turned-investor Lori Fena, "we had a choice between continuing to self-fund and taking some outside investment. And when I was meeting with some [prospective] investors, they actually asked the question 'What is your plan as far as family?' It was clear that they weren't sure, based on my answer, how that was going to affect the investment decision, but if I was a male entrepreneur, this is not something that would have come up."

Of course, not every female entrepreneur is questioned about her reproductive plans. "We were never once asked anything inappropriate," says Internet entrepreneur Rosaline Gulati, whose company, Viveca, has just raised $14.4 million from a handful of top-tier venture firms. "I don't feel that we were treated differently because we were female. I think you have to understand how the game is played, but anyone can learn the rules." Besides, she says, "the hallmark of a good entrepreneur is that you don't let external factors stop you. If you don't have the right VCs, go find the right ones."

It's one thing to talk about not letting external factors get in the way of running a company, but it's another thing to deal with the reality of a pregnancy while struggling to start a new high-tech company. If a female entrepreneur becomes pregnant while in the process of running a young company, her pregnancy can be viewed by VCs—even by female VCs— as a reason to remove her from the company.

One female VC offered the following anecdote about an entrepreneur who decided to push her luck: "She subsequently got pregnant with her second child, and I knew that it was going to be too much for her to grow this company and have two infants in the house. By this time, she and I were not getting along particularly well because she needed more and more money and didn't want my input, but she thought I should just give her the money and go away.

"I had already invested more money than the company was worth, but she thought I was trying to steal her company. Like a lot of entrepreneurs, she just didn't understand corporate valuations. She was using a five-year-down-the-road valuation instead of today's valuation. She kept saying, 'This is going to be a big company; it's going to be worth millions of dollars.' And I kept saying, 'Yeah, but we're not there yet, and it isn't.'

"After she had the baby, I offered to go to her town for two days a week, at my own expense, to help her get this company launched, and she turned me down flat. And then we had an enormous back-and-forth with lawyers and lawyers' fees and lots of accusations flying, and I finally had to take the company over."

Once the pregnancy-prone entrepreneur was finally purged, the VC was able to take the company to new heights. "It was an absolutely good experience overall," the VC says, looking back. "The company ended up being quite a good success."

It is instructive to contrast the situation of the pregnancy-prone female entrepreneur, who needed to be purged from her own company, with the situation of NBX cofounder Alex Laats, who, together with his wife, Laura, dared to have baby number two during the most stressful days of the formation of NBX Corporation.

"When Jake was born, Erik was two," Laats remembers. "And Laura was working, too, because we needed the money. So now, all of a sudden, things went up a notch. Erik needed attention, and Jake needed Mommy, so it was imperative that I be home between six P.M. and eight P.M."

To balance the demands of his new infant with the demands of his new company, Laats reorganized his work schedule. "I got to work at six A.M. and worked until six P.M. so that I could be home at six-thirty and help get the kids to bed at eight o'clock," Laats remembers. "I would read stories, do baths, and then, after eight o'clock, do some more work."

Listening to Laats talk about his busy schedule, I get the impression that it is possible for an entrepreneur to do everything—and to do it well. And after speaking with several of the most influential behind-the-scenes players at NBX, I get the impression that if they thought about it at all, nearly everyone involved with NBX viewed the birth of Laats's second child as more of a behind-the-scenes time-management challenge than as an event that would cast doubt over Laats's ability to manage his company.

It remains to be seen whether the venture capital community will ever grant female entrepreneurs the same degree of personal autonomy that is presently granted to their male peers. Given the fact that female entrepreneurs receive less than five percent of venture capital investment dollars, it is clear that this subject requires additional investigation.

Who Will Drive You to the Mountain?

Although the sport of hang gliding often seems like a rather solitary endeavor, if you drive to the mountain in New Hampshire where Pehr and Semyon took their lessons, you will notice that the shady area just outside the hangar is crowded with the gliders' families. Just inside the metal doorway you can see little boys and girls playing with Game Boys and toy cars while their nongliding parents discuss wind conditions or simply chat.

To a casual observer, this community of rather sedentary individuals may not look as if it is doing much to support the sport of hang gliding. But if you pay attention to the social dynamics, you will notice that the child-care services being provided at the base of the mountain play a huge role in the hang gliders' ability to excel at their sport.

Likewise, Alex Laats's ability to juggle both a growing family and a growing high-tech start-up was heavily dependent on the support he received from his wife, Laura. And it is important to note that before Laats ever made the decision to quit his job and start the new high-tech company, he made absolutely certain to win his wife's approval. "That was a key moment," Laats remembers. "Laura and I had been talking about doing a start-up eventually, and I had been working with MIT start-ups on a consulting basis. So I went to Laura and I said, 'Are you willing to deal with me here? Because it is going to be nuts. I am going to need you to do everything—run the house and run everything other than work.' And she said, 'Yeah!' She never was concerned about risk, and neither was I, because it was a good space, and it seemed like if we went fast, we could make a difference. She made the deal that she was willing to put up with incredible hours."

When Chuck Ramsey was starting the executive-search firm Ramsey Beirne, his wife, Dianne, was working at a job that she abhorred. Mrs. Ramsey recalls that her office environment was so terrible that it was not uncommon for employees to take breaks from their work to speculate whether the new secretaries would last an hour, a day, or a week.

There were many occasions when Mrs. Ramsey thought about leaving her job and looking for a more pleasant work environment. But with a son in college and a husband who wanted to start his own business, she felt obliged to make the best of her situation. "You stay because the money is good," Mrs. Ramsey explains.

"I was able to do my career change because the money was good,"

Chuck Ramsey echoes. "I would come home and bitch about my day, and Dianne would say, 'You haven't heard anything.'"

Both Chuck Ramsey and his business partner, David Beirne, understood that during Ramsey Beirne's most fragile period, the continued existence of their executive-search firm was heavily dependent on Mrs. Ramsey's continued willingness to put up with a job that she detested. "David always wanted to make sure that I approved of everything," Mrs. Ramsey remembers.

Of course, David Beirne did not actually ask for Mrs. Ramsey's approval on *everything*. When, for example, the company changed its billing structure from a contingency-based model to a retained model, Beirne didn't get around to running the decision past Dianne for fear that she would not approve. "The year it was really bad, I did not know how close they were to needing my salary," Mrs. Ramsey reflects. "I knew it was rough; I just didn't know how rough."

But although there were occasions when Mrs. Ramsey doubted whether or not her husband's company would eventually become a success, there was one individual who could always be counted on to greet new developments with unbridled enthusiasm: Candace the Wonder Dog.

"You always knew I would be successful, didn't you, Candace?" Chuck says, reaching down to scratch the Wonder Dog on her wonder neck. "Didn't you know I was going to be successful. Candace? Didn't you?"

Candace the Wonder Dog rolls her eyes.

Apparently, part of the entrepreneurial process is finding encouragement wherever possible.

Entrepreneurship as a Family Affair

It is important for entrepreneurs to feel they are being supported by the key people in their lives, but this support can take a number of different forms. During the earliest days of Color Kinetics Corporation, George Mueller went out on a limb financially. "I went ten months without a salary, spent the $13K in life savings in my bank account, and accrued $44K in credit-card debt on nine or ten credit cards," Mueller recalls.

Seven months into his entrepreneurial experience, when Mueller's bank account was down to just $16, he received a letter from the Internal Revenue Service (IRS) containing a tax return of $1,300. "I distinctly remember opening my mailbox that day and immediately tearing open the IRS envelope to realize that I was no longer broke," Mueller recalls. That very day, Mueller signed the IRS check over to his landlord. "That kept me in business through the next month, a month without financing rewards," Mueller recalls.

Fortunately, Mueller's mother lived in the apartment next door to him, and as a retired entrepreneur herself, she understood her son's predicament. When she learned of Mueller's financial crisis, she volunteered to pay his rent for the next two months, until he could close on his first round of VC financing.

When Mueller decided to max out his credit cards to finance his eccentric semiconductor lighting business, he was taking a significant financial risk, since there was no guarantee that he would ever get the money back. But Mueller believed that even if his company tanked, he would be better off for having had the experience of becoming an entrepreneur. "I've hired maybe seventy-five or a hundred people already in my life, I've opened up offices in twelve countries, and I've raised more than twenty million dollars," Mueller says. "For a high-tech entrepreneur like myself, the safety net is so large that you could always turn around and get a six-digit starting salary with a $30K to $40K signing bonus. Your frame of mind is that, sure, if you risk all that money, you could always make it back in a high-paying job. And if not, you can always start another company."

Although it seems clear that George Mueller's decision to wager $44,000 on Color Kinetics was an exceptionally good investment, all too often entrepreneurs discover that there is a reason why high-tech start-ups are considered risky. Because of the high probability of failure, it is extremely important for entrepreneurs to come to terms with the possibility that they may well lose whatever it is they are putting on the line.

What Happens If Your Safety Net Cannot Support Your Weight?

A hang glider's worst nightmare involves having his safety harness break in mid-flight, feeling himself break away from the glider, and plunging headlong into oblivion. Likewise, an entrepreneur's worst-case scenario involves having the safety net of venture capital, customers, and employees break apart and watching the company tumble into oblivion.

I wish I could say that this kind of thing only happens in B movies and the imaginations of risk-averse persons such as myself. But the truth is that this kind of thing really does happen all the time.

When I was researching the question of what it was really like to start a high-tech company, one of my contacts at the MIT Entrepreneur's Club told me to call Jeff Osborn and ask him for some stories. I didn't know much about Osborn before I placed the call aside from the fact that he had been involved with a number of high-tech companies that experienced varying degrees of success, so I started the conversation by asking him whether he could recollect any particularly stressful moments.

This made Jeff Osborn laugh. "You want a stressful moment?" he asked. "I've got a stressful moment." It took him a while to stop laughing, but when he did, he told me the following story.

In 1992, Osborn was president of a high-tech start-up called Wilder Systems, which, during the term of Osborn's presidency, went from making $120,000 per year to making zero dollars per year (although the company later recovered and ultimately became a successful business). To keep Wilder solvent during this difficult period, Osborn was obliged to cut employee salaries—including his own—to just $100 per month.

At that time, Osborn's personal savings account was no gold mine, and the loss of his salary strained his family's finances. Although Osborn recalls that he and his wife did try to reduce their standard of living, they were unable to meet the demands of their various creditors. And so, as time went on, the creditors started coming around to repossess various objects.

Jeff Osborn didn't worry too much when the people came to take his car, since he lived close enough to Wilder Systems to be able to walk to work. But he was concerned about the possibility that the bank might foreclose on his house.

Still, Osborn clung to the belief that before anything truly bad happened, he would be able to fight his way out of this particular pool of financial quicksand. Not wanting to reveal the true situation to his wife, Osborn gambled that before the sheriffs came, he would be able to collect on a $40,000 invoice, pay himself and his fellow employees a substantial amount of back salary, and catch up on his mortgage payments. But Osborn soon discovered that no amount of creative bill collecting could induce the $40,000 debtor to come up with the cash, since the customer could no more afford to pay Wilder than Osborn could afford to pay the bank.

Hearing that the customer would not be able to pay him made Osborn feel his world was beginning to collapse. But although he racked his brain to come up with alternatives, there simply was no way out. Foreclosure was imminent, and the only thing left for Osborn to do was break the news to his wife.

As Osborn walked home from work on the day of the foreclosure, he rehearsed all sorts of different ways to explain what was about to happen. But as it turned out, he didn't have to say a word. "When I walked up to the house," Osborn recalls, "the sheriffs were already there, taping a foreclosure notice to the front door."

Osborn found his wife in the kitchen, staring into space.

"I'm just so sorry," Osborn said.

At this critical moment, Osborn's wife did not lose her temper. She did not scream or yell, and most importantly, she did not demand a divorce. She simply stared off into the middle distance and collected her thoughts.

Finally, after what seemed like an eternity, she turned to face her husband. "Is this what you wanted?" she asked.

"Yes," Osborn replied.

At that point, Osborn's wife put her arms around him and kissed him. "Well, then," she said, "I guess this is what I wanted, too."

When the sheriffs and the bankers were finished auctioning off the Osborns' possessions, all they had left was a ten-year-old Jeep, a pile of old clothing, and their dogs. A friend telephoned Osborn with an offer for a job in Virginia. Being penniless, Osborn was obliged to accept.

The job Osborn took was at a high-tech start-up known as UUNet Technologies, Inc., which, during the time Osborn worked there, grew from a market capitalization of $30 million to a market capitalization of nearly $3 billion. And this increase proved very good for Osborn's bottom line: Just four years after he joined UUNet, Osborn was able to retire from the company and buy himself a house in the Florida Keys. With his excess cash, Osborn set up his own angel investment company, Osborn Capital. And this decision has also been financially rewarding: One of Osborn Capital's investments, ArrowPoint Communications, was acquired by Cisco Systems for $5.7 billion in Cisco stock.

Still, Osborn says that regardless of how much money he accumulates, he will never forget what it felt like to come home from work and see a sheriff taping a foreclosure notice to his front door.

Every so often, Osborn receives a computer-generated letter from a credit-card company inviting him to apply for a new line of credit. And every now and again, Osborn takes the time to fill out the application and send it back. Invariably, Osborn reports, the request for an additional line of credit is turned down. And invariably, when Osborn receives word that he has been turned down yet again for an additional credit line that he does not need, he thinks of a line from John Kennedy Toole: "A man of vision will always find himself opposed by a confederacy of dunces."

Chapter Three

SETTING UP SHOP:

Establishing Your Company's Image

As the old saying goes, you never get a second chance to make a first impression. And as many entrepreneurs find out, this saying is as true about offices as it is about personal appearances. You may save some time at the outset by starting your company in an extremely modest facility, but if your space prevents people from taking you seriously, it could have dire effects on your ability to build a healthy business.

Two entrepreneurs, whom I'll call Stephen and Henry, were so pressed for cash when they were starting their Internet-based financial-services company that they decided to start the business in a residential apartment that would double as their living space. Determined to get the largest possible space for the lowest possible price, the friends moved into a $700-a-month three-bedroom apartment in one of Philadelphia's worst slums.

"It was a mess," Stephen says of the apartment. The walls looked as though they had not been painted in years, and the decomposing plaster bore an uncanny resemblance to vomit. There were so many cockroaches scurrying over the apartment's floors that Stephen could not sleep through the night without worrying about being attacked. "Our table was a card table, and our bookshelves were boxes," Stephen remembers. To elevate himself above the level of the cockroaches, Stephen pinched some cushions from his parents' couch and crafted a makeshift bed out of plywood boards. "That was the one thing I did to improve my standard of living," he remembers.

Although their living conditions were less than ideal, the boys worked frantically to develop their Web site as quickly as possible. While Stephen blasted through *Teach Yourself HTML in 21 Days or Less,* Henry made phone calls to major financial-services firms, trying to set up strategic partnerships. "We tried to convince them to give us the data for free, in exchange for a massive upside in a year's time," Stephen remembers. Reflecting on the various promises that he and Henry made to the representatives of financial-services firms, Stephen says, "We basically lied to these people. The amazing thing was, it actually worked."

Using his strong telephone voice, Henry convinced a director of new-business development at a major financial institution to agree to a face-to-face meeting, where they would discuss a possible business relationship. But when Henry proposed holding the meeting at the director's Wall Street office, the man demurred. The director said that he *was* interested in finding out what Stephen and Henry had to offer, but he wanted to see the company in its proper context. And so there came a day when Stephen found himself rushing around the dirty apartment, stuffing his plywood bed into the hall closet and trying to make the place presentable.

Clearly, this was no small task.

A few weeks earlier, Stephen had looked up from his computer screen to see a twelve-inch-long rat enter the apartment via the fire escape and scuttle across the living-room floor. Determined to get rid of this unwelcome guest, Stephen chased the animal around the apartment with a broom. But instead of exiting via the fire escape or the front door, the rat sought shelter beneath the apartment's ancient stove.

Stephen quickly learned that no amount of poking or cajoling could convince the rat to give up its hiding place. After a quarter of an hour of useless thwacking, Stephen hit upon the idea of simply turning the oven on.

Although the stove's advanced age prevented Stephen from turning it up more than 200 degrees, "eventually it got pretty hot under there." Before long the rat crawled out and went scuttling down the hall. "I thought that was pretty good, knowing enough to turn the oven on," Stephen reflects.

It seemed unlikely that the twelve-inch-long rat would show up for a second visit on the day of the big meeting, but rat or no rat, Stephen knew it was going to be difficult to convince the director of new-business development from one of Wall Street's most prestigious firms to set up a lopsided business relationship with a company that had nothing to show for itself except enthusiasm.

The more Stephen thought about it, the less he believed that the director would show up at all. But when the hour came, the director did appear, clad in full business regalia: three-piece suit, starched collar, wing-tipped shoes, and cuff links.

With his fancy duds and impressive résumé, the director of new-business development was not prepared for the decrepit hovel that was the boys' apartment. But something impelled him to climb the apartment's rickety stairs, knock on the open door, and take a seat on one of the metal folding chairs.

"I thought I would break the ice by asking him if he wanted anything to drink," Stephen remembers, "but I hoped he would say no." Unfortunately, the director of new business development said yes, and Stephen was obliged to go into the kitchen and search for an appropriate drinking vessel. "We didn't have any glasses, so I grabbed a big plastic cup with a dinosaur on it that I had gotten free from Burger King," Stephen recalls.

There wasn't enough time to actually *wash* the plastic cup, but Stephen did take a moment to rinse it out, fill it with cloudy tap water, and bring it back to the living room. Unfortunately, once Stephen delivered the dirty dinosaur cup to the director of new business development, the meeting was essentially over. "When he got back to the office after our meeting, he told one of his coworkers that I had served him water in a dirty cup," Stephen said. "That was all he said about the meeting—that I had served him in a dirty cup. After that, we never heard from him again."

How to Get People to Call You Back

Unsolicited telephone calls from desperate-sounding entrepreneurs are often ignored by the captains of industry, but there are ways to increase the likelihood of being listened to. Muddy Charles regular Gregg Favalora provided the following tips for making contact with busy executives. (Favalora credits one of his financiers with dreaming up this particular technique.)

"When you call up a large company, you usually don't even know the phone number of the person you're supposed to be talking to, so you end up talking to a receptionist," Favalora says. "You have to be very nice to the receptionist, since this is the person who controls the interface to the people within that company.

"To make it easier for that person on the other side of the phone who doesn't want to talk to us, anyway, we made a one-page fax." Favalora's fax explains who he is, what he is doing, and who has agreed to support his effort. The fax goes on to announce that Favalora would like to conduct a brief demonstration of his product and ends by saying that Favalora is planning to call the individual in a couple of days.

"When I talk to secretaries, I say, 'Look, I know you're really busy, but I want to talk to Mr. So-and-So. I'm going to send you this simple one-page fax, and you don't even have to worry about it. If you could just put it on his desk, that would be great.' "

Although Favalora reports that this technique has worked very well for him and his colleagues, he admits that even with the one-page fax, there are times when he feels as if no one wants to return his phone calls. "After a while it becomes hellish, but it's very important to keep the pipeline full," Favalora says. "It's really easy to spend two weeks working really hard and setting up lots of meetings, and then all of a sudden you're completely empty for a week or two, and it's depressing. The way you avoid that is by constantly pushing new events into the pipeline."

To do this, Favalora recommends building a "gigantic database of who you want to talk to, from what industry, and why. You have to keep track of who you called, whether or not they called you back, what secretary you talked to, and so on. You make about forty phone calls, and maybe five of them will wind up in actual meetings about a month later."

Cleanliness Is Next to Profitability

Clearly, there are many things that Stephen and Henry could have done to improve their chances of making a good impression on the director. They could have rented a temporary office suite for the day, for example, or they could have simply gone to the store and bought themselves a set of clean glasses. But when I talked to Stephen, I got the feeling that the dirty dinosaur cup was only the most memorable of an entire series of embarrassing incidents that stemmed from the fact that Stephen simply *did not like* where he was working.

"We lived in such squalor, it was depressing," Stephen remembers. "My ex-girlfriend called me up and said she wanted to come down and check it out, but I was just like, 'No!' I didn't want her to see what it was like. I was in a state of massive despair, because I realized that we had no idea what we were doing."

The stress of working round-the-clock in a cockroach-infested apartment took such a toll on Stephen's emotional reserves that he eventually decided to abandon the enterprise and go back home to live with his parents. But although he acknowledges that there was no possible way he could have spent any more time in the horrendous apartment, Stephen has had a hard time letting go of his Internet dreams. "The thing that keeps me up at night," Stephen says, "is, what if Henry makes this thing a success? But then I realize that I couldn't have spent any more time with this guy—it was killing me."

Can You Succeed on Your Own?

As Stephen and Henry discovered, it can be a daunting task to set up a new Internet business when one lacks critical elements like money, technological know-how, and an understanding of basic business etiquette. But there are some places that will help entrepreneurs develop their ideas and get their new businesses up to speed no matter where they are starting from. If an entrepreneur finds that he is overwhelmed by the prospect of locating an office and establishing strategic partnerships, he may find it useful to join a business incubator.

A number of the so-called business incubators that have been created by the government to promote the development of certain neighborhoods or to stimulate the transfer of new technologies from government-sponsored research programs to industry are little more than collections of office suites featuring lower-than-average rent and an occasional networking event. But the business incubators that are receiving most of the media attention these days are for-profit enterprises that offer everything from investment dollars to assistance with recruiting new employees.

To learn more about the kind of services that are provided by for-profit business incubators, I paid a visit to Tim Rowe, founder and CEO of the Cambridge Incubator, which is located inside an MIT-owned building just steps from the Sloan School of Management and the Muddy Charles Pub.

My main reason for going to see Rowe was to find out how the Cambridge Incubator, which invests substantial amounts of money—perhaps as much as a half-million dollars—in each of the companies that move into its venture campus, is different from the angel investors and "seed stage" VCs who also make this type of investment.

It didn't take long to figure out that this was exactly the right question to ask.

According to Rowe, there is a huge difference between the half-million dollars provided by the Cambridge Incubator and the half-million dollars provided by traditional sources of VC. And this difference goes way beyond the simple fact that at an incubator the VC firm and the start-up are both housed in the same building.

"The distance between the investor and the entrepreneur, which was perhaps helpful, historically, as a way of keeping perspective, has become untenable in this next generation of the Internet competitive environment," Rowe tells me. "You can't wait until you can convince somebody to fund you. You need to get funding immediately if your idea is ready for it. You need significantly more resources, significantly earlier in the development of your business, if you are going to be competitive in the current environment."

According to Rowe, the success or failure of an Internet start-up often depends on how quickly the start-up is able to obtain the resources it needs to grow. "As lots of people are fond of saying," Rowe tells me, "if your idea is any good, then there are five other people who have that idea and are pursuing it right now. And the question is, really, can you execute? Can you build a business? Can you find a CEO? Can you resolve the intellectual-property issues? Whatever it is, it needs to happen immediately."

To ensure that the companies that move into the incubator will be able to obtain the resources they need as soon as they need them, the incubator fixes the company up with a few members of its special "leadership team" as soon as the company moves in.

"It may be that a business comes in and it's a guy, a girl, and a dog," Rowe says. "It's a fantastic idea, and we say, 'Great! We're going to invest in you, and we're also going to give you access to ten people who are experts in each of their functional areas.'"

If a team needs help with its marketing, for example, "David Sack will sit down and join that team until they can hire a director of marketing," Rowe says. Rowe assures me that Sack is particularly qualified to help a company develop its marketing strategy because he has acted as the director of marketing for several dot-coms and is well versed in the business of "getting the buzz going." "He's not an adviser," Rowe emphasizes. "He's not a consultant. He's a doer while you build your team. And eventually you will have your own director of marketing who will learn from David how to play that role if they haven't played it before."

If a team needs help with its technology, Rowe might introduce the team to a technology wizard by the name of Bill. "We might put half of Bill on a new start-up until they could get a chief technology officer," Rowe says, "and we might put half of Bill on another project, depending on what it needs. Bill is not cheap, but we invest the money necessary for that company to be able to afford Bill. And what we charge for Bill is what we pay for Bill. We don't have any markup on Bill.

"We don't make money putting people on teams. We make money if the investment we make becomes worth a lot because the company has an IPO or is acquired or something like that."

The idea of having someone on hand who can anticipate and avoid the kind of technological problems that plague high-tech start-ups sounds comforting at first. But when I start to think about the mechanics of accepting help from someone like Bill, I get a bit nervous. Because Bill is, after all, "not cheap," it seems clear that Bill's contributions would be monitored quite closely by the rest of the incubator's staff, who do, after all, control both the supply of money that is being used to pay Bill and the amount that Bill is being paid.

I wonder how much control an entrepreneur would have over the business that he was trying to build when the people who control his purse strings are sitting right on the other side of the office. And then I wonder how a new entrepreneur—a person who has quit his job and assumed the significant financial risk of starting his own company—would feel about sharing the control of his company with ten "experts."

When Alex d'Arbeloff and Nick DeWolf were starting Teradyne Corporation back in the 1960s, they recruited a board of advisers, "but we had a tendency to think that we were smarter," d'Arbeloff says. Instead of asking other people for help at the outset, d'Arbeloff recalls that he would take time to get things straight in his own mind first. And when the advisers did give him advice, he didn't always want to accept it. "The best advice is from your customers," d'Arbeloff explains. "And even better advice is a purchase order, right?"

Biotech entrepreneur Petra Krauledat shares d'Arbeloff's belief that the best way to learn is through trial and error. "There is a certain amount of experience you need to start a new business and not fall flat on your face," she says. "So my advice is, fall flat on your face and then you will have the experience."

Other entrepreneurs express concern about the price of an incubator's services. "We never considered using an incubator," Internet entrepreneur Rosaline Gulati tells me. "It was too expensive. If you're a resourceful person, you'll find a way to get things done."

Entrepreneur Alex Laats agrees. "Anybody thinking about incubators should be very careful to think about what you're actually going to get," Laats instructs. "You're going to get some advice; you're going to get some facilities assistance. And how much do you want to pay for that in the equity side of your business?

"Incubators are not going to make companies more likely to be successful, in my opinion, unless the people running the incubators are really dedicated toward doing the work necessary to help them out. Some of them are—obviously. But if all they're giving you is a place to put down your PC, what are you really getting?"

Don't Waste Your Money

Petra Krauledat believes that it is very important to remain frugal during a company's earliest days. To save money, she performed the preliminary research for her first biotech company, Sienna Biotech, in a laboratory she had constructed in the basement of her New Jersey house. "We thought it was more important to hire than to find space, so we focused on hiring first," Krauledat remembers. "We were able to get some lab space from Rutgers University that was sort of an adjunct to the chemistry labs. The lab space was not free—we certainly paid them for that—but we didn't have to worry about outfitting a laboratory."

Although Krauledat's company spent its early days literally inside Rutgers University, Krauledat assures me that the university did not have any claim to the research being done at Sienna Biotech. "It was just extra lab space that they had: an old biochemistry lab that was fairly large and wasn't being utilized anymore. We called Rutgers's administrative office, and they said they were doing things like this because some of their older facilities were too large. We paid the professor a small research grant, so we had the right to use the lab space."

When the time came for Krauledat to locate office space for her second biotech start-up, she had enough money (from the sale of Sienna Biotech) to pay for whatever kind of space she needed. But Krauledat chose to start Union Biometrica in an extremely modest facility. "The space here is very low-key, very inexpensive," she says, noting that "we picked it because we wanted cheap space. If you bootstrap a business, it is very important that you don't waste a nickel on the trappings of the high and mighty."

Still, Krauledat cautions that "you want to give people the feeling that they can trust you, so your space has to be somehow under control. But I think you can make up for less luxurious space with neatness and organization.

"My recommendation to young people that are starting businesses is: Be modest with your space. Make it clean and well kept, but you don't have to go into the fanciest buildings that have all of the modern high-tech trappings; it is not necessary. And the investors that I have spoken to have confirmed that they like to see a reasonable rent expenditure."

Describe Your Ideal Vacation

The difference between starting a company on one's own and taking a spot inside a business incubator is like the difference between planning one's own vacation and spending one's holiday on board a luxury cruise ship. It's clearly cheaper to do things on your own, and there is no doubt that planning your own trip means having more control over the way you spend your time and money. But there's something soothing about being able to sit back and let someone make all of your decisions for you.

Judging from the number of tours that are booked each year, a significant fraction of the population believes that the phrase "packaged adventure" is not an oxymoron. But an equally significant fraction of the population is put off by the idea of paying someone to tell them how to spend their free time.

David Foster Wallace has written an especially clever essay entitled "A Supposedly Fun Thing I'll Never Do Again," explaining why he will never again subject himself to a "7 Nights Luxury Cruise in the Caribbean." In this essay, Wallace spends a hundred pages figuring out why the "supposedly fun" experience of traveling on board a luxury cruise ship filled him with despair, made him want to jump overboard, and caused him to experience real fear about his subsequent reentry into the real world.

It's perfectly fine to take your vacation on board a cruise ship, and it's perfectly fine to start your company inside a business incubator. But once you make the decision to go on a cruise or join an incubator, there is no going back. You can't just jump off the ship once it has left port. Still, you might be able to predict whether or not you would enjoy starting your business inside an incubator by seeing how well you like the idea of having someone else plan your vacation.

I know from reading the Sloan alumni Web site that Rowe's wife, Amy, who founded the travel-related e-business known as Etineraries, has "a passion for travel." And I also know that Ms. Rowe's travel-related business, which provides customized information to travelers as well as a platform for targeted e-commerce, was one of the first companies to join the incubator. But I don't know whether Mrs. Rowe's personal travel preferences involve group tours or solo travel. And I don't know anything at all about the incubator's other entrepreneurs.

To find out how the people who start businesses inside the Cambridge Incubator like to spend their vacations, I accept an invitation to attend the Cambridge Incubator's combination housewarming party/public-relations fair, which has been dubbed the "Liquid Launch

Party." I am especially interested in going to this party because Rowe has told me that the incubator's new office suites (or bays, as they are called) have been custom designed by a handful of prominent architects, including the design genius "who is building Gap 2000 Tokyo."

Knowing that the Cambridge Incubator was designed by the architectural mastermind behind a major retail establishment in the literal ground zero of what is, quite possibly, the most presentation-obsessed society on earth, I am not at all surprised, when I walk into the incubator, that I feel the same buy-everything-in-sight impulse that I experience whenever I step inside the Gap. Although the rational part of my brain knows that I could probably get along just as well without yet another plain white T-shirt, the irrational part of my brain desperately wants to buy whatever it is that they're selling.

The party is crowded with investors and incubees, all of whom appear to be healthy, wealthy, and well educated. Every party guest has straight white teeth, shiny hair, and perfect posture, and every party guest seems to be as beautiful and popular and confident as the models in the Gap ads. Every guest seems to be bursting with excitement about the incredible things that are just on the verge of happening. But although it seems clear that everyone has an awful lot to say, none of the incubees seems to want to talk to me about their businesses. They are happy to pass out public-relations blurb sheets, which are filled with words like "content" and "information" and "people on the go." But although one company claims that its entire purpose for existing is to allow users to "easily stay in touch with friends, family, colleagues, and vendors," I am unable to find anyone who can tell me what that means.

Frustrated with my inability to get any of the Cambridge Incubator's incubees to give me the time of day, much less tell me about their vacation preferences, I go across town to a place called Newcogen and speak with an entrepreneur named Sanjeev Datta. Datta is more than willing to tell me about Blue Ripple, the Internet infrastructure company he cofounded about eight months back. And he's even willing to answer my question about whether he sees any similarities between starting a business in an incubator and taking a vacation on board a cruise ship. "The cruise can be a lot of fun as long as you have the freedom to do what you like," Datta says. "You have all sorts of help to make sure that the ship is going in the right direction and all the logistics are taken care of—the safety net is there, et cetera. But it's all a question of balance."

When a vacationer decides to spend his holiday on board a cruise ship, he must pay a certain fraction of his hard-earned dollars to the folks who charter the ship, cook his meals, and clean up his tiny stateroom. Similarly, when an entrepreneur makes the decision to start his company inside a business incubator, "you do give up something," Datta admits. "You give up equity to join Newcogen. And it's a question of, is it too little? Is it too much? That's debatable. But I think at the end of the day we can build a really successful company, and that equity is not going to matter a whole lot."

Datta understands my concern about entrepreneurs wanting to retain control over their own companies, but he insists that at Newcogen, control isn't an issue. In fact, before Datta agreed to join Newcogen, he asked Newcogen's founder, Dr. Noubar Afeyan, whether he appreciated Datta's desire to remain independent. Datta recalls saying to Afeyan, "'The reason I'm leaving a pretty comfortable position back at Fidelity Investments is to start my own company.' And his assurance was 'Absolutely. It's your company, you name it, you run it.' That's been their attitude. Their help has been there when we wanted it."

Besides, Datta says, Newcogen does not actually consider itself a business incubator. "They are sort of an incubator plus," Datta says. "They bring a lot more value than a typical incubator." Instead of calling itself a business incubator, Newcogen markets itself as a "joint venture partnership," which means that instead of investing their VC dollars "on the same basis that any venture capitalist would," by buying a chunk of the company up front, Newcogen gives its entrepreneurs money in the form of a convertible note. Datta explains that at Newcogen, "they put money in, but they don't do a valuation until we've built the company together."

So far, Newcogen's investors have put approximately $4 million into Blue Ripple. But Datta cannot say how much of the company this represents. "The idea is that when we go out for our first external round, which would be some time in the beginning of next year, someone—an external investor—is going to put a valuation on the company," Datta says. "That's when they figure out what percentage of the company they get. Before that we are all growing in the same direction, trying to increase the valuation of the company."

When the time comes to solicit financing from an external investor, Datta is certain that the folks at Newcogen will help him obtain the best possible deal. "The way the deal is structured, it's in their interest to get a good valuation for us in the next round," he says. "And not only that; they have connections with lots of other VCs in the area. We've already had some informal meetings, and when the time is right, we'll make our pitch to them."

In addition to providing Datta with the cash he needs to get started and introductions to the folks who can give him more, Newcogen has provided Datta with a completely networked office space on the tenth floor of a building in Cambridge—a piece of real estate that, Datta says, is "not easy to find." Newcogen has also provided Datta with the services of a vice president of human resources, the services of Newcogen's in-house legal counsel, the services of Newcogen's various administrative assistants, and the collective wisdom of the Newcogen board.

I asked Datta whether he was comfortable with the level of coaching he was receiving from the Newcogen board, who were, after all, located just on the other side of the building. I was surprised by his answer. "Lately I wish we could spend more time with them," Datta says wistfully. "But I would assume that's just a temporary phenomenon that they're really tied up. Other than that it's been great. They have been very responsive, and very supportive."

The Joys of Finding Your Own Office

Entrepreneur Geeta Sankappanavar, who decided to start her medical administrative-services outsourcing company, Intellirecords, without the help of an on-site business incubator, is amused by my cruise-ship analogy.

"When you do a start-up on your own, it's kind of like planning your own trip to Kenya," Sankappanavar says. "It's cheap, because you buy your own plane tickets, but you never have enough money, and you can never find the right people to travel with at the same time." Although Sankappanavar acknowledges that it would be much easier to simply book a slot with a tour group, she prefers solo travel because "the experiences that you find are so remote and so wonderful and when you get there you are so, so happy.

"Regardless of whether your trip is good or not, it's the experience of getting there that makes you develop as a person."

When Sankappanavar was choosing the physical location for Intellirecords, she made the decision to forgo business incubators in favor of learning as much as she could about her various real-estate options. Because Sankappanavar and her partners were already living in New York City, she began her search by investigating a "plain vanilla" office space in New Rochelle, New York, just thirty minutes from Manhattan by train. But although the unspectacular office met Sankappanavar's budgetary requirements, the building's dull gray carpeting gave the place "a rather industrial feel" and created an atmosphere that was somewhat dreary. "It was just what I envisioned a start-up to be," Sankappanavar says. "Nothing."

Determined to find a space that would be "open to the exchange of ideas," Sankappanavar checked out an "absolutely gorgeous" space in Jersey City, which "seemed to be the epitome of what a high-tech start-up should look like." The suite had high ceilings, funky iMac computers, and "all this metal everywhere." It was, in Sankappanavar's opinion, "exciting and sexy and thrilling." But the office was also very expensive, so Sankappanavar ruled it out.

Noticing that the area around Wall Street was becoming "an up-and-coming mecca for high-tech start-ups," Sankappanavar paid a visit to an Internet company in that region. But when she set foot inside the company's offices, the idea of being located just steps from the nation's big investment houses lost most of its appeal. "It was scary," Sankappanavar remembers. "All the overhead lights were dimmed, so it was completely dark—the only light in the office was the glow from the computer screens." The company's founders had arranged five desks in an area about the size of a suburban living room and separated the work stations with white curtains. "People were hunched over their desks, and they would peer over their shoulders to look at us," Sankappanavar remembers. "We thought to ourselves, *We are not like this—no way in hell. We are an Internet-enabled start-up company, but we are not the kind of dot-com where the only relationship that defines the company is the one between the employee and his computer."*

Frustrated with the spaces she had been seeing in and around New York City, Sankappanavar returned to New Rochelle to investigate an office space in "a creaky old building" that looked out upon Long Island Sound. The office was "a combination of high-tech and Old World," with plenty of light, tasteful moldings, and a "very comforting and womblike" atmosphere. It wasn't exactly the high-impact environment that Sankappanavar had originally envisioned, but the old building had a certain charm, and Sankappanavar could see herself being happy there. Satisfied that this office represented the best she was going to get for her price range, Sankappanavar forked over the down payment and signed a lease.

"It sounds stupid to notice these things," Sankappanavar says, "but when you work eighteen or twenty hours a day, it's important that your office be somewhere you like."

Because the decisions one makes about where to position a company at the earliest stages of the start-up process are going to have a huge effect on the rest of the start-up experience, it's important to spend some time covering all the bases. And most entrepreneurs do a relatively decent job figuring out where their offices should be located and how they are going to arrange their desks.

It's the intellectual side of setting up shop that throws people for a loop.

Who Makes the Decisions?

Founders of high-tech businesses are notorious for saying that every person who has been recognized as an official member of the company's founding team will have an equal voice in the decision-making process. But more often than not, this nonhierarchical corporate framework winds up being more trouble than it's worth. "Equal partners don't make decisions well," an entrepreneur explained. "Without a captain, you can't steer."

Engineers Mark Eichin and Christopher "Monty" Montgomery considered themselves extremely fortunate when they were putting the finishing touches on their company's new Internet acceleration product,

Fast Serv 2.0, because they did not have to make a decision about who was going to have control over the product's design. The lucky break occurred when Monty went off to get married, since this gave Eichin a chance to come up with a single overall vision for the entire system.

Monty's decision to effectively disappear for three weeks "was really convenient," Eichin says, because "that meant that I could take everything that we had learned by working on it together and all the stuff that he had written up and hammer it out. When Monty came back, he was able to say, 'Okay, I recognize bits of this, and I can fill in the rest.' He still got credit for the design, so he was happy with that, and at the same time I got the control I needed to get it consistent.

"At the end we got basic agreement on everything, and I didn't have to worry about convincing him to support me on the things that were details. I could just be arbitrary and pick."

The situation with Fast Serv 2.0 provides a rare example of a case where things just fell into place, but in most situations it's a good idea to spend some time thinking about how decisions are going to be made.

Most entrepreneurs are aware of how important it is to sit down with a corporate lawyer and fill out the legal documents that will protect their company from hostile forces in the outside world. But few entrepreneurs understand that it is just as important to protect their companies from the nasty competitive forces—things like jealousy, egotism, pettiness, and even fatigue-related memory loss—that can erode start-ups from within. It is unfortunately the case that some entrepreneurs get so excited about setting up their new businesses that they don't even bother to draw up a comprehensive business plan.

Entrepreneur-turned-angel investor Ed Zyszkowski told me about an Internet entrepreneur who was in such a hurry to start building his world-changing Internet company that he asked Zyszkowski to write his business plan for him. "He was like, 'How about I just dictate it while we have buffalo wings over at the sports club?'" Zyszkowski remembers, chuckling.

Although some angels like Zyszkowski are happy to accommodate such behavior ("I wrote most of it, actually," Zyszkowski admits), most professional investors wish that entrepreneurs would devote more time and energy to the planning process. C. B. Health Ventures' Linda Ystueta wishes that before entrepreneurs asked her to provide funding for their health-related high-tech businesses, they would spend some time putting together a so-called project plan—a simple one-page document stating where the company is today and where they want to be in five years. "Granted," Ystueta says, "you will have higher detail later on than you will have at the beginning, but you had better have step-by-step plans."

When entrepreneurs take the time to develop a simple project plan, "all of a sudden you know how many employees you need when," Ystueta says. "Then you can tell people, 'In six months I'll be looking for someone to do this.'"

Many entrepreneurs prefer not to create written records of their start-up plans, since the only thing they know for certain is that their plans are bound to change. "But if you don't have that plan in mind, you lose your focus and end up running around in circles," Ystueta says. "Change it, fine. But then know *what* you changed and *why* you changed it. Some people constantly get wishy-washy, but you can't afford that as an entrepreneur. You need to be efficient and effective."

Ystueta's comments are echoed by MIT chairman and Teradyne co-founder Alex d'Arbeloff. "My recommendation is to have very focused objectives and know exactly what you are doing," d'Arbeloff says. "Know exactly who your customer is, and know exactly what product you're going to build. If you know exactly what you want to do, then you can test the idea quickly. If it's not working, you can change it. On the other hand, if the idea is vague, then it's very hard to check, and you might not find out you're in trouble until it's too late."

But coming up with a comprehensive idea about what needs to happen when is only the most obvious step in the planning process. It's no less important to figure out how a company is going to address those irksome issues that have to do with human nature.

Does Anyone Else Understand What You're Doing?

Quite often, high-tech entrepreneurs enjoy the fact that at their company's earliest stages, they are the only ones who can understand the technological innovation that they are developing. But as a company grows and takes on more people, these new people will have to learn how to work with the systems that are being created.

Some entrepreneurs have a problem with the fact that growing a company means figuring out how to communicate with other people. Additionally, some techies don't want anyone else to know what they are up to, because this makes them worry that they may eventually lose control over the technological aspects of their own corporations.

Clearly, some communication problems stem from the fact that technologists in general are not terribly compelling communicators. Even when they do try to express themselves, people don't always understand what they are saying. But every now and again a founder will try to solidify his position as the most valuable contributor in the company by taking steps to ensure that no one else will ever be able to follow in his footsteps.

One engineer created a completely proprietary set of software tools, which were unlike anything that was available on the open market, and used these tools to develop his company's entire technological framework. Although the engineer himself had no trouble working with his homemade tool kit, the person in charge of hiring new programmers found it extremely difficult to find anyone who could work with this fellow, since no one else had any idea how to duplicate his results.

Whenever a new employee would ask questions about the unusual tool kit, the engineer would either ignore him entirely or inform him that the answers were intuitively obvious.

As time went on, the company discovered that teaching new employees how to use the programmer's homemade tool kit was an extremely expensive proposition, especially when they considered that it hadn't been necessary in the first place. Although it had seemed obvious in the beginning that it would be in everyone's best interests to allow the engineer to use his special tools, it would have been better in the long run if the engineer had constructed the Web site using a set of tools that other people knew how to work with.

This is the kind of problem you can avoid by making a project plan and forcing yourself to consider not only where you want to go but how you are going to get there.

Chapter Four

PROTECTING YOUR INTELLECTUAL PROPERTY

W hen I visited entrepreneur Gregg Favalora at his new office on Route 128, he wasn't able to talk with me immediately because he was on the phone with his patent lawyer. While I was waiting, I noticed that he had the book *Patent It Yourself,* by patent attorney David Pressman, sitting on his bookshelf. Knowing that Favalora was, at that moment, speaking with a patent attorney, it seemed odd that he would have a do-it-yourself book sitting on his bookshelf. But when I asked Favalora about this anomaly, he explained that he had used the book to reduce the number of hours he needed to spend with his legal counsel.

Instead of paying the lawyer to give him a crash course in the basics of patent law, Favalora could use the book, and others like it, to learn basic facts about filing patents, registering trademarks, and keeping trade secrets before his lawyer's clock started running. By making up his own mind about what he wanted to do before he got on the phone with his patent lawyer, Favalora could use the lawyer's expertise to double-check the decisions that he had already made and provide advice about things he was unsure about.

The world of patenting is, after all, filled with a huge number of esoteric legal documents that need to be filled out correctly the first time and a multitude of mysterious-sounding adjectives that were never covered in high school English class. But even if you are very good at filling out legal documents and already know the definitions of "adder" and "bezel" and "xerotic," it's still a good idea to run your application past an experienced patent attorney.

The reason it is so important to check, and double-check, the educated guesses you make about how to protect your intellectual property is that if the representatives of a large and not-particularly-scrupulous corporation decide that you have come up with an extremely valuable innovation, you may find yourself in the undesirable position of having to defend your patent while simultaneously creating a market for your product. To understand how difficult this can be, one need only consider the case of Philo T. Farnsworth, who spent the years 1921–1949 inventing, patenting, and attempting to profit from the electronic television.

Philo Farnsworth was just fourteen when he came up with the idea for electronic television. Legend has it that at the exact moment when the idea came to him, Farnsworth was plowing a potato field on his family's farm in Idaho. However the idea actually came to Farnsworth, it had lodged itself firmly in his mind by 1922, when the teenager finally worked up the courage to share his invention with his high school chemistry teacher, Justin Tolman.

Tolman was impressed with the idea that Farnsworth had come up with and listened carefully to the boy's ideas. But filing for a patent was expensive, and the income from Farnsworth's family's potato farm was not enough to justify the high costs of hiring an attorney and filing an official patent application. And so Philo Farnsworth did not seek legal protection for his "image dissector tube" until 1927, after a community-chest fund-raiser named George Everson had invested $6,000 of his own money to help Farnsworth flesh out his idea.

After Farnsworth had developed a rudimentary model of his invention, Everson raised $25,000 from a collection of wealthy San Francisco bankers and set Farnsworth up in a proper laboratory. But this initial $25,000 investment was only the beginning. In his book *The Story of Television*, Everson reports that it actually took more than thirteen years, and $1 million, before Farnsworth's television was ready for commercialization.

Unfortunately, the thirteen-year period during which Farnsworth worked around the clock to invent, and perfect, his electronic television happened to coincide with the Great Depression. Not surprisingly, there were many occasions when the Farnsworth Television Corporation, like many other corporations of the same period, ran extremely low on funds. During these uncertain times, there were a number of occasions when Farnsworth's backers decided to put the Farnsworth system, together with all of the associated patents and inventions, up for sale.

When the Farnsworth company was for sale, Farnsworth's backers often invited representatives of rival corporations to tour the Farnsworth laboratories. Everson recalls that the company gave tours of its offices in March 1928, shortly after the stock market crash of 1929, and again in 1931. And it seems that a number of the large corporations that toured Farnsworth's offices did express interest in buying the Farnsworth patent portfolio. But the dollar amounts that the companies offered were always much less than Farnsworth's investors had hoped to receive, and so these bids were always rejected.

It is not clear what the representatives of rival corporations actually learned when they toured the Farnsworth laboratories, but it seems clear they were given a thorough demonstration of everything that had been invented to date. Historians report that Farnsworth was extremely candid about sharing the scientific details of his inventions with his fellow engineers and with members of the press.

Some entrepreneurs go out of their way to avoid sharing the details of their innovations with anyone outside their corporation, but Farnsworth seems to have believed that fame would be good for business. "There were many reasons Farnsworth wanted as much publicity as possible for his system," Farnsworth's widow, Elma, explains in her book *Distant Vision*. "Not the least of these was the continuing desire of his backers to find a buyer for their costly venture."

Later, when it became clear that Farnsworth's rivals were pursuing patent applications in similar scientific areas, some members of the Farnsworth Television Corporation began to wonder whether they had made the right decision in allowing representatives of rival corporations to tour their laboratories and in publishing detailed articles about Farnsworth's inventions in various scientific journals. But it is hard to say what would have been the ideal course of action, given the circumstances.

On the one hand, the publicity did serve to advertise the Farnsworth patent portfolio, which Farnsworth's backers hoped to license to their competitors. On the other hand, the tours, the interviews, and the various other public disclosures allowed Farnsworth's rivals to get a clear view of the corporation's various weaknesses, including the fact that the company often seemed to be short of cash.

"Throughout the 1930s, Philo found his time divided between defending his patents, continuing to refine his system, and haggling with his own backers for adequate funding," Mrs. Farnsworth writes.

Starting a television corporation during the nineteen twenties was, after all, an extremely expensive proposition. To make a profit on television, it was necessary to build a television receiver that could show images on par with those that were being shown in movie theaters, develop a nationwide network of television broadcasting stations, and produce programs to show on these stations. A company like RCA had the financial resources necessary to investigate these various business opportunities simultaneously. The Farnsworth Television Corporation did not. But Farnsworth's investors felt that the patent protection they had obtained from the U. S. government would allow them to obtain a return on their investment.

"We were of the opinion that our company would achieve its greatest success by simply sticking to the research-and-development program, deriving our revenues almost exclusively from royalties on patents," Everson wrote, noting that "the terms of such [a patent licensing] agreement would determine the measure of success of our venture."

Unfortunately, there was a problem with this plan. The patent portfolio that Farnsworth's investors hoped to take advantage of was begun back in 1927, and during the period in question, U.S. patents were only good for seventeen years from the date the patents were issued. (These days, U.S. patents are good for twenty years from the date that they are filed.)

As Everson goes on to write in *The Story of Television,* in September 1939, the Farnsworth Television Corporation finally reached an agreement with their "chief competitor in television," the Radio Corporation of America (RCA), and Farnsworth's backers breathed a tremendous sigh of relief. The agreement stipulated that RCA would pay royalties for the use of Farnsworth's various television patents and that Farnsworth's company would receive a license to use some of RCA's patents as well. But the good feeling was short-lived: In April 1941, the war in Europe became so ominous that the U.S. government ordered American industries to discontinue manufacturing commercial radio sets (and television receivers) until further notice. "This meant that television was indefinitely delayed," Everson wrote.

Those corporations that had been involved in manufacturing commercial radio sets and television receivers were encouraged to try their hand at building essential war material and to compete with fellow corporations for a finite number of wartime contracts. And Everson reports that the principle behind the Farnsworth dissector tube was put to good use in various military projects, including the Sniperscope, which allowed soldiers to see in the dark.

But as time went on, Farnsworth's television patents began to expire, one by one.

Finally, in 1949, some twenty-two years after Farnsworth had filed his first patent application, the Farnsworth Television and Radio Corporation was acquired by the International Telephone and Telegraph Corporation (ITT).

A Patent Is Only the Beginning

The case of Philo T. Farnsworth illustrates that simply obtaining a patent on one's invention may not be enough to ensure that one will be able to derive profit from his or her invention. It is certainly possible for inventors to make money by obtaining patents and licensing these patents to rival corporations. But if you look closely, you will notice that the individuals who use this strategy are often closely affiliated with university technology licensing offices or the intellectual-property offices located inside large institutions.

It is very difficult for individual entrepreneurs to fend off hostile patent attacks on their own, even if they do have the backing of some wealthy bankers. In most cases, it is much easier for an individual entrepreneur to simply develop a reputation in the marketplace for selling quality products.

How to Protect Yourself

The first thing you should do when you come up with an innovative idea is to write it down on a piece of paper, get two trustworthy individuals to sign and date this piece of paper, and then store it in a safe place. The second thing you should do is figure out whether there is any possible way for you to make money from this innovation. If it looks as though it would be possible to do so, you should learn as much as you can about the costs and benefits of filing patent applications, registering trademarks, and keeping trade secrets. Once you have decided which of these options is best for your innovation, you should test this strategy by talking it over with an experienced patent attorney.

If you decide that you are going to keep your invention a trade secret, you should practice talking about what you are up to without giving away any of your trade secrets. (This might be difficult.) You should prepare various speeches for potential employees, potential business partners, potential customers, and interested journalists, and you should rehearse these speeches with every member of your founding team. When you practice these speeches, you should remind your cofounders to make eye contact and smile a lot so that the potential employees, customers, business partners, and journalists do not get offended when they realize that you are not giving them any real information.

Although it is extremely tricky to convince potential employees, customers, business partners, and journalists to spend time thinking about your high-tech business when you are simultaneously trying to avoid disclosing any trade secrets, some entrepreneurs do choose to protect their intellectual property by treating their innovations as trade secrets. After all, protecting your innovation in the other way, by filing a patent application, means revealing to the world exactly what you are trying to do, as explicitly as possible, so that when your patent expires, everyone else will be able to use your innovation.

If you plan to use your innovation for more than twenty years and you want to keep everyone else from benefiting from it, you may decide to classify your innovation as a trade secret. However, if you ever attempt to raise VC financing, you may be forced to choose another path.

When entrepreneur Yonald Chery was looking for financing for the digital whiteboard company known as Virtual Ink, he discovered that having a patent application on file was a necessary prerequisite to obtaining his first round of venture capital. When Chery began to show his design for a digital whiteboard to various investors, the investors asked, "Can you legally build this thing without infringing on someone else's patent space?" Since Chery had come up with his invention on his own and not copied it from anyone else, it seemed to him that he should have the right to build his product. But if, unbeknownst to Chery, someone else had already filed a patent for a similar digital whiteboard, there would be trouble. The other worry was that even though Chery's innovation did not then infringe on any of his competitors' patents, if Chery did not either protect or publish his innovation, it might be possible for a future competitor to obtain a patent for the invention later on.

The investors were so insistent, Chery reports, that in order for Chery to raise VC financing, "it essentially became a requirement to be able to show some sort of freedom to operate in this area and to show a strategy for protecting yourself."

Although Chery's investors knew that the entrepreneur would have to spend a great deal of time and effort to file a patent application, they felt that this time would be well spent, since the research he would do to file his patent application would teach him a great deal about his competition. "As you start to look into what other people have done in terms of patents, you find people who you wouldn't expect to be in that space, and you see that maybe someone else has thought of your idea before," Chery explains. "Seeing competing approaches helps you define your interpretation of your own innovation and refine your own strategy."

If, for example, a patent search revealed that an entrepreneur's competition was all going in one direction with regard to a particular problem, a savvy entrepreneur could make the decision to secure intellectual property in a slightly different area and build his company around an idea that was truly novel, worth protecting, and different from prior art.

To keep abreast of the rapidly changing patent landscape, Chery consults a wide variety of information sources, including the Delphion Intellectual Property Network (formerly the IBM Intellectual Property Network), located at www.delphion.com; the U.S. Patent and Trademark Office, located at www.uspto.gov; and the World Intellectual Property Organization, located at www.wipo.org. All of these information sources provide an excellent place to start learning about what one's potential competitors are up to. But Chery has discovered that the most useful information about the individuals who are trying to compete directly with his company's products is already stored on his company's own computers.

"If you pay specific attention to who is looking at your press releases and getting your data sheets on a daily basis and if you notice that they're also trying to access Web pages that aren't directly pointed to by your home page or they are making up directories to probe around unpublished pages accessible from your Web site, you can find out who is trying to snoop and how intense they are about it," Chery says. "There is a very high correlation between these particular things and the people who are trying to grab information. We have found people that we didn't realize were indirect competitors, but we found out that they had downloaded the press release. You can also find out who is interested in your product either as a partner or a customer."

The best way to deal with the knowledge that some people are downloading press releases and accessing various portions of your Web site is to assume that these people are potential customers, potential business partners, or interested journalists. "We get all the logs, and we see what pages people were looking at, and then we call them up," Chery says. "It helps in business development, it helps in sales, and it helps our research-and-development group."

What Lawyers Can Do

Although books like *Patent It Yourself* contain much of the information you need to get going, they can't second-guess your uninformed legal decisions or give you the kind of clearheaded emotional support you need when the going gets rough. More importantly, they can't tell you how to proceed in the event of an actual lawsuit.

Another thing that books like *Patent It Yourself* can't do is refer entrepreneurs to wealthy individuals who have a history of investing in new high-tech companies. And as any entrepreneur who is trying to raise VC financing will gladly tell you, this can be a valuable service.

When entrepreneur Geeta Sankappanavar was searching for a law firm for her medical administrative services outsourcing company, Intellirecords, she conducted six different interviews and evaluated lawyers based on several criteria. Because she had not yet found a VC investor, she wanted to choose a firm that had the ability to introduce her to both potential clients and potential VCs.

But more important than the question of whether the firm could introduce her to potential VC partners was the question of whether the law firms' previous clients were happy with the firms' services.

Sankappanavar asked the lawyers how many start-ups they had worked with, what funding stage the companies were at when they first retained the lawyers' services, and how long the start-up companies stayed. Finally, Sankappanavar asked whether her company could expect to receive attention from a named partner or from someone with less experience.

The firm Sankappanavar eventually chose had a history of dealing not only with new high-tech start-ups but with new electronic health ventures. And Sankappanavar reports that in addition to having a thorough understanding of the kinds of problems these companies face, the firm has distinguished itself by going out of its way to promote strategic relationships between the companies it serves. While Sankappanavar was in the process of interviewing the firm's previous clients to find out how well they were treated, she was introduced to a number of companies with whom she might eventually form strategic partnerships.

During my discussions with entrepreneurs, I learned that it is quite common for corporate lawyers—who spend their days drawing up term sheets for, and making friends with, wealthy angel investors and VCs—to serve as scouts for these wealthy clients by introducing them to entrepreneurs who are seeking funding.

This practice is so widespread that some entrepreneurs will take a law firm's network of established business connections into account when they decide whether or not to work with a particular firm. But although many entrepreneurs decide that it is worth paying extra money to have access to the connections of a top-tier law firm, there is no guarantee that a lawyer will introduce an entrepreneur to any of her wealthy clients. And a struggling entrepreneur who does not presently have any money connections should not delude himself into thinking that a named partner at a prestigious law firm is going to give a small start-up company as much attention as she would give to a major account, especially if the lawyer knows that the entrepreneur does not have the money to pay her. A lawyer at a smaller firm may have less influence, but she may be more willing to use her connections to assist a new client.

It Pays to Be Picky

"An entrepreneur always wants to work with a lawyer who is familiar with that area of industry," says independent consultant Lori Pressman, who spent eleven years working with entrepreneurs inside MIT's TLO. Pressman believes it's a good idea for entrepreneurs to choose patent attorneys with prior training in the entrepreneur's particular research area because "someone with experience will file much quicker than someone who has to buy a book." To put it more simply, "if an attorney shows up with a book he just bought, be prepared for really high bills," Pressman warns.

During her days at the TLO, Pressman came up with a number of opinions about the various ways that patent attorneys can help inventors. "The really good patent lawyers help their clients think about strategy," Pressman says. For example, a good patent attorney will encourage an entrepreneur to frame his patent application around what the entrepreneur is trying to sell rather than what the entrepreneur originally dreamed up. And the really good patent attorneys will encourage entrepreneurs to consider not only *what* they plan to produce but also *where* they plan to do business.

If an entrepreneur's market research tells him that 90 percent of his market is inside the United States, he may not want to bother applying for patent protection outside this country. But if it turns out that 50 percent of the entrepreneur's products will be sold in Europe and the other 50 percent will be sold in Japan, it may be worthwhile to consider filing abroad.

There are a number of reasons why filing for a patent protection outside the United States is different from filing domestically. In the United States, entrepreneurs have one year from any publicly enabling disclosure to seek legal protection for their invention. But if a person is hoping to obtain patent protection outside the United States, being too open about one's innovation can have adverse consequences. "The instant you disclose your idea in an enabling way, patent protection is not available outside the U.S.," Pressman warns.

There are, of course, many ways to talk about one's invention without "disclosing" it in an "enabling" way. "If you say, 'I have an invention that allows me to leap tall buildings in a single bound,' but you don't say *how*, the disclosure is not enabling," Pressman explains. But many entrepreneurs find it difficult to talk about their inventions without revealing all of the technical details.

If an entrepreneur really wants to talk about his invention but does not feel that it would be possible to conduct any conversations without explaining how the product works, he might consider asking his friends to sign confidentiality agreements. (An example of such a confidentiality agreement is available in the Appendix.)

How to Reduce Your Legal Fees

If an entrepreneur decides to pay the extra money and work with the world's best patent attorney, there are a number of things he can do to bring down his costs. Before going to visit the patent lawyer, the entrepreneur should figure out how his invention is different from other inventions in the same space and come up with specific examples of already-existing patents, or "prior art."

Later, after the entrepreneur has established a working relationship with his patent lawyer, the best thing he can do to reduce his legal fees is to *return the attorney's phone calls*. "Help your attorney," Pressman advises. "Attorneys are under legal deadlines to make responses to the patent office. And frequently your expert input is a real time and money saver."

Some entrepreneurs refuse to read the reams of legal documents that they receive from their attorneys, "because that's the legal stuff." However, Pressman says, "You can get much better patents if you communicate with your attorney."

Confidentiality agreements are not for everyone. But those entrepreneurs who do not take the time to obtain confidentiality agreements in writing may have a difficult time proving that their disclosures were protected by verbal confidentiality agreements—and therefore were not "public"—if they run into problems later on. "As a practical matter, it's really a matter of trust," Pressman says, noting that "once a patent application is on file, you can make all of the disclosures you want without patent-law consequences, though one should still consider the business consequences."

What a Patent Is Not

According to the U.S. Patent and Trademark Office's (USPTO) official Web site, "a patent is a type of property right. It gives the patent holder the right, for a limited time, to exclude others from making, using, or selling the subject matter that is within the scope of protection granted by the patent."

If an inventor continues to pay the necessary fees, his patent could last for twenty years from the date on which he filed his initial application. But simply owning a patent on an invention does not give the inventor the ability to make a profit from his invention. And if the patent is ever challenged in a court of law, "it is up to the patent holder to enforce his or her own rights," the Web site says.

If an inventor is considering filing an application for a utility patent but he is not sure that he can afford to pay the fees, he may want to consider filing a provisional application. The USPTO Web site reveals that in the United States, a provisional patent application "can be filed up to one year following the date of first sale, offer for sale, public use, or publication of the invention."

The filing fee for a provisional patent application is much less than the filing fee for a nonprovisional, or standard, patent application, but many patent experts try to discourage their clients from filing a provisional application. Provisional patent applications do not, after all, mature into full patents unless an inventor files a standard patent application within one year after the provisional patent is filed. And provisional patent applications are not necessarily any easier to file, since in both cases, inventors are encouraged to make their disclosures as complete as possible.

"Whether a patent will be granted is determined, in large measure, by the choice of wording of the claims," the government Web site reveals. And if an entrepreneur is going to go to the trouble of making the very best patent application that he possibly can, he may want to file the standard application right away and get the whole process over with.

Another reason to think twice about filing a provisional application is that it is often difficult for busy entrepreneurs to keep track of when the provisional application is going to expire. And if an entrepreneur allows his provisional application to lapse and his "patent pending" invention is already in use, or on sale, in the United States, the inventor may lose the right to ever patent the invention.

Most entrepreneurs agree that filing for a patent is both stressful and expensive. The "fees" section of uspto.gov reveals that in addition to the original filing fees, an entrepreneur could find himself paying late fees, surcharges for additional claims, and additional fees when the patent issues. As time goes on, the inventor may need to pay to maintain his patent or to extend his patent's scope. Then, of course, after all of these governmental fees have been paid, an entrepreneur still has to find some way to pay his lawyer. But most entrepreneurs agree that this is money well spent.

Paying Your Lawyer

Regardless of whether an entrepreneur decides to go with a large, established law firm or a small, emerging firm, the most important question that an entrepreneur should ask when interviewing prospective lawyers is how the entrepreneur will be billed for the first year of legal service. Specifically, entrepreneurs should consider asking their lawyer whether there is any possibility that the law firm will accept shares in the company in lieu of cash during the first year. Many entrepreneurs find it advantageous to make their lawyers part owners of their businesses, because this provides an extra incentive for the lawyers to open doors on the company's behalf.

After an entrepreneur has explored the possibility of paying his lawyer with equity in his young company, he should ask the lawyer about his hourly rate. When considering the possibility of paying one's lawyer with cash, entrepreneurs should keep in mind that law firms with a history of working with high-tech start-ups will generally offer more affordable billing systems to their start-up clients, since their entire operation is optimized to provide cost-effective services to start-ups.

One way that some law firms bring down the price of legal advice during a company's first year is by using standardized legal documents to fulfill a company's legal needs. But billing systems can vary greatly from law firm to law firm. In the old days, corporate lawyer Andrew Updegrove tells me, some law firms delivered formal bills to their start-up clients every month, "but how hard you tried to collect varied on the circumstances and the firm and that sort of thing." Updegrove's own solution to a start-up client's problem of not being able to pay their legal bills is to avoid running up gigantic bills in the first place. "The typical start-up with nothing but a business plan might only need a couple of thousand dollars of legal services before they get financed, if you do it right," he says.

Some law firms allow clients to run up $10,000 worth of services before they send out a bill and then assume that the start-up will avoid paying this bill until they get financed. Other law firms will give entrepreneurs an "introductory rate," which is substantially discounted from their normal rate, until the start-up receives a significant amount of financing. Still other law firms offer something called a "deferred payment with 25 percent uptake," where they refrain from charging anything at all until the start-up receives financing and then send a bill for the full fee plus 25 percent. This additional fee acknowledges the fact that in choosing to work with a start-up company, the law firm is taking the risk that the start-up may never receive financing and that the law firm may never get paid.

Because it is definitely in an entrepreneur's best interests to have a lawyer on his side looking for unforeseen legal glitches, an entrepreneur would do well to have an honest dialogue with their lawyers *before* the clock starts ticking.

Choose an Unpopular Research Area

Sometime ago, entrepreneur Tim Cargol decided to start a company to sell hardware supplies over the Internet. He named his business toolmill.com, he gathered together a couple of friends, and he entered his plan into MIT's $50,000 business-plan competition. But when the team finally had their chance to stand before the judges, Cargol realized that his on-line hardware business didn't have a whole lot going for it.

"The $50K review team asked all the right questions, and we didn't have the right answers," Cargol remembers. When Cargol was asked, "Why are you two the best people in the world to do what you're doing?" he didn't know what to answer. "And the real answer was, we weren't," Cargol says.

Shortly thereafter, Cargol abandoned his plans for starting an Internet hardware store and devoted himself to finishing his master's degree.

Cargol's master's thesis involved figuring out a way to solve a particularly vexing problem that has been plaguing the electric-power industry for years. The problem has to do with an extremely nasty box called a load tap changer, or LTC, which has a tendency to break without warning. When an LTC breaks down, the electric-power utility loses between $250,000 and $1 million per hour until the box is repaired. But that's not the worst part. When a box that routes a million dollars' worth of electricity per hour breaks down, the consequences can be devastating.

One need only examine recent news reports from the state of California to see how society at large is affected by the loss of power. And it is not unheard of for innocent bystanders to be maimed, or even killed, when an LTC explodes. "If you've ever seen one of those pictures on TV, with the camera focused on a metal box that has flames shooting out the top," you've seen the remains of an LTC, Cargol says. "The shrapnel from the exploding metal can cause other transformers and other circuit breakers to explode. And then the oil inside catches fire, of course, and that's bad.

"Sometimes they'll let it burn for a day or two until it's cool enough for them to come in and size up the situation. But in the meantime, they may be paying that quarter of a million dollars an hour to reroute the electricity."

To help electric-power utilities predict when their LTCs will need to be replaced, Cargol and his partner, Dr. Chat Cooke, developed a special device called a nondestructive breakdown oil tester. Cargol designed his device to sit inside an LTC and monitor the quality of the oil. Once it has been installed, the device will send information about the state of the load tap changer back to the start-up's computers for analysis. The utilities can then access information about how the equipment is doing.

Given the fact that 50 percent of all electric-utility failures have to do with the failure of an LTC, Tim Cargol believes that there will be a big demand for his company's devices.

But he doesn't expect to have much competition.

Speaking of the actual process of creating his nondestructive breakdown oil tester, Cargol says, "You work with oil, and it's physically dirty. You get oil all over your clothes a lot of the time." Additionally, the physical process of getting these devices into the field can be rather treacherous.

To test the device, Cargol was obliged to climb up a ten-foot fiberglass ladder, physically stand within several feet of quarter-million volt transmission lines, and make contact with the dangerous LTC.

"The first time I was up there, I realized that that's not a place that most engineers are going to want to do a lot of work," Cargol says. "It's scary, it's dangerous, and you'd best know what you're doing, unless you're crazy."

Standing on the fiberglass ladder, Cargol could literally feel the volts rushing past. "The hair on your arms is standing up, and you need to maintain contact with the transformer so that you don't charge up and get a nasty shock when you touch it again," Cargol says.

Given the extreme danger of working with LTCs, Cargol estimates that there are few people in the world who would try to compete with him. But if anyone does, they are likely to be scared away by the math.

"The technology is a difficult blend of space-shuttle electronics," Cargol says. "It's not some kind of consumer-grade 'let's just throw in a couple of transistors and hope that it works' system. You have to work with submicrosecond pulse technology, and there is a tremendous amount of electromagnetic noise that you have to deal with."

Most of the people on planet Earth simply don't have the right combination of knowledge and guts to replicate what Cargol and Cooke are doing. But if anyone tries to compete with them, "there is the patented technology," Cargol says. "Which you can read about if you want, but it's kind of technical. And we're confident that there isn't another solution."

Shout It from the Mountaintop

The biggest reason why it's a good idea to apply for one or more patents and to pay top dollar for the kind of attorneys who know how to fill out the applications properly is so that an entrepreneur can feel more comfortable talking about his idea. And as the case of Direct Hit attests, it is extremely valuable to feel comfortable talking about your idea.

When the Internet search engine Direct Hit first went into business, cofounder Gary Culliss made it his job to tell everyone he knew what he was doing. Because Culliss had already filed several patent applications, he wasn't worried about having his idea stolen. And because he was not concerned about having his idea stolen, Culliss was able to speak freely to journalists, telling them whatever they wanted to know about his company.

As part of his awareness-raising campaign, Culliss paid a visit to a professor at Harvard Law School who was regarded as an expert on the Internet. "I sat down with him for about thirty minutes," Culliss said, "and I said, 'Hey, you're interested in the Internet. This is what we're doing. Do you know anybody that I should be talking to?'"

Shortly after Culliss told the professor about his idea, the professor was contacted by a reporter from the *Wall Street Journal* who wanted information about the latest developments on the World Wide Web. Impressed by his recent visit with the enthusiastic Gary Culliss, the professor mentioned Direct Hit, and shortly thereafter the company was featured in a prominent article. "In some ways you could say that this was entirely accidental," Culliss admits, "but I don't think it was accidental because of my pitch."

On another occasion, Culliss sent an E-mail to a researcher who had released a study about the size of the World Wide Web. Culliss's E-mail congratulated the man on his important work and explained how Direct

Hit was helping to solve the problem of information overload. The researcher responded favorably to Cullis's E-mail, and Culliss sealed the friendship by offering to let the researcher try out his new demo. Shortly thereafter, the researcher received a call from the *Industry Standard*, asking for his opinion on search engines. "The first thing he did was mention Direct Hit," Culliss says, "and we ended up being one of three search technologies featured in an *Industry Standard* cover story."

When he wasn't cultivating friendships with independent consultants, Culliss tried to establish relationships with journalists directly. If Culliss noticed that a journalist had written an article about Internet search engines, he would send the journalist an E-mail referencing the article and mentioning something about Direct Hit. He made a list of between fifty and one hundred journalists that he would contact on a regular basis, often with little more than a postcard describing something that Direct Hit had recently done.

Culliss emphasizes that there is a difference between mass-mailing postcards and developing a strategic publicity program. "It can be done in an intelligent way that makes sense," he instructs. Instead of trusting the job to a public-relations agency, Culliss took the time to put the journalist's first name on each postcard and to personally sign each one.

"I think that journalists are very hardened and turned off by the PR agencies," Culliss muses, noting that with one PR team handling between five and seven different companies, "it's impossible for them to really concentrate on what they do, which is to build those relationships with the journalists interested in your specific area." Culliss himself is a strong proponent of developing one-on-one relationships with journalists and trying to understand them as human beings. "Personal attention is really appreciated by journalists," he says. "They are so used to just receiving shotgun press releases that when they get somebody on the phone who can intelligently discuss the technology or the product, they are very appreciative. That tends to be reflected in the amount of ink that they dedicate to the product or the technology."

When Direct Hit was ultimately acquired by rival search engine Ask Jeeves, the "presence" that the company had managed to establish for itself in the "marketplace" of people who used search engines was one of the key factors used to determine the company's value. The other key factor, Culliss says, was Direct Hit's ability to "compete for, and win, new business."

It would have been much harder for Direct Hit to compete for new business if its fundamental search methods had been less robust or if its engineering team had been less effective. But it seems clear that the company's ability to win new business was directly tied to its knack for garnering favorable press coverage.

Indeed, when Cullis was asked what specific things had the greatest impact on the company's eventual success, he referred not to his four patents or to the long hours he had worked but rather to the awards that the company had won and to the articles in which the company had been favorably mentioned.

One article in particular, which listed the winners of CNET's 1999 "Search Engine Shootout," seemed to have a particularly profound effect on the development of the Direct Hit presence. "People who are interested in search engines read those announcements of the awards, and it just continues to feed upon itself," Culliss explains, "because then people want to use your technology more. That gets you more mind share in the marketplace and more consideration for more search-engine shoot-outs, and it just goes on from there. If you maintain the quality of the product, you end up winning."

Chapter Five

IT'S THE PEOPLE

How to Attract Dynamic Individuals to
Your High-Tech Start-up—And Keep
Them from Burning Out

T he first time I met Andy Mulkerin I was at a party in Cambridge
with a bunch of high-tech start-up employees. I asked Mulkerin
what he did for a living, and he told me he was a process manager
for E Ink Corporation. And then something strange happened. As Mulkerin began to talk about his job, his eyes grew wide, and he took on the
glazed, unfocused look of a religious ecstatic. Apparently, Andy Mulkerin
loves his work.

"Today you should have seen us," he gushed. "We were on fire.
Everyone was moving fast, all cylinders were firing, and it was just going
perfectly. Everyone was happy and smiling and joking around." But as
Mulkerin described his day, his rapture was replaced by pangs of guilt for
having left the office to come to the party. Although Mulkerin was happy
to discuss the joys of being process manager, it seemed clear that he
would be more comfortable if we continued our conversation at E Ink itself.

I scheduled my visit for 7:00 P.M. the following Thursday—twelve
hours after Mulkerin had arrived at the office. But even though I had
gone out of my way to choose a time of day when Mulkerin was supposed to be resting, I get the feeling that my presence is slowing him

down. As I scan through my list of questions and set up my tape recorder, Mulkerin jumps up from the table, removes a pepperoni pizza from the company's refrigerator, and pops it into the microwave.

"You'll have to excuse me while I eat my dinner," he says.

Not a problem, I reply. Actually, I am intrigued by the fact that Mulkerin is choosing to eat his dinner here in the E Ink break room after having spent the previous twelve hours in the same building. Is it normal for him to eat all of his meals at E Ink?

Mulkerin replies by describing the elaborate lengths to which he goes to avoid setting foot outside the building. "I discovered that there are two main reasons why I would want to leave work," he explains. "The first is that I start to get a little bit tired, and the second is that I want to change my socks. So, to extend my day, I bought myself a bunch of clean socks." But even with the supply of clean socks, Mulkerin admits there are some times when he just has to go home. "If I could work more than twelve hours a day, I would," he explains. "The problem is that I just stop making sense after a while. My problem-solving skills go down, and my body functions start malfunctioning. You can only work so much during a day."

With that said, Mulkerin has discovered that if he does a little advance planning, he can put in more hours. "I'm planning on getting out of here early tonight so I can get to bed early, knowing that I'm going to be here all tomorrow night, but you've got to pick and choose your battles," he warns. And when Mulkerin does pull an all-nighter, "you end up losing focus at like ten A.M."

When Mulkerin feels himself beginning to lose focus, "I go get myself a large coffee," he says. "I don't know if it's too healthy, but I love it. It gets me a second wind, and I'm zipping around again." As if to prove his point, he zips over to the microwave and removes the now-hot pepperoni pizza. "It may just be the caffeine, but it's something. I just feel like it extends my day, if only psychologically. And that's good."

Although Mulkerin is doing everything he can think of to increase the amount of time he is able to work, he can only do so much. Fortunately, he has received clearance to hire several new employees.

The employees in Mulkerin's manufacturing group are unique among E Ink employees because the work they are doing—manually assembling the company's electronic signs—does not require a great deal of previous training. And this means that Mulkerin can choose his new employees based on their attitude rather than their previous experience. "I'm really just looking for a sharp pair of eyes," he explains. "I'm very confident that I can teach people everything they need to know as long as they are willing to listen and not jump to conclusions."

The practice of hiring people based on their willingness to learn rather than on their previous experience is not all that common among companies that hire unskilled and semiskilled workers. "The temp agencies aren't used to people who are willing to take a chance on anyone who has the interest," Mulkerin says. "I tell them not to worry about the person's experience. I just need people with good energy. The number one criterion for someone to come to work in my group is that the person has to care and want to be there. I can do so much with a person like that."

Mulkerin has watched more than one person transition from a jaded temporary worker to a highly motivated member of his manufacturing group once they understand that their stock options make them part owners of the business. "Some of them have been told what to do for years and years, but now they have a stake in the company," he says. "When the signs don't come out right, they try to figure out how to make them better. They really do care about what they're doing because they see that we're all in this together."

Attitude Really Does Matter

Unlike Mulkerin, when entrepreneur Vanu Bose is looking for new employees for his software radio company, Vanu, Inc., he looks for recruits with vast amounts of engineering experience. But Bose shares Mulkerin's belief in the importance of locating employees with the right attitude.

"When I went around and talked to the various people that I knew I wanted to work with, I had a very strict filter," Bose said. If the interviewee was interested but was concerned about potential obstacles to the start-up, Bose automatically put him into the "maybe later" category. Conversely: "Anyone who said it sounded like a good idea, acknowledged that there were obstacles, but knew that together we could figure it out, was an immediate hire."

Bose's hiring strategy provides him with ample opportunity to screen out those individuals who do not share his attitude toward risk taking. "If they're analyzing ways it might fail, it's not the right mentality," Bose says. "When you're presented with something, you can do two things. You can look at the positives, or you can look at the negatives. I look at the positives first. If the positives don't add up to something that is worthwhile, you don't even have to look at the negatives. But if the positives are really high, you might say you want to do it, anyway, even if the negatives were also high."

If a person looks at the negatives first, it will spoil their opinion of the entire project. "You'll say, 'Oh, no, there are all these problems,' and you won't analyze the positives properly," Bose warns. "I was looking for people who were looking at the upside. And in the process of that, they were thinking about things not as problems but as challenges we were going to have to overcome."

One of the first people that Bose talked to after making the decision to start his company was a high school friend named Andy Beard. Bose's goal in talking to Beard was simply to get some legal advice, but Beard surprised him by volunteering to join the company. "I never would have considered asking him because I didn't think he was the kind of person with the right attitude," Bose said. "But his answer gave me the right attitude when I wasn't even looking for it."

The answer that Beard gave was that although the company could benefit from some good legal advice, it could benefit even more from the addition of a full-time lawyer. "He basically said that it was a great idea and that he would be a great asset," Bose recalls. Instead of listening to the company's potential pitfalls and evaluating them one by one, "it was almost him selling me on the thing."

When Bose thought about Beard's family situation (married with two children) and career situation (on the partner track at a prestigious law firm), he didn't think that his friend would want to drop everything and start a company.

"I was dumbfounded," Bose says. "I didn't think he was the start-up kind of person. But as soon as I explained the idea to him, he said, 'Look, I'm in if you want to go ahead with this.'"

Get It Right the First Time

When Vanu Bose was deciding who to choose as his cofounders, he consulted the book *Hiring Smart! How to Predict Winners & Losers in the Incredibly Expensive People-Reading Game* by Dr. Pierre Mornell. The book is filled with all sorts of useful bits of information gleaned from Mornell's years as a psychiatrist and hiring consultant. For example, "It's illegal to ask about a candidate's marital status, but the practice is widespread, especially with candidates for top executive positions."

When considering a person for a high-tech start-up, it is useful to approach them in the way that Bose did, as a friend asking for some free advice, rather than as a potential employer. Getting to know a potential hire outside the context of an official job interview—say, by inviting the person to have a beer with you at the Muddy Charles Pub—allows you to gauge how much effort the person is willing to spend on their career without breaking any employment laws.

Avoid the Bad Apples

Bose and Mulkerin both know what they are looking for, but they also know—almost intuitively—what they don't want. Likewise, any successful entrepreneur has to learn to identify the warning signs of an unsuitable employee.

The kind of person who is wrong for a high-tech start-up is a person who has an extremely large ego. "You have a lot of people in this space who can be very technically competent but are ruled out because of how they are going to interact with the team," warns high-tech headhunter Eileen Foley. According to Foley, a person who has been top dog at a large and established company for a number of years is likely to have a difficult time adjusting to the crazy world of a high-tech start-up. "Most of the companies that are putting together their team for the first time are incredibly sensitive to this personality type," Foley says, "because there is only so much room for big egos."

Experienced entrepreneurs emphasize the importance of checking references to avoid getting involved with the wrong person. When someone says that they didn't have a good relationship with their partner, entrepreneurs stress the importance of finding out *why* their last relationship didn't work out. They suggest asking questions like "How is this person in a tough situation? How does this person respond to other people's suggestions? When the chips are down, does he blame other people, or does he take responsibility?"

Checking References

In his book *Hiring Smart,* hiring expert Dr. Pierre Mornell recommends calling references during their lunchtime, with the intention of reaching an assistant or a voice mail, and asking the reference to return your call. "If the candidate is outstanding or excellent, I guarantee that eight out of ten people will respond quickly and want to help," Mornell writes. "However, if only two or three of the ten references selected by the candidate return your call, this message is also loud and clear."

When you do speak with the reference, it's a good idea to give the reference as much time as he needs to say what he wants to say. If you get the feeling that your reference may be unwilling to share some critical information, consider asking the reference for additional references.

All of this reference checking may yield information that you do not want to hear, but it's much better to hear this negative information before you commit to hiring the candidate than after you have entered into a binding legal contract.

Is the Candidate a Team Player?

When Mark Eichin was interviewing techies for the high-tech startup known as Fast Engines, he developed certain tests to figure out whether or not the candidates would be able to work in a team environment. "You just ask them about some project they've worked on, get them to describe it, and start asking them about what problems they've had," Eichin instructs.

By asking candidates to describe the different problems they have run into, Eichin can tell how much experience the engineers have had working in a given area. But more importantly, if the engineer is able to describe the problems he has previously dealt with, Eichin can get a sense of the person's ability to communicate in general. (It is not unusual to find someone who is a very gifted individual programmer but who cannot communicate with other people in a useful way. And although it is possible to hire these people, Eichin feels that it is better to keep them as single-project subcontractors, rather than members of the team.)

Lessons from the MIT Blackjack Team

Before a would-be blackjack player is allowed to play with the MIT team, he must pass a variety of tests, or "checkouts." The checkouts allow team leaders to judge players not only on their ability to count cards but also on their ability to respond to unforeseen circumstances. "We try to simulate the casino environment as much as possible, including distracting the players," says Andy Bloch, a Harvard-educated attorney-at-law and former MIT team leader. Occasionally, members of the MIT blackjack team will attempt to cheat the players either by paying them too little or trying to take the money when they have won their bets.

"We probably have some of the hardest tests of any blackjack team," Bloch says proudly.

The MIT blackjack team has at least three different levels of checkouts, designed to determine whether a person is ready for the role of "back counter," "spotter," or "big player." Before a person can assume the role of back counter, he must prove his ability to keep track of the relative supply of high and low cards as the dealer works his way through fifteen different decks.

"You can make maybe three mistakes," Bloch says. "If you make too many mistakes, you have to start over from the beginning."

Before a would-be player is allowed to serve as a spotter and actually gamble with the team's money, he must demonstrate his ability to count cards and play blackjack at the same time. For this checkout, "if you made any strategy errors, it was an automatic failure," Bloch says. "If you got cheated once, it was an automatic failure. If you made too many counting mistakes, you failed and had to start over from the beginning. Usually that meant waiting until the next week to try again."

The most difficult tests of all were reserved for those who wished to serve as big players: carrying large amounts of cash and betting the maximum amount when the count was good. The big-player checkout required candidates to keep a running count through twenty-five decks of cards, to make bets, to vary their bets depending on the count, and to utilize a variety of different strategies to prevent the dealer from figuring out that they were counting cards.

"I don't know anyone who ever passed that the first time they tried," Bloch says. "People have taken months and months to pass that test. Some people give up eventually."

During the highest-level checkout, team leaders typically bring in a couple of extra team members whose sole job is to distract the player who is taking the test.

"We probably used to go a little overboard in our checkouts," Bloch says. "But I think it's very important to do at least some level of checkout and know how many mistakes you are making."

There are good reasons why the members of the MIT blackjack team are so picky about who is, and is not, allowed to gamble with the team's money. Team leaders understand that even if a card counter tests well, plays well, and reports all of his winnings, he could still lose money on a given trip. "If they have an expectation on a trip of, let's say, $10,000, they could win or lose $50,000," Bloch says. "If they came back saying that they lost $20,000 or won $30,000, you wouldn't know if those numbers are accurate or not."

In other words, even with the elaborate checkout process, the team leaders still have no way of knowing how a given gambler is going to do in a given weekend. "You can never really predict exactly what the outcome is going to be," Bloch says. "You can know that on the average we expect to make $5,000, $10,000, $50,000, or $2,000 on a trip, but you never really know."

The team leaders have no way of predicting whether their players are going to have their pockets picked while they are counting cards or whether the team will have its communal pocket picked by players who do not report their winnings. "You're not going to be able to supervise them," Bloch says. "You never really know whether they are even playing. Maybe they go and drink, which is against our team's rules. Or maybe they are playing well but they are stealing from the team. You really don't know. You have to trust them."

Make Your Company's Presence Known

Before an entrepreneur can determine which candidates seem trustworthy and which do not, he needs to attract some job applicants in the first place. But with the amount of money flowing into high-tech startups these days, good help is becoming harder and harder to find.

One obvious place to look for top-notch high-tech talent is at the career fairs sponsored by prestigious universities. But entrepreneurs must employ a wide variety of creative strategies if they want to stand out from all the other high-tech companies that are also vying for the students' attention. To increase their company's visibility at the MIT Career Fair, engineers from E Ink hung up one of the company's new electronic signs and programmed it to flash the message "E Ink is hiring." But the flashing sign, and the booth that went with it were only the tip of the iceberg.

The Monday before the career fair, representatives of E Ink arranged to have a slide of the company's logo displayed during the previews before the movie *Fight Club,* which was shown on the MIT campus. To increase the company's appeal among the *Fight Club* audience, the engineers positioned the E Ink logo on the side of a rubber-band-powered Styrofoam rocket. When the image of the company's logo, attached to a Styrofoam "finger blaster," was shown on the big screen, a representative of E Ink fired an identical rocket into the air above the audience. This three-dimensional rocket broke the beam of light coming from the movie projector and informed everyone present that E Ink was standing by. The day of the MIT career fair, the company distributed hundreds of these same finger blasters, all equipped with the words "E Ink is hiring," to anyone who stopped by their booth.

Sometime later, engineer Holly Gates figured out a way to use MIT's prestigious robot-design contest, 6.270, to promote the company. Gates knew that the electrical engineers who turned out for the robot-design contest were likely to possess the skills that E Ink was looking for. To gain their attention, Gates brought an E Ink sign to the contest and set it up next to the stage. Throughout the evening, whenever a robot was eliminated, Gates would put a message on the screen telling the audience what had happened.

When E Ink cofounder Barrett Comiskey tried to reserve a booth at

Stanford University's career fair, he found out that all of the spots had already been taken by Silicon Valley Internet companies. But that didn't stop him from recruiting at the fair. Although the university's two official white tents were already filled to capacity, he was able to set up his own personal camping tent in an empty space in front of a decorative fountain. After programming an electronic sign to flash the message "E Ink is hiring," he started to collect résumés.

When one of the event's official organizers came over to the makeshift "booth" and told Comiskey that it was unfair to the Internet companies for him to collect résumés without paying any money, Comiskey amended the situation by paying the registration fee on the spot. After the money had changed hands, the event organizer walked away satisfied, allowing Comiskey to keep right on collecting résumés in the prime spot between the two official tents.

The Importance of Being Scientific

Piggybacking on university-sponsored events is a good way to attract student engineers to a high-tech start-up, but when a company wants to attract employees with industry experience, it needs to go out into the real world. When Comiskey wanted to collect résumés from experienced colloid scientists, he left the world of university career fairs and went straight to the annual meeting of the American Chemical Society.

Figuring that the American Chemical Society would be happy to help a company that was going out of its way to attract attention to the field of colloid science, Comiskey predicted that the event's leaders would not mind if he borrowed a bulletin board during the conference's official "poster session" from a colloid scientist who had forgotten to show up.

To make it easier for conference organizers to approve his unusual poster, Comiskey waited until the woman in charge was busy before asking for permission to use the vacant space. After a yes answer had been obtained, Comiskey fastened his sign to the bulletin board and programmed it to flash the message "E Ink is hiring." (To validate his claim that E Ink signs were, in fact, both important and scientific, Comiskey hung up an article from the scientific journal *Nature* that had highlighted the company's unique contribution to the field of colloid science.)

The response that Comiskey received was overwhelming. Nearly everyone who visited the poster session stopped to look at the E Ink sign and glance at the reprint from *Nature* magazine. And just as Comiskey had predicted, most of the people who happened by had the kind of backgrounds that E Ink had been looking for, and a number of them expressed interest in setting up an interview.

Although E Ink's innovative recruiting strategies were useful in raising the company's profile among prospective hires, Comiskey admits that part of the reason why E Ink's hiring efforts have been so effective is that the company has established its reputation through more conventional channels. "We've had a consistent amount of good press," Comiskey says, "and it has been increasing because we pay people to make sure it happens. So when we go and cut deals or when we do recruiting, I'm not this nobody from MIT trying to explain what the hell we do. When I meet someone, they have already read about us in the *Journal* or *Nature* or *USA Today* or *Wired* or *Popular Science*. They say, 'Oh, yeah, you are the guys who do this.' Even if they get it technically wrong, I'm starting from a huge advantage. I don't have to do any selling of the original explanation of what's going on because they already know the basic story."

Nothing Succeeds Like Success

Once an entrepreneur succeeds at obtaining some favorable press, raising VC financing from a prestigious VC firm, or convincing a prominent individual to take a seat on his board of directors, it becomes a great deal easier to hire the next group of employees. Likewise, once a start-up has established a reputation as a hot new company, it becomes easier to convince recruiters to hire employees on the company's behalf.

Headhunters take pride in their ability to figure out which companies are going to be the most successful and in their ability to fill those companies with the most dynamic individuals in their databases. "Candidates come to us because they believe that we have access to the best jobs," says recruiter Eileen Foley. "If you can get people access to what they consider the hot jobs in Boston, the ones that are giving the most options and the best packages, it puts you ahead."

To figure out which companies are hot, headhunters study which VC firm bothered to invest in the start-up and who the founders have convinced to serve on their board of directors. "Who are the people in play over there?" asks recruiter Scott Dunlop. "Are these people who have been there and done that, or are these twenty-two-year-old guys who have done this in their basement? That sometimes works as well, but it's important that they have some 'name-brand' people."

The name-brand people that Dunlop refers to are people who have come out of companies that have already become household names. The implication is that if start-ups can attract experienced talent from their more established counterparts, they can be forgiven for having a founder who lacks experience.

To ensure that a high-tech start-up will receive access to the best résumés in a headhunter's database, it's a good idea to woo recruiters in the same way that one would woo an employee or VC. Recruiters can be influenced by news articles about the company, recommendations from previous clients, and compelling demonstrations of the product or service that is being developed. If these things don't work, they can also be influenced by outright bribery.

One headhunter told a story about a company that was trying very hard to attract employees in preparation for its initial public offering, just weeks away. The company was offering phenomenal compensation packages, but it was not content to let money alone do the talking. To ensure that it would receive the best candidates around, the company declared that the headhunter who brought in the most candidates within a certain number of weeks would receive her very own Porsche.

"Are you talking about a *car*?" the headhunter asked the company's representative when she first learned of the unusual offer. "Because the only kind of Porsche I know about is a car."

Yes, the rep assured her, his company was indeed offering a bona-fide, adult-sized Porsche car to the headhunter who could bring in the most employees.

The offer of the Porsche certainly got the headhunter's attention, but I got the impression that she was not planning to go out of her way to steer candidates toward that particular company.

A Fun Place to Work

To gain mind share in an increasingly competitive environment, high-tech start-ups are going out of their way to offer their employees a "cool" work environment. At high-tech start-up Abuzz, employee Dan Dunn delights in the fact that he is allowed to bring his German shepherd to the office. Foosball tables, table tennis, basketball hoops, and scaled-down hockey rinks are common sights within high-tech start-ups. And if you pay a visit to Color Kinetics Corporation, "you can't miss a Nerf tennis match," laughs founder George Mueller. "We haven't come up with a prize yet, but we're thinking of a vacation day or maybe a flight somewhere."

Mueller takes great pride in the games, gadgets, and foodstuffs that he has procured for his employees at Color Kinetics. "We have a Tempest game, and we also have a gigantic green ball," he brags. He describes a peculiar sporting event, the Green Ball Game, that seems to amuse him as much as it entertains his employees. "You take the ball, and you try to roll it down the main aisleway," Mueller instructs. Participants in the green ball championships can compete in various categories, according to their gender and age. "There is the WGBA, the Women's Green Ball Association; the GBA; the Green Ball Association; and the Senior League, for the people over thirty. That shows you how young we are."

If employees become hungry throwing the green ball around the office, they can head over to the Color Kinetics kitchenette, where the supply of food appears to be infinite. "We have so much food that you could eat here full-time," Mueller says. "We do lunches on a regular basis, and we have HomeRuns deliver food to our office every other week. We've had every different kind of chip and snack and chocolate that's around: dark chocolate, Pepsi, Coke, pizza, Fluff, Nutrigrain waffles." Gesturing toward a second cupboard, he continues: "Nilla wafers, Air Crisps, peanut butter and jelly." As if that were not enough, the company gets fresh bagels delivered several times a month.

How Much Is a Stock Option Worth?

The more money a company has, the more it can afford to spend on its employees. But the cookies, candies, and office games only help to obscure what is already a very confusing process: figuring out which company is right for whom.

Some start-up employees are extremely savvy about evaluating the different offers they receive from high-tech start-ups, which almost always include the opportunity to buy the company's stock at a heavily discounted rate. But since many more employees have only a vague understanding of what is meant by the phrase "stock options," it's a good idea for entrepreneurs to make certain that candidates understand what they are being offered.

It's easy to understand the difference between a salary of $70,000 and a salary of $110,000, but it's much harder to figure out whether 2,500 stock options from company A will be worth more, or less, than 8,000 stock options from company B. There is no law saying that every company must issue the same number of shares of stock; in fact, the number of shares that are issued by new high-tech companies varies drastically from company to company.

To make matters even more confusing, there is no way to tell what these stock options are going to be worth when it comes time to redeem the options. A company that was incorporated only yesterday could be filing for bankruptcy in twelve months' time, or it could be worth billions of dollars. (If this comment seems unbelievable, consider the case of Akamai Technologies. Incorporated on August 20, 1998, the company filed for its IPO on August 20, 1999, a year to the day after it was incorporated. At the end of the first day of trading, Akamai's stock had a market capitalization of approximately $10 billion.)

Because things are so uncertain, start-up employees often rely on certain preconceived notions, based on rumors and past experiences, to help them decide which offers to accept. To illustrate this point, head-hunter Eileen Foley tells a story about an Internet company that was providing excellent offers in terms of money but only giving between 2,500 and 5,000 stock options. "All of the candidates were very young guys in their early twenties, coming out of Fidelity and SIG and these start-up companies, and they turned down the offers based on the amount of shares alone," Foley remembers. "They all felt like they should be getting 30,000 or 40,000 options. The company kept saying, 'You know, we're so close to going public, there aren't those kinds of shares.' Well, today that stock is trading at $227 a share, and it's already split, so they would have made millions on their stock. But they were naive to the difference in where the stocks were priced."

To make certain that high-tech employees understand exactly how much potential value they are being offered, entrepreneurs should talk with candidates about stock-option packages before the candidates have had a chance to make up their minds. The start-up world is filled with stories of employees who walked away from extremely lucrative options packages either because they did not understand the real value or were not willing to take the risk that the options would ever become liquid.

Recruiter Scott Dunlop tells a story about a candidate who had to choose between working at an Internet start-up and taking a job at the consulting firm Ernst & Young. The base salaries being offered by the two companies were relatively similar; the chief difference was that the start-up was offering 7,000 stock options. Try as he might, Dunlop was unable to make it clear to the candidate that $2,000, after taxes, was likely to be worth a great deal less than the 7,000 stock options he was being offered at the start-up. In the end, Dunlop remembers, the candidate traded 7,000 shares of a highly valuable stock for $2,000 more in base salary at Ernst & Young. "He probably, realistically, had been sitting on $500,000 or $700,000 worth of options," Dunlop explains. "We were speaking a language that he didn't understand."

Because it is so difficult to figure out how much a given stock option is going to be worth, savvy employees focus on those aspects of the start-up experience that cannot readily be quantified. For example: "I didn't work at Fast Engines because I was getting a biweekly salary," says start-up employee Mark Eichin. "I worked on it because it was interesting. I put a lot of my spare time into the project, too, because I was convinced that people needed it and that it would be successful."

Control, Freedom, and Recognition

The people who hang out at the Muddy Charles Pub agree that the most important part of one's high-tech experience is not the salary that one takes home but rather the way that one is treated by one's fellow employees. Instead of bragging about the size of their paychecks, high-tech employees boast about how much control they have over their workday.

Employees want to have the freedom to decorate their offices as they like, to eat when and where they choose, and to dress in whatever clothing makes them most comfortable. They want the freedom to choose the type of computer that they will work on, the kind of operating system they will work in, and the programming language they will use to write their code.

If the high-tech employee uses these freedoms to create something that is better than what was there before, he wants to be recognized for this accomplishment. "To me, recognition is more important than money," says senior design architect Nancy Nangeroni. "My personal philosophy is that what most of us really need and want in this world is attention. We need to know that other people care about us."

The kind of attention that Nangeroni values most does not cost anything to administer, but it does require a certain perceptiveness on the part of one's management team. "Tell other people that this employee did something good," Nangeroni suggests. "But you don't want to make more of a big deal about it than whatever was done was worth. If somebody contributed a nice little technical innovation, say, 'Hey, that was a great little technical innovation.' And maybe you mention it in a meeting. But that's enough, probably."

On the other hand, if somebody really does make a major contribution to the team's progress, "then maybe you trumpet it a little bit, and maybe you take a bunch of people out to dinner. Free meals, where everybody goes out and has dinner together, are a great thing."

When Mark Eichin and his friends talk about their ideal work environment, they emphasize the amount of freedom that is given to each engineer. When evaluating a particular high-tech start-up, Eichin and his friends pay attention to "how restrictive it is, how much they care, and how much they trust you. Do they allow telecommuting? Do they believe that if you're logged in from home you're actually getting work done? Do they believe that you get more stuff done on your own time than you do when you're sitting in the office, anyway?

"For some types of work, you really have to be there because you're interacting with the rest of the group. But when you're doing stuff that you can do off on your own, anyway, when you've gotten the specs and you're just going to be spending the next three weeks coding, you don't need to deal with anyone else for that." During those periods, Eichin says, "if I get inspired, I can sit there and work for eight or ten hours at a stretch and then decide, at two o'clock in the morning, I guess I'll sleep late tomorrow. I will get as much, or more, done than someone who comes in nine to five and says, 'Oh, it's five o'clock. I guess I'll stop thinking about the problem now.' "

Even more important is whether a company's employees appear to believe in, or "buy into," the product or service that the company is selling. "Does the company get buy-in?" Eichin asks. "And at some levels, do they own your soul?"

How to Close on an Employee

This need for freedom provides a convenient opportunity for employers who are trying to lure potential engineers to their high-tech start-up. For example, when Randy Chan is trying to convince people to join his engineering group at E Ink Corporation, he emphasizes the amount of freedom they will have over their working environment. "I look to expand people," Chan says. "I allow employees to do whatever they want as long as we set milestones and goals and they meet them." Instead of requiring employees to ask him to sign off on all their projects, Randy tells them to simply go ahead and take some risks. Chan's attitude toward management is: "Don't ask me for permission. I want you to just go do it. I'll let you know if you're headed in the wrong direction."

Since E Ink is a start-up, Chan cannot promise his employees that the company is going to be around forever. "But I can provide them with what they never had: autonomy, the ability to make their own decisions and the go-do-it attitude, rather than five layers of management."

When Chan brings in new employees, he shows them what he means about giving them access to all levels of the corporation. A typical job interview involves individual chats with six to eight E Ink employees from diverse areas, such as technology, marketing, and manufacturing. Next, Chan shows candidates his own desk, located in the middle of the technology "bench" area. "I sit right here in the middle," Chan says. By showing candidates that his desk will be located in the employee's direct line of sight, he conveys the message that he will be truly accessible on a daily basis.

Chan's ulterior motive in giving employees the freedom to structure their workday in whatever way they like and in making himself available on a daily basis is to expose his engineers to something beyond the world of engineering. He tries to emphasize the benefits of this unique managerial style when he is trying to convince someone to accept a job. Working at E Ink, Chan says, means "sitting in an open space, ten feet away from one of the corporate officers and V.P.s, and knowing exactly, real time, why we are doing something with regard to our business and technical strategy.

"I actually let people read contracts that we're writing," Chan continues. "Proposals, joint ventures, et cetera, so that everybody understands why we're doing things. Because of my role in both technology and business development, I truly show them that they will also be in on the business aspects of the company."

Apparently, Chan's strategy of describing the company as a place to learn new skills has had the desired effect. "We had a software guy who had people throwing money at him to go to Texas and other places," Chan says. "Why did he join E Ink? Part of it was that he knew one of the engineers, and part of it was our technology, which he thought was cool. But one of the things he told me was that it's a place to learn. This start-up wasn't just going to stick him in a corner and feed him a bunch of doughnuts and tell him to hack. We were going to allow him to go out with the marketing people, we were going to allow him to go out with the technical people, and we were going to allow him to do a lot of things that he would never be able to do at a large, established company."

Chan is well aware of the fact that if he is going to recruit the most sought after high-tech employees, he will have to give them exactly what they are looking for. "The playing field is now leveled," he says. "You have kids coming out of school that are so smart and so ambitious that if I don't teach them this, they'll find somebody else to do it."

The rationale behind introducing engineers to all of the different parts of the organization is to provide them with the skills they will need to start their own companies someday. "All of them have told me this,"

Chan says. "They said, 'Randy, besides E Ink technology, we want to know what you know, quickly, so that when we go out and start companies of our own, we'll know what to do.'" Chan claims that he will rate his success as a manager by the number of calls he gets from his former employees asking him to come to work in their own start-up companies. "That's my scale," Chan explains. "Did I actually impact people enough to get calls? If I don't get any calls, that means that I've failed."

Burnout

After entrepreneurs have gone to the trouble of locating dynamic employees and getting them to sign on the bottom line, the last thing they want to deal with is losing these employees to engineering burnout. Unfortunately, the behaviors that cause engineers to burn out are the same behaviors that cause high-tech start-ups to succeed.

"Burnout is when you lose your ability to manage the pressure," says start-up veteran Nancy Nangeroni. "When you start reacting to every demand that comes to you, you wind up being consumed by the demand. You start falling behind, and pretty soon you're just going to break if you come to work anymore."

Once an employee has burned out, it becomes impossible for him to understand how to act in either his own best interests or those of the organization. To recover from burnout, it may be necessary for the employee to quit his job and immerse himself in an entirely different activity.

When Ed Zyszkowski was starting a high-tech company called Torrent, he operated on a schedule that was not sustainable. "To avoid traffic," Zyszkowski remembers, "I would jump in my car between six and six-thirty A.M. and get to the office just before seven. I would work until two or two-thirty in the morning, get back in the car, get home at three A.M., jump into bed, and wake up again at five A.M. or so. That went on for three years, and interspersed with that was a lot of travel. You just need to have the ability to do that. I would say that's a part of the process."

"You end up with periods of sleep deprivation," warns Zyszkowski's wife, entrepreneur and angel investor Lori Fena. "That affects them adversely later on, because as the company grows, they just can't handle it. They can't stretch themselves, and they get replaced."

After three years of twenty-hour days, Zyszkowski was obliged to hand the reins over to someone else. "When I left my company, it was sort of painful, but I knew I had to do it," Zyszkowski says. "I was dying. I couldn't handle it anymore. Now I realize that this is part of the natural order of things. You wind up being there, but at a certain point you have to let go. It's kind of like when kids grow up and it's time for them to go to college and you can't baby-sit them anymore."

It's Like Blowing a Fuse Inside Your Head

"I got burned out by NBX," Pehr Anderson remembers. "I got so incredibly burned out from NBX that when I left the company, I spent a month in bed, trying to figure out what I was going to do with what was left of my life. As I was lying there in bed, my fingers would twitch as if I was going to write more code."

Before Pehr acknowledged his burnout and left NBX Corporation, there were some extremely stressful moments. One particular stressful moment occurred on a muggy evening during the month of August 1997. I was able to observe the incident firsthand because I had spent the evening hanging around the start-up—reading magazines, surfing the Internet, and washing our clothes at a Laundromat two blocks away.

Pehr and his colleagues were gathered behind closed doors in the NBX conference room, having an official meeting, but I could see their heads through a glass window. At around seven-fifteen P.M., I passed by this glass window on my way to the Laundromat to move our wet clothing from the washer to the dryer. But as soon as I got outside, I noticed something rather strange: There were no lights in the windows of any of the buildings along Kirkland Street. Apparently, the city of Cambridge was experiencing a power outage.

When I got to the Laundromat, I found our clothes at the bottom of the washing machine, still sopping wet. All around me people were stuffing wet clothes into plastic garbage bags and cursing about the lack of power. Because it was so late in the evening, it seemed clear that even if the power did come back on, it would not be possible to get the clothes dry before the Laundromat closed its doors.

The prospect of stuffing wet clothing into plastic garbage bags and carrying them across the street to our car seemed so demoralizing that I decided to ask Pehr for help.

Looking up and down the street at all of the darkened buildings, I assumed that it would be no trouble for Pehr to leave his meeting for a few minutes. But when I emerged from the Laundromat and turned right, I saw the glowing lights on the third floor of 120 Beacon Street.

As I walked toward NBX, I tried to decide whether I really wanted to interrupt Pehr's meeting to ask him to come help me move the laundry. And when I got to the third floor, I spent a few minutes lingering outside the conference room, deciding whether or not to make my presence known. I wasn't sure how Pehr would feel about my adding my laundry difficulties to the already tense atmosphere of the office meeting.

Earlier, Pehr had told me that the meeting's purpose was to allow all interested parties to voice their opinions about a certain software tool that the company was thinking of adopting. Pehr opposed this tool for a wide variety of extremely technical reasons, not the least of which was the fact that the tool was extremely expensive.

Before the meeting started, Pehr had tried to tell me why he was so vehemently opposed to the adoption of the software tool, but this explanation didn't make much sense to me. Although it was apparent that Pehr had developed a list of reasons why he was opposed to the new tool, in his burned-out state he could hardly articulate them. He didn't have the patience to translate his jargon-filled explanations into the kind of English that I understood, and he became annoyed when I proved unable to read his mind.

It seemed clear to me that if Pehr were unable to convince his wife that the software tool was a bad idea, he would be even less successful in dealing with his coworkers. To make matters worse, I could see that he didn't have the emotional reserves required to pay attention to anyone else's suggestions. His nerves were frayed, his eyes were bloodshot, and he was starting to become irritable.

Pehr believed that most of the people at the meeting had already decided to vote in favor of the new tool. Even worse, he also knew that in his burned-out state, he would not be able to convince them to change their minds. Pehr saw the meeting as a formality, designed to make the foregone conclusion seem like a group decision.

When I finally worked up the courage to tap on the glass window and ask Pehr to help me move the laundry, Pehr surprised me by jumping out of his chair and running out of the conference room.

Apparently, the meeting was going as badly as I had anticipated.

"I had said, 'Look, this is dangerous,'" Pehr recalls about the meeting. "I was worried about the future of the company being based on this thing because we didn't know whether it would work and we wouldn't have known for a very long period of time." However, others at NBX believed that although the untested software tools were likely to have some problems, they still represented the most efficient way to get the product out the door. Faced with the knowledge that his opinion was about to be overruled, Pehr was all too willing to duck out of the meeting and find out what I wanted. And when I told him about the streetwide power outage, his face brightened. The notion of an electrical power outage appealed to something at the core of Pehr's identity as an electrical engineer. An electrical-power outage meant that the rules of logic no longer applied. To Pehr, the loss of electrical power represented the loss of power itself. If the grid was off, there was no possible way for events to occur the way they were supposed to.

Sitting in the meeting, Pehr had felt his own personal power draining away from him. Now, presented with hard evidence that the entire grid had been disrupted, he saw an opportunity to make a comeback.

Pehr's attempts at rhetoric had gotten him nowhere. But he knew he could always count on the gigantic metal levers that were located behind the elevator in the building's electrical closet. If someone shut off the building's electricity, Pehr reasoned, the meeting would have to end. And if the meeting were to end, Pehr would be able to go home and recharge his psychological batteries. Finally, since the power was already out in every building along Kirkland Street, no one would suspect foul play.

Pehr could not make the trip to the electrical closet and do the job himself, since Pehr was supposed to be in the meeting. But if I snuck into the electrical closet and flipped the switch, no one would be able to figure out what had happened.

I didn't like the sound of Pehr's idea, and I told him as much. But Pehr would not let go of what he perceived as his one remaining chance to regain control of the technical side of NBX Corporation.

"Please," Pehr begged, "you've got to help me. There is no other solution!"

Pehr was desperate, but I was not, and in the end I decided against performing the act of sabotage.

In my opinion, turning off the lights at NBX would not have had any effect on the company's decision whether or not to use the software tool; it would only have served to postpone the inevitable. From my perspective, it was better to face facts and get the whole thing over with.

But from Pehr's perspective, every minute that he could delay the adoption of the heinous software package meant another minute that he retained control of the technical future of his beloved company.

In the end, Pehr was forced to make his case according to the normal rules of spoken English. And in the end, the meeting went as badly as Pehr had feared. "They said, 'Okay, hearing these arguments, we disagree with you, and we believe that we should use these untested software tools,'" Pehr remembers. "'That's what we're going to do. Thank you for your input.'"

Since Pehr did not have any experience using the new set of software tools, he felt that their introduction "pretty much killed my ability to contribute in any way to the future of the company." And once his ability to contribute to the future of the company had been removed, he felt that he had no choice but to leave.

Deciding to leave NBX was an extremely painful decision for Pehr to make, but in the long run it was the best thing both for Pehr and for the company. Physically, Pehr was so exhausted that he was no longer able to get his work done. Emotionally, he was so demoralized that he no longer cared about performing the political maneuvers that would earn him the respect of his fellowmen.

When an entrepreneur becomes so burned out that he is no longer able to act in a manner that is consistent with the company's best interests, we say that the company has "founder's poison." A founder can poison a company if he pursues goals that contradict the goals that are being pursued by the company's managers and uses his leverage to create dissent in the ranks.

The thing to do under these circumstances is to ask the founder, in the most polite way possible, to take a little break and to come back when he is well rested. (In practice, most burned-out founders do not wind up coming back to their companies, but instead go on to other challenges.)

Leaving a high-tech company can be a painful experience for a burned-out founder, and he is likely to complain a great deal during this extremely stressful period. But sticking around and continuing to work when one is clearly burned out can have consequences that are even worse.

The Importance of Taking a Break

"I had a boss who dropped dead," says start-up veteran Nancy Nangeroni. "Literally. I had a boss who did not take care of his body and did not take care of himself. He was walking up the stairs at home, and he dropped dead.

"He would push himself tremendously. He would pull all-nighters, and he was just too old to be doing it. He was in his fifties, but he was very young in his mind. He was just working, working, working, pushing himself harder and harder."

ChiliSoft founder Charles Crystle told a reporter from CNET News.com that at the very end of his term with ChiliSoft, he felt he was headed in the same direction. "I was just dying," Crystle said. "I weighed over 250 pounds and felt like hell. I was in a bad mood all the time. That was for a year and a half."

Burnout is so common among the founders of high-tech start-ups that it almost seems to be an inevitable part of the job. Just as we expect a certain percentage of professional tennis players to suffer from the affliction known as tennis elbow and a certain percentage of professional hockey players to lose their front teeth, so, too, we should expect a certain fraction of high-tech entrepreneurs to suffer from the neurological affliction known as burnout.

But certain precautions can be taken to make burnout less likely.

To avoid engineering burnout, Nancy Nangeroni recommends emphasizing the importance of having a life outside of work. "Kick people out if you find people spending too much time at the office," she advises. "Or take them out for a beer and make sure that they laugh a little bit. As the leader of a company, you need to play, and you need to make sure that your people are playing, too. You need to stay alert for when it ceases to be play for people, and you need to intervene when you see that it is moving from play to drudgery. If it's becoming that way for yourself, then you need to do something to change that."

The bottom line, Nangeroni says, is to recognize a person's need to relax. "If I'm running a business," Nangeroni said, "I want my people to have lives outside of work. I want people to remain balanced so that they remain emotionally healthy enough to be stable and centered on the job."

Nangeroni recommends keeping an eye out for these early indicators of engineering burnout:

- red eyes or other obvious physical symptoms of overwork
- making more mistakes than usual
- inability to delegate tasks effectively
- inability to prioritize
- working more than eighty hours per week
- a sense that work is beginning to feel like drudgery

To avoid losing people to engineering burnout, Nangeroni recommends the following:

- Encourage employees to make efficient use of the time they spend at the office instead of encouraging them to stay late and work weekends.
- Keep track of the employees who are pulling all-nighters.
- Remind employees to go home if it's clear that they've been working too hard.
- Include employees' significant others in work-related social activities.
- Keep healthy food in the office refrigerator.
- Provide employees with a budget for ordering sandwiches and pizza.
- Resolve employee conflicts as soon as they arise.

- Ask employees whether or not they are able to perform a task instead of telling them they must do something.
- Understand that a new high-tech company is like a partnership.
- Realize that employee/boss and founder/cofounder relationships can be as complicated and frustrating as any personal relationship.
- Manage by consensus.
- Find ways to play at work.
- Give employees some creative latitude with the product they are building.
- Realize that founders of high-tech companies often lack crucial people skills.
- Compensate for a founder's lack of people skills by inviting one or more "emotionally intelligent" individuals to join the management team.

And most importantly,

- Try to get employees to laugh.

Chapter Six

What Venture Capitalists Look for When They Evaluate New Proposals

During the last days of the twentieth century, some venture capitalists (VCs) went to great lengths to make themselves available to would-be entrepreneurs. They gave lectures at entrepreneurial conferences, they drank beers at the Muddy Charles Pub, and they told elaborate stories to explain why their particular firm was better than all the rest. But as the twenty-first century began, many of those same VCs who had formerly gone out of their way to meet new entrepreneurs began to hide in their offices and shun all contact with the very people who most needed their assistance.

When I did my first round of interviews for this chapter, I spent a particularly illuminating hour with an extremely enthusiastic VC who seemed eager to meet as many entrepreneurs as possible. But when I went back to visit him a second time, shortly before this book went to press, I got the impression that his goals had changed.

Instead of emphasizing all the things his firm could do for entrepreneurs, the VC told me how difficult it was becoming to arrange a liquidity event.

"Right now, there are going to be a limited number of companies that go public," the VC said. "And those companies that get acquired are going to get acquired for smaller sums."

It seems that when the stock prices of the world's largest technology firms are valued at 30 percent of their peak price, those large technology firms are much less likely to use their remaining cash to purchase high-tech start-ups. Additionally, when the stock prices of the largest technology firms are somewhat depressed, the individual investors who speculate on technology stocks have a great deal less wealth to spend on the stock offerings of newly public companies.

When VCs observe that there are very few initial public offerings (IPOs) taking place, they start to worry about whether they will be able to cash out of the companies they have invested in.

When venture capitalists start to worry about the likelihood of cashing out of their investments, they become much more selective about the companies that they put their money into.

Under these circumstances, the VC tells me, "We just don't have the time to look at new projects, because we are forced to spend our time addressing issues within our existing portfolio companies. And if we are focused on working with our existing portfolio companies, it's academic that we can't be looking for new projects."

A year ago, the VC gave me ten reasons why his firm was better than all the rest. But this year, the thing that the VC is most proud of is the fact that he only has seats on a couple of different boards of directors.

The VC has heard horror stories about other VCs who got so caught up with the Internet madness that they spread their firm's wealth much too thinly. "Some of those people are finding themselves on fifteen different boards now," the VC says. "When you have fifteen different companies, it's like raising fifteen sick children, you know? It's true. You think I'm kidding? You got a CEO on the other end of the line who's got a major problem a day. Every one. I don't know how they manage."

When a VC becomes overwhelmed by the number of problems that are being faced by his current flock of entrepreneurs, he becomes much less interested in accepting unsolicited phone calls from cash-strapped would-be entrepreneurs. But the VC is quick to point out that in a bear market, the extreme difficulty of getting funded means that those companies that do get funded are more likely to become winners. "I think that in the end we are going to have healthier venture firms and healthier start-up companies," the VC says. "If you can get through the process in this environment, you have a higher likelihood of success. It's a high bar these days to get funded."

Another VC, Jonathan Goldstein, of TA Associates, agrees. "If you have a good idea, this is a great time to be an entrepreneur," Goldstein says. "If you've got some lousy idea that would have gotten funded three years ago or two years ago or one year ago, sure you perceive it's a bad time to be an entrepreneur. But you've got a lousy idea.

"I assure you, somebody who's got a great idea is going to get funded."

It's Hard for Them, Too

VCs are elusive. Tired of being chased down, pounced upon, and asked to fund a million different deals, the group of individuals known as VCs have developed an elaborate array of defense mechanisms that can make it nearly impossible for an entrepreneur to obtain even five minutes of their time. "I get more than a hundred E-mails or phone calls per day," says Venrock's Pat Latterell. "It's coming at us like a fire hose. I try to be as responsive as I can, but it's almost impossible to react to one hundred queries a day." Although it can be extremely difficult to make contact with an influential VC (who is probably trying his best to make himself as available as he can), the worst thing a high-tech entrepreneur can do is give up. A healthy relationship with a well-connected VC can make the difference between being able to meet one's first-year goals and being forced to declare bankruptcy. A bungled face-to-face interview or a botched telephone call can put an entrepreneur on the list of America's Least Wanted.

Few people agree on the best way to make a good impression on a VC. What people do agree upon is that the VC industry is notorious for its reliance on gossip, hearsay, and gut feelings to make multimillion-dollar investment decisions. To have the best chance of impressing a jaded VC who has already seen every business idea under the sun, an entrepreneur needs to understand the subtle rules of VC etiquette.

Start with the Angel Investors

The road to VC does not always begin with a VC. In fact, relatively few VC firms invest in seed-stage companies. An entrepreneur looking for between $50,000 and $750,000 will generally obtain that funding through "angels" or wealthy individuals with a penchant for investing in brand-new companies.

There are several reasons why an entrepreneur would want to obtain seed-stage funding from an angel investor rather than a VC. The most obvious reason is that most VCs are looking to invest more than a seed-stage company can handle. If an entrepreneur accepts too much money too soon, he might give away too much stock and lose control of the company. Or worse: If the entrepreneur accepts millions from a VC who is looking to cash out in eighteen months but the entrepreneur knows he needs to spend at least a year developing his idea, they could get into an ugly wrangle. If an entrepreneur greatly exaggerates the value of his brand-new company so that he can attract financing from a first-round VC rather than a seed-stage angel investor, he might run into some major headaches when he tries to raise additional financing later on.

A VC on the other hand, has every reason to invest large sums of money to obtain a significant fraction of a young high-growth company. Guy Bradley of CMGI's @Ventures says that the amount a given firm would like to invest in a single company is dependent on how much money the firm has and how many partners there are. "You can only watch over a certain number of companies," Bradley said. "Given that, you take the number of partners and the amount of free time they already have and multiply it out by the number of deals that they can reasonably handle on a full-time basis. This leads you to the amount that a firm needs to invest in each company." At the time that I interviewed Bradley, CMGI had approximately $285 million to invest, and Bradley was looking to make initial investments of between one and ten million. "The sweet spot is probably in the three-to-five-million-dollar range, figuring that we're going to be investing at least as much in follow-on rounds for the same company," Bradley says. But as more and more money is being pumped into VC funds, the size of a VC's preferred initial investment is growing, too.

A well-capitalized fund that makes investments in gigantic increments is not appropriate for most companies at the idea stage. As Bradley explains, "You don't want to go to a fund that is looking to invest three to five million if you are at the pure seed stage unless you have truly a spectacular lineup in terms of the management, business opportunity, and the advantages that you will bring to the picture." Angel investors and seed-stage VCs are useful for filling the gap between the tail end of an entrepreneur's accumulated life savings and the well-capitalized venture funds that are looking to invest in huge increments.

Another reason why entrepreneurs might prefer angel funding to professional VC during their company's earliest stages is that angels have a reputation for being more active and less obtrusive than VCs. Thus, the founder of an entirely angel funded company is likely to have more control over the company's direction than he would have if he were to, say, join a VC-backed incubator. Although angel investors may go out of their way to pull strings for a new company, they probably won't demand a seat on the board of directors. While it *is* a good idea to ask one's angel investors to earn their investments by serving as advisers to the young company, entrepreneurs should reserve board seats for people who can bring significant industry contacts or management expertise.

Angels and VCs at the Muddy Charles Pub

While professional VCs are generally unlikely to invest at a company's earliest stages, they might be willing to give an entrepreneur something even more valuable than money: advice about building a successful business. VC Jonathan Goldstein spends his time trying to help TA Associates invest the $5 billion that the company has in committed or invested equity capital. And with so much money to look after, he and his partners can only make investments of between $25 million and $250 million. But although Goldstein knows that most of the entrepreneurs at the Muddy Charles Pub aren't ready for that kind of money, he is still willing to hang out and play the networking game.

"I get a lot of calls and a lot of inquiries from people looking for advice," Goldstein says. "I just can't handle the volume and do my job—focusing on new and existing investments—at the same time. This allows me to go to one place and meet many of the same people in a couple of hours. In addition, I get to learn about emerging technologies from the folks on the front lines, drink some beer, and eat some pizza." Although Goldstein doesn't always understand the technological innovations that are being discussed at the Muddy Charles Pub, he says he's always willing to learn and to make suggestions about commercializing the innovation. "If I can give the budding entrepreneurs some useful advice, that would be great. But at a minimum, I enjoy meeting with people who have similar goals and ambitions."

The third reason why angel investors are more helpful at the seed stage is that in most cases they invest sooner than their professional counterparts. Angel investor Barry Unger believes he makes a psychological deal with the entrepreneurs he decides to support. "I'm not going to mess you up with due diligence, I'm not going to take six months to make a decision, and I'm not going to tie up both our lawyers with four hundred pages of documentation," he says. While angel investors have the freedom to make decisions based on intuition, professional VCs are obliged to spend time gathering information about an entrepreneur's background and the size of the potential market so that they can justify their investment decisions to the university endowments, pension plans, and wealthy private individuals who give them money to invest.

Nearly everyone has heard stories about entrepreneurs who were "this close" to closing on a round of financing, only to have the VC firm back out at the last minute. Such eleventh-hour changes of heart can be devastating to an entrepreneur who has forgone paychecks, strained relationships, and even mortgaged his home in an attempt to make ends meet until he could close on his venture financing.

Unger tells the story of an unsuspecting entrepreneur who was abused by a VC. The VC told the entrepreneur he was extremely interested in investing in his new company, but he didn't want the round to be diluted by too many other investors. The VC offered a term sheet with a "no shop" clause that specifically forbade the entrepreneur from taking money from any angel investors. Then he spent three months performing due diligence before deciding not to invest in his start-up.

While the entrepreneur was waiting for the VC to make up his mind, he turned away millions of dollars in additional funding that could have paid employee salaries. The entrepreneur aged very quickly during the waiting period, going from a young man of twenty-eight to a middle-aged man of forty-five in just three short months. At the end of the three-month period, he nearly went bankrupt. He was forced to lay off most of his employees and revisit the original would-be angel investors "with his tail between his legs." Many of these original angels were annoyed at having been spurned earlier and decided not to invest in the reopened round. The angels who did invest did so at a lower valuation than they would have agreed to earlier.

Part of Unger's code of ethics for investing in high-tech start-ups involves "not doing secret stuff" and "not stringing anyone along." Some investors will offer an entrepreneur a fantastic deal on their company—provided the entrepreneur signs a confidentiality agreement and promises to discuss the terms of the deal with no one. Unger advises en-

That Certain Something

"The thing about entrepreneurs is that they have their own energy source," says entrepreneur-turned-angel investor Lori Fena. "There is a certain drive that goes on inside of them that is self-propelling. Nobody has to wake them up in the morning. Whereas with some other people everything looks good on paper, when you get away from it, you say, 'I don't think they have the energy internally, to drive, to complete it.' They may have a great business plan and an incredibly analytic mind, and they might be the best salesperson in the world, but they just don't have that internal combustion process."

Fena's husband and coinvestor, Ed Zyszkowski, agrees. "We look for the people who have the maturity, the drive, and the vigor. It doesn't have to be youthfulness, in fact, sometimes people who are older and who have done this for a long time are as enthusiastic and as vigorous as anyone else."

Fena continues: "But the real question is, are they driven? Because no matter how good the market is, no matter how much money there is, it's hard. And you've got to make sure that you've got someone who is going to continue to do what it takes to make this thing happen."

"It could be something as simple as putting up with these crazy travel schedules," Zyszkowski offers. "We were sitting in the last board meeting for Voter.com, and the assistant for Justin, the young CEO, came in and handed him the schedule. After the board meeting he was going to have to get on a plane and get to Washington because he had an eight o'clock breakfast meeting, but that afternoon he had a meeting in California. So he got onto a plane in Dulles and flew out to California for dinner that evening. The next day, he was up in Boston, and the following day, he was back in D.C. He was willing to do this.

"That's what it takes to succeed: You have to meet with the right people and make the right things happen. You have to have the personal discipline to be able to do that and not kill yourself."

trepreneurs to be extremely skeptical of investors who threaten to withdraw offers if an entrepreneur discusses their deals with a third party, since "secrecy is a way to hide abuse" and asking around is the only way for entrepreneurs to learn about the kinds of valuations that are being given to similarly sized companies in the same industry.

Our Money Is Better Than Theirs

VCs quickly point out the disadvantages of taking investment money from angel investors instead of commercial VC firms. Most angel investors do not have the "deep pockets" normally associated with an established venture fund, which means that once a typical angel investor has written a check, he probably won't be able to come up with any more "follow-on" capital to invest. With that said, the universe of angel investors is changing rapidly. According to R. Gregg Stone of Kestrel Venture Management, the angels have gotten so wealthy over the last few years, it is getting harder and harder to distinguish between angels and professional VCs.

"Traditionally, individual investors were good for $50,000 to $200,000 each, so maybe a group of them would be worth as much as half a million," Stone says. "That number has gone up because of the number of successful entrepreneurs who are putting in as much as forty million to work at a throw. Most institutional firms want to get at least a million to work in a round and more typically two or three in a round and ultimately five to ten in a company." Smaller VC firms, such as Kestrel, are happy to invest as little as $350,000 in a round and ideally about $2 million in a company. "We're still between these two groups, but the lines have blurred," Stone says.

Most early-stage investors understand that when they see a deal, they have a small window of opportunity to put money into the company, but later on, Unger warned, "they can't play with the big boys." Angels understand that a company's valuation will change significantly over time; the price of a share of stock is likely to rise significantly, and the only valuation that matters is the one agreed to most recently. For example, an angel investor who puts in $50,000 at the very beginning might not have the $900,000 he needs to keep his percentage in a later round. With each successive round, the percentage of the company owned by the firm's initial investors becomes smaller and smaller—unless they invest more money.

If a single angel investor cannot give an entrepreneur what's needed to reach solvency, the angel may at least be able to direct the entrepreneur to an established network of other angel investors. Rumor has it that the United States is filled with informal networks of angel investors. The trick is to find one in the right geographic area and to obtain a personal introduction.

Entrepreneurs discover the vast majority of angel backers through personal networks of "friends, family, and fools." If an entrepreneur's family cannot provide the necessary cash or connections to keep the company going, the entrepreneur might try to obtain leads from university professors who teach classes on entrepreneurship or from local entrepreneurs who have cashed out of their respective business ventures.

Entrepreneurs who do not receive invitations to private groups of angel investors are welcome to show up at the public cattle shows or get in contact with the folks at the Muddy Charles Pub.

What Investors Look For

Charles Harris of the Harris & Harris Group tries to "spot talent at a very early stage" and then "put that talent into an environment in which it can achieve its potential.

"I don't for a moment think that I am smart enough to know exactly what that potential can be, but if I sense that it can be significant, then the fun for me is trying to provide an environment whereby that talent can flourish. Then I have the satisfaction of being able to see the end product, if successful.

"I'll give you an analogy. For more than a quarter of a century I've been involved as an owner in the Thoroughbred-horse business. The end of it that I have chosen is where I go to the auctions and look at all the baby horses and try to pick out ones that I think are promising. I try to pick the ones where the promise is not completely obvious, because if it is, then that's reflected in the price. I buy them and put them in the hands of facilities, trainers, and so on, and give them every opportunity to reach their potential.

"It's natural that I gravitated into the early-stage, high-technology VC business, because that gives me an even greater sense of getting to do the same things with people. Here, young people instead of young horses.

"Naturally, you have to make money on some of these things, because otherwise you couldn't afford to pay all the expenses and make up for the losses on the ones that don't work out. You're getting involved in a business venture at the very highest risk stage and also the stage where you have to do the most work yourself relative to the amount of money you can employ. It runs counter to a good economic policy of money management if you're just after the economics, which is having the highest ratio of financial capital to the lowest ratio of skilled professionals putting that capital to work.

"In the early-stage venture-capital business, it's exactly the opposite. You have the lowest ratio of venture capital to the highest ratio of highly skilled professionals putting it to work. The other thing that works against the very early stage venture-capital business is that, like anything else, your success is measured by the present value of your return. The longer something takes to pan out, the higher your absolute dollar return has to be relative to your investment in order to produce a present value which is competitive."

Guy Bradley of CMGI's @Ventures has a different set of requirements. "Most first-tier VCs look for companies which have the potential to do an initial public offering (IPO)," he says. "There's a shifting definition over time about what makes a company IPOable, but one rule of thumb is that if a company isn't projecting that it's going to be able to do fifty million in net revenue within five years, then it's probably not IPOable. The other rule of thumb is that this fifty million in net revenue can't be more than 5 or 10 percent of the total estimated market for that product or service or set of products or services. In other words, you've got to be in a billion-dollar market segment for you to have an IPOable company. That's not entirely true, but I don't want to invest in a company where I'm relying on them achieving monopoly status in order to be able to do an IPO.

"An entrepreneur might wonder why we focus on companies which are IPOable. The reason is that we like to have more than one possible exit strategy. Otherwise we're stuck with having to find somebody to buy the company. And in some senses we're putting our fate into somebody else's hands. All other things being equal, we would rather back a company which has at least the potential of doing its own public offering as well as having an exit through an acquisition.

"One of the side effects of having as many business plans as we have is that there are lots of companies which are worthwhile investing in that one doesn't, for volume reasons, get a chance to invest in. And so I apply an additional factor when deciding whether or not to invest in a company, and that's whether or not I like the people. I have passed on investments which struck me as being really good investments, but I just didn't like the guys. And when you're seeing as many plans as we are, there are plenty of fish in the sea."

How to Decide Which VC Firm to Approach

It's a good idea to spend time researching VC companies before deciding where to send your business plan. "Entrepreneurs want to work with reputable, established organizations that are going to have access to additional capital and access to top people in order to help them recruit more people to their management team," says Tim Healy of Commonwealth Capital Ventures. "Top-tier firms are going to have access to other contacts throughout the industry, whether that be opening up the doors to companies that are going to need this product or service, making introductions, or bringing more top-tier venture-capital firms to the group.

"You should ask what a given venture-capital professional brings to the table that another venture capitalist doesn't. A good firm will have expertise in your area, or they'll have access to seven or eight other venture-capital firms that you might want to work with in the future. Most importantly, they'll have access to a continuing stream of capital. This isn't a one-time-only fund of Joe Smith's money that he made in his hotshot, whiz-bang technology company that he just sold for fifty million dollars, and so now he has twenty-five million in the bank that he's putting to work in some high-risk, high-growth opportunities. This is money that should have a regular stream in the future. You're not going to get money once; you're going to get money a second time and a third time, and you can't do this process over and over again. You need to know you're going to be able to go back and make it easier to get money a second time and a third time and a fourth time."

Think Like a VC

When Venrock's Joe Casey receives letters from entrepreneurs seeking VC funding, he pays more attention if an entrepreneur mentions something specific about his firm's investment focus or Casey's professional background. "It certainly has more relevance when someone comes to me and says, 'We think you could be particularly effective because of your product-management skills at Intel,'" Casey says. "It shows that the person has not only done their homework but is thinking appropriately about the expertise or insight they're seeking from investors. Not only does that build the credibility of the entrepreneur, but all other things being equal, the companies where we can offer the greatest impact are often the most fun and engaging projects as well.

"We don't invest in companies unless we can add value, either based on individual expertise or the collective wisdom of the firm. When I see one of our portfolio companies referenced, I know that the person has gone out of the way to ask, 'What is it that this individual can specifically bring to my company?'

"If they're making those linkages, it starts to initiate the thought processes that we like to undertake on our own. It also just shows more effort and initiative and that this person's approach to the funding of their business is a very mature, well-orchestrated process."

If Joe Casey were an entrepreneur, he would perform a great deal of market research before showing his business plan to any VC. "I would ask, 'Who are the firms that are most likely to fund this entity, and how do I get an introduction to those firms?'

"You say, 'I'm going to work every angle I can. But I'm going to work every angle I can on the six firms who are most likely to fund me, and I'm not going to spend energy on those firms that wouldn't fund me even if I got an introduction from the best man of the senior partner. They'd take a meeting with you, but it would be a waste of time for both parties.'" Writing a highly targeted cover letter is extremely important, Casey says, because "you don't work with a firm; you work with an individual." Therefore, before an entrepreneur can establish a relationship with a particular VC firm, Casey recommends asking, "Is there a partner at that firm that you think can be particularly effective?"

VCs earn the right to invest their money in an entrepreneur's company by demonstrating that they have specific knowledge about the industry in question, relevant operating experiences they can impart, and/or meaningful relationships with significant industry players. Likewise, entrepreneurs earn the right to develop relationships with specific VC firms by demonstrating that their product or service will complement and extend the firm's existing body of knowledge.

"Be selective and screen the choice of partner with the scrutiny sufficient for any long-term relationship," Casey says. "There's a higher likelihood of success if you can say, 'You've done projects in this area before; here's a new one, here's how it fits your portfolio, and here's how other companies in the portfolio might benefit from working with us.'

"Of course, if you can outline the path to a massive financial return, that might get their attention as well."

An entrepreneur who can demonstrate this type of logic is particularly attractive to a VC, Casey says, because "they're thinking the exact same way that we do, about extending the franchise beyond the successes we've already had in a market sector."

According to Casey, each project is considered a composite of many attributes. "We look at a combination of the market, the technology, and the team," Casey says. "We're most driven by the desire to help create leaders in new, large markets, but we like to remain close to our discipline." If Casey were looking at a new business plan in the field of optical networking, for example, he would begin the review process by asking himself how much he and the other members of his firm knew about optical networking. Then, once it was clear that his firm did indeed have some relevant expertise in that area, Casey would try to figure out whether or not his firm could introduce the company to employees or other resources that would help the company gain a competitive advantage.

"There are some fundamentals that people just don't consider sufficiently in advance," Casey says. "But by spending a little more time in the selection and targeting process, I think they could make their approach to the firms far more effective."

How to Approach a Venture Capitalist

"I saved that from the wastebasket for this book," a VC said during an interview. "We get crap like that all the time." He held up a single-page query letter riddled with spelling errors. The letter made grandiose projections about the astronomical returns a VC could expect if he gave the entrepreneur a few hundred grand, but there was no mention of the kind of business the entrepreneur was hoping to start.

"I don't think this thing is real," the VC said.

Through the years, the VC has received countless letters from would-be entrepreneurs, all of whom promise to deliver fantastic returns on the VC's investment. But all too frequently, the VC gets the feeling that the would-be entrepreneurs he hears from don't have any idea how to run a good business.

It is, after all, relatively easy to walk into the library of a prominent business school, take *Pratt's Guide to Venture Capital Sources* off the shelf, write down the names and addresses of a few VC firms, and slap together an enthusiastic cover letter.

In fact, it's too easy.

The situation has gotten so bad in recent years that many VCs will refuse to read business plans from entrepreneurs who have not bothered to obtain a referral from anyone in the VC's circle of contacts.

Once an entrepreneur has obtained a referral, it's a good idea to spend some time figuring out how the entrepreneur's business idea would fit in with the VC's present portfolio. Then, as a final step before the entrepreneur makes contact with a given VC, he should find out how that particular VC prefers to interact with the outside world. (The best way to obtain this information is by talking to entrepreneurs who have already received financing from the VC in question.)

If an entrepreneur was looking for an initial investment of between $350,000 and $2 million from R. Gregg Stone of Kestrel Venture Management, for example, "the wrong technique is to send a business plan in the mail," Stone says. "Although we and every other venture firm try to be dutiful and read every business plan that comes in, the fact is that a lot come in. Particularly if it's a thick plan, it never seems to move." If a plan sits on Stone's floor for more than a month, "then you look at it and say, 'Gee, I haven't done anything for a month or two, and no one else in the country has done it, so it couldn't be a good deal, anyway.' It's the wrong approach.

"The right approach would be to get a referral in through one of our entrepreneurs or one of our limited partners. But if not a referral, one should call or try to make contact by phone and have ready that elevator speech."

An elevator speech, Stone says, is a sales pitch that lasts "sixty seconds. No more than sixty seconds on why this is a good opportunity. And really focus on the value equation: that my company does X, and it's going to solve the Y problem. With Z amount of money I can carry it to this step, and this is what I expect to happen at that step. Really, a very short equation. We try to encourage our entrepreneurs to do this, but no one does it very well. In a very short time frame, capture what is the essence of the company and explain why an investment makes sense."

If Stone is intrigued by an entrepreneur's elevator pitch, he will ask them about the length of their business plan. If the entrepreneur says, "Oh, it's only eighty pages," Stone will tell them to send an executive summary. "I don't want something that's too detailed," Stone says. "For one thing, lots of parts aren't going to interest me at first, and the second thing is, I don't want to be holding any proprietary materials that I don't want to make use of. What I really want is a five- to six-page executive summary, the résumés of the key members of the management team, and a one-page spreadsheet of the financials."

Anthony Cirurgiano of Argo Global also discourages spending too much time on a business plan. He once received a box containing four one-and-one-half-inch tomes comprising the physical representation of an entrepreneur's gigantic vision. "If he had just been that diligent in inventing his product, maybe I would have been interested in his idea," Cirurgiano says.

Guy Bradley of CMGI's @Ventures is much more receptive to E-mail queries than he is to either postal mail or unsolicited telephone calls. "The best thing is not to send it through the mail; the best thing would be to send me an E-mail with a two- to three-page summary. I get to E-mails a lot faster than I get to the physical business plans."

If an entrepreneur sends Bradley an E-mail query and he does not hear a response for a while, he should not interpret this silence as a sign that his plan has been rejected. "I try to respond within a couple of days to E-mails," he says. "If I haven't been able to get around to it, generally stuff is piled up enough that I work the most recent going back rather than the oldest going forward. The relevant advice to all those poor entrepreneurs out there is if you don't hear back in a week's time, feel free to send it again or send a reminder; it will just bring it to the top of the stack again.

"And don't be offended by not hearing a response. Chances are it's due to the VC's just being too busy. Personally I am never troubled by entrepreneurs who continue to send E-mails. If I were an entrepreneur, I think my attitude would be that if you haven't said no, I don't know that it isn't yes. Keep asking."

Entrepreneurs should not assume that a creative presentation will cause a VC to spend more time with a given business plan than with the one below it. Instead of binding one's plan between the pages of a children's coloring book or dressing it up with expensive gift wrap—as some people have done—entrepreneurs should figure out how a particular VC most likes to be approached.

Like Stone, Anthony Cirurgiano recommends that entrepreneurs obtain a referral from someone within his network of contacts before sending their physical business plan. But Arthur Snyder of Citizens Capital Inc. prefers direct voice solicitation.

"Never get a referral," he instructs. "Call me up! Pick up the phone! Who the hell are you and what do you want? I'm a busy executive. What are you bothering me for?" He laughs. "You find out if he can accept that and kid back with you without getting mad.

"Some people don't see that I'm kidding with them. I just want to find out how seriously they take themselves. We can't take ourselves seriously. Everybody we meet has got something that we don't have."

Going to Arthur Snyder for VC financing is a bit like going into a ring with an angry bull. In both cases, it's a good idea to be well aware of one's own weaknesses. It's also a good idea to be psychologically prepared for anything.

"I have never made a loan to a company in my life," Snyder says. "You make investments in people. You look at people, and you judge who they are. Just the way they walk in the room. You look at the way they're dressed, what they say, what's important to them. If you're going to run a business, you're going to have to be able to take humor and events as they happen and not get bent out of shape about them.

"At the New England Merchant's Bank, I used to have three telephones and a secretary. The telephone would ring, and I always picked up my own phone. 'Hi. I'm Bill Jones.' 'What do you want, Bill?' 'I want to borrow some money.' And I'd say, 'Fine. Make an appointment with my secretary.' He'd say, 'First I want to send you some figures.' I'd say, 'Don't bother, because if you send them, I won't read them.'

"Three days later, my secretary would say, 'Mr. Jones is here.' He'd come into the office, and I would say, 'Sit down. What do you want?' He'd say, 'You know what I want. I called you and asked for a loan!' I'd say, 'Fella, twenty-five people have called me and asked for a loan since you called, and I haven't the faintest idea who you are.'

"I'd say to him, 'Where were you born?' And he'd tell me. And I'd say, 'Where did you go to school?' And he'd tell me what college he went to. And I'd say, 'No, where did you go to *school?*' Then I'd say, 'Where did you go to college? When did you graduate? What was your degree in? After you graduated from college, what was your first job? How long were you there? Why did you leave?' And I can tell by looking at his eyes that he left because he got fired because he was playing with the boss's secretary.

"You know. You can tell by looking at their eyes and how he reacted to that. Does he take this as humor? Is he offended by being challenged on everything he says? I challenge everything he says. I want to find if this guy can take it. Because business is not easy.

"Then he'd say he was working at Raytheon, and he wanted to leave to start a company. I'd say, 'What business do you want to start?' Then I'd say, 'What kind of salary do you want?' And if he said, 'I haven't the vaguest idea,' that would be good. If he said, 'I think I should get fifty thousand dollars,' I'd say, 'What are you earning at Raytheon?' I'm going back a few years in salary. He'd say, 'I get thirty-five.' I'd say, 'Why the hell should some new business pay you fifteen thousand more because you're president of it?' If he'd say, 'Because I'm president of it,' he had no chance of getting that loan. Done. Forget it. Because when a guy is in business and he thinks because he's the president of some company that he set up he has the right to get a big salary, who is he kidding? If he overpays himself, he overpays the people working for him and everybody else in the organization."

Frugality is admired by many people who invest in early-stage companies. The following anecdote, shared by Jerry Bird of Claflin Capital Management, Inc., illustrates how important it is for entrepreneurs to convince VCs that they are frugal. At the time that this anecdote was related, Bird was eating lunch—a handful of roasted peanuts—in the Claflin break room.

"This entrepreneur had been a disc jockey, and he had a loud, booming voice. He doesn't hear well. I've noticed that people who don't hear well generally tend to speak very loudly. In any event, he was that kind of a guy, and no sooner did we make that first investment, which was a million and a half dollars in '83, he knows that he can go out and rent a car, and what does he rent? He rents a Cadillac. A big Cadillac. And this was at the second board meeting. He said, 'What did you think of that car I rented, Jerry?' I said, 'It's just awful.' Because it's this little peanut company, and they're not making any money. I don't know who they're trying to impress by this, but it's just awful. Sends the wrong signal.

"So he said, 'What should I do about it? I just rented it.' And I said, 'Trade it in. Get something else.' He said, 'That will cost a lot of money.' I said, 'Don't worry about it. Just trade it in for something else.' He blew half the money that he raised in the first round.

"After he went public, we had the right to go to Mamma Maria's, which is the hottest restaurant in the North End. The entrepreneur called up and said, 'You need a ride?' I said, 'Sure.' He said, 'I'll meet you outside.' So there he was, driving some Mercedes. Whatever it was, it was a special one—$120,000 or $180,000. I said to him, 'What a great car.' He said, 'Do you like this car?' We were driving over, and he turned to me and said, 'Can I keep it?'

"I said, 'You can do whatever you like.'"

Expensive cars and elaborate restaurant dinners should be postponed until a company has achieved liquidity, or at least until it has broken even. As long as an entrepreneur is using someone else's money to pay his bills, he should keep in mind that his expenditures will be monitored closely.

The Office Meeting

It is standard for entrepreneurs to present a twenty-minute electronic slide presentation at an introductory meeting in a VC's office. Kestrel's R. Gregg Stone gave the following advice: "It doesn't have to be on the laptop and on PowerPoint, but once you get by the elevator conversation, the next step is the twenty-minute bullet-point presentation. This speech describes who they are, how they got there, what the business model is, and why together you are going to make money for your limited partners.

"Entrepreneurs can invent their own business model, but they had better know an established company that has succeeded with that model. I have had terrible luck investing in companies that say, 'We've got a different business model that no one has ever seen before.' There is a model out there that's worked, so they really ought to think carefully about how the business is going to function.

"How do the direct sales work? Do they use dealers and distributors? Are they going to use marketing dollars, or are they going to do it another way? How are they going to discount the product? They had better understand all those issues and have some pretty good reasons."

Try It Out on Your Friends First

Entrepreneurs should take the time to practice their presentations with friends, family, and fellow entrepreneurs before they meet with a VC, and they should pay close attention to the questions asked and the advice that is offered. If an entrepreneur screws up at a place like the Muddy Charles Pub, it's not that big a deal. However, if an entrepreneur screws up in front of a professional VC firm, the VCs are likely to tell all their VC friends about how foolish the entrepreneur looked.

"If a venture capitalist says no," an entrepreneur tells me, "the rest of the world will just hear the no, they don't hear the reason why. And that no starts to spread through the whole world, and then no one wants to talk to you because they're all scared that something must be wrong." Because of the VCs' propensity for gossip, it's a good idea to have rehearsed all possible questions, and all possible responses, before going into a VC's office.

The Formal Interview

The formal interview inside a VC's office allows the VC to show off to his partners by asking all sorts of nosy questions about the risks that the company is likely to face. Therefore, when presenting a company's risks, an entrepreneur should be as realistic as possible. "I really don't want to see a business plan that's filled with baloney risks where the entrepreneur's lawyer thinks up these things like: 'One risk: lots of competition from well-capitalized companies. Second risk: reliance on management, which is thin,'" Stone says "Blah blah blah. All those things are known with small companies, and those are not real risks; this is just the mumbo jumbo that you see. I think it's insulting. It shows lack of sophistication for the entrepreneurs to put that in.

"What investors really want to hear about is what keeps entrepreneurs awake at night, not what their lawyers tell them to put into the prospectus. And those things are probably, in a technology-based company, 'Can I make it work?' In an execution company it's 'Can I get the people to execute [the business plan]?' I don't have to see these risks outlined in the plan, but I want them to talk about it—so they might put it as a bullet point in their presentation."

A VC's Attitude Toward Confidentiality

Some VC firms have been rumored to steal ideas from entrepreneurs and to incorporate these ideas into business plans drawn up by their closest friends. Unfortunately, once a business plan has been presented, there is very little an entrepreneur can do to protect himself from the theft of his intellectual property. Court cases are long and expensive, and it is highly likely that a VC firm will be able to pay more to retain better lawyers. Although none of the firms mentioned in this book have a reputation for stealing intellectual property, nearly every VC has heard stories about *other* firms that are less than scrupulous.

Still, there are some things working in an entrepreneur's favor. Given the fact that most VC firms rely upon good reputations to attract new business plans, developing a reputation as an intellectual property thief would be devastating to a VC's business. A second reason why entrepreneurs should not worry about having their ideas stolen is that the odds are in their favor. VCs receive too many business plans to steal the good ideas and set up their own rival businesses.

VC Anthony Cirurgiano believes that entrepreneurs should accept his word that business plans discussed in his office will remain confidential. "A handshake should be sufficient," he says. If having a VC sign a letter of confidentiality is absolutely essential, an entrepreneur should allow the VC to sign a boilerplate letter of confidentiality that has already been approved by the VC's lawyers. Entrepreneurs should not demand that VCs sign their own particular nondisclosure agreement (NDA), since VCs do not have time to have every single NDA approved by legal counsel.

If this situation seems a bit unfair, entrepreneurs should keep in mind that the VCs are the ones with the money. The more hoops a VC has to jump through in order to read a given business plan, the less likely it is that he will actually look at the plan.

"There is a pretty simple reason why most VCs won't sign confidentiality agreements," says CMGI's Guy Bradley. "We see so many business plans that basically, regardless of our ethics, sooner or later somebody is going to sue us. And when it happens, we'd like them to have as little ammunition as possible. If an entrepreneur doesn't feel comfortable about proceeding without an NDA, then the plenty-of-fish-in-the-sea principle applies. One wishes him all the best and moves on to the next of the thousand business plans that month.

"Some people have the illusion they are in possession of a great idea that no one else has had. That's almost always incorrect. Generally speaking, the phrase 'an idea whose time has come' is true. One doesn't generally see anything having to do with pets, let's say, and then all of a sudden you see eight business plans in six weeks having to do with pets on the 'Net. Stuff just comes in waves. And usually when you have an idea about something, chances are good that somebody else has also had that idea. Your idea is not as valuable as you think it is.

"Now, it may sound somewhat harsh from the entrepreneur's perspective, but what is working in the entrepreneur's favor is that, to the extent that a VC gets a reputation of not maintaining confidentiality, sooner or later that's going to get around. If that happens, the VC's supply of business plans, and particularly good business plans with savvy CEOs, is going to go down. There is something of a self-policing aspect to the entrepreneurial/VC community in the sense that your best assurance as an entrepreneur is that the VC is not going to want to get a bad reputation."

The Site Visit

Most investors, whether they are angel investors or professional VCs, will want to visit an entrepreneur's work space before they decide to invest in a new company. This site visit can be somewhat embarrassing to an entrepreneur of modest means, since a successful VC or angel investor will obviously have a much higher standard of living. But entrepreneurs should not worry about inviting a potential investor into a cramped urban apartment or a modest suburban home. One investor told me that part of the charm of being an angel is getting to see the "before" aspect of a "before and after" high-tech success story.

Seed-stage investors who provide funding to home-based entrepreneurs want to feel as if they are getting in on the ground floor of an enterprise that has not yet taken off. Therefore, before an entrepreneur obtains funding from a VC, he should maintain a "zero burn rate" for as long as possible. This means that entrepreneurs should not sign a lease on expensive office space before they obtain their initial round of seed financing.

Regardless of the size and condition of the work space, entrepreneurs who are about to host a potential investor should make certain their environment is clean and tidy. This means cleaning up all visible garbage and throwing away leftover food containers. Regarding an entrepreneur's ability to keep a clean house, Stone says: "I really want to see a company that even at an early stage is running itself professionally and cleanly.

"Winners come in all shapes and sizes, but there are certainly things that I don't want to see. I've looked at companies where they've sent me a great business plan, and you get to the company and you realize it's just dirty. Or the parking lots are marked out with the founder closest to the door. I arrived at one company and noticed that all the cars had Windsurfer racks on them. I went in and talked not to the CEO but someone else, and I said, 'When are you going windsurfing?' And he said, 'Oh, we take them off the cars when people are coming down to look at the company.'"

VCs visit start-up offices so they can get a better feel for the people who work there. Although a VC will want to meet only the CEO and the right-hand guy, he will want a tour of the office. It's a good idea to make certain a majority of the employees are in the office on the day the VC comes to visit. If a VC comes to an office and sees nothing but empty desks, he will get a "queasy feeling." That said, an entrepreneur should not ask circuit-board-building engineers to come to work sporting cuff links and a tie.

To Invest or Not to Invest: That Is the Question

When it gets right down to it, most VCs and angel investors will make their investment decisions based on the personal chemistry between themselves and the founding team. When John Hegan of Claflin Capital Management was asked why he invested in a particular company, he replied, "I just liked the guy." Aside from getting referrals from inside a VC's network, dressing neatly, showing genuine passion for one's idea, and presenting a business plan appropriate for the investor in question, there is very little an entrepreneur can do to ensure that a particular VC will respond favorably to his personality. For this reason, entrepreneurs should not take it personally if a VC decides not to invest in a new company. Sometimes random events cause investors to go one way or another.

Ross Sherbrooke of Investor Associates recalled one such incident: "I remember I came out of a meeting with my pal Nate Corning over at Kilby Street one day, and we were walking out there on the sidewalk. There was this company going around, and we thought it was so terrific. We were just about to cross the street when a delivery van parked right in front of me. I was right on the fence about investing. On the side of the delivery van was painted: 'XYZ Express Service. If it's too hot, put it down and call us.' So I thought, *That is the answer; I'm not going to do the project!* It was too hot to handle. That is a true story."

With 20/20 hindsight Mr. Sherbrooke felt he made the right decision.

"I don't remember the company, but it was the right thing to do. I don't even remember whether the company turned out to be a success or not. I have no idea. Eighty percent of the decisions that you make in life are not important, except that it is important to have made them. It is much more important to have said yes or no and to get on with it than it is to hem and haw. And you can be right saying yes, or you can be right saying no."

To avoid falling victim to these random twists of fate, an entrepreneur should maintain parallel discussions with a number of different VCs. If one investor backs out for no good reason, an entrepreneur who planned ahead can simply move on to the next source of funding.

Chapter Seven

PERSEVERANCE:

The Story of One Core Financial Network

I n the mythology of high-tech start-up companies, there is no place for a man like Barry Star. He does not drink or smoke, and he does not seem to be afflicted with that peculiar disease of the endocrine system that causes men to drive too fast, swear at subordinates, and rack up sexual conquests. Whereas some entrepreneurs spend their Sunday afternoons jumping off cliffs and shopping for the latest-model sports car, Star spends his Sunday afternoons taking his kids to the latest animated movie. "Did you see the movie *Toy Story*?" Star asks. "*A Bug's Life*? Great movies. And the guy John Lasseter—he's the creative genius behind those movies."

To be fair, I should point out that Star's fascination with the latest releases from Pixar Studios probably has something to do with the fact that he used to work for Steve Jobs at Apple Computer. But it's not just the fact that he watches a lot of children's movies. The "soccer dad" image goes all the way to the core of Star's personality.

For a VC who has been trained to look for the brassiest, most obnoxious, most insane person around, it's a little disorienting to think that someone as normal as Barry Star might be able to start a successful high-tech company. Star did not drop out of college, and he did well enough in his job at Fidelity Investments to be promoted to the level of executive. But like most high-tech entrepreneurs, there was something about the large-company atmosphere that bothered Star.

"I was once managed by somebody whom I affectionately called a houseplant," Star says. "Ever been managed by a houseplant? A houseplant is somebody who just basically does nothing and grows—you water them once in a while. He was a nice enough guy, but he just sat there. And I said, 'Gee, I can do better.'"

Star complained about his "houseplant" boss for a long time, and when he finally became vested at Fidelity, he talked to his wife, Heidi, about going off to start a new high-tech company. "She said, 'Just go do it, because I don't want to hear about it anymore,'" Star recalls. But not everyone was as supportive as Heidi.

"I had a lot of people say, 'Leave Fidelity and go out and run your own business? What, are you crazy? How risky is that?' But for some of us, what you're doing is you're reducing risk by going to work for yourself. How much risk do you think there is for my career when I have to work for somebody who I call the houseplant? When I am working for myself, I have complete control over my destiny."

Star's first foray into entrepreneurship was a consulting company called the Star Development Group, which specialized in the electronic distribution of financial services. And the Star Development Group did pretty well, creating electronic products for the likes of Charles Schwab, Ameritrade, and Waterhouse Securities.

One day, one of Star's clients gave him a check for $100,000, which was to him, at the time, a lot of money. "I walked it down to the local bank, and I deposited it, and I realized that the bank charged me eighty-five cents for the privilege of putting in my money," Star remembers. "It turns out that corporate bank accounts don't pay any interest, either. So there I was, putting a hundred grand into a corporate bank account that earned zero interest. Now, having come out of Fidelity, I knew that I was getting taken."

Worse than the fact that he was being charged eighty-five cents to deposit money in his own bank account was the fact that the bank didn't seem to respect Star as an individual. "A traditional bank looks down on their clients," Star says. "You ever walk into a bank? More often than not, there is a picture of a bank officer looking down on you."

Star was proud of the money he was earning in his electronic consulting business and annoyed that the bank did not seem to value his money as much as he did. So he came up with an idea to create an alternative banking option that would provide small-business owners with the kind of services they could not get at a large bank. Having worked to develop electronic banking facilities for wealthy individuals, Star knew how convenient it was to be able to move money around at any hour of the day or night. So he decided to apply some of the ideas he had been thinking about to small business and develop a service that would allow small-business owners to take advantage of the convenience of around-the-clock banking.

"A mind-set that a lot of small-business people have is that during your business hours you are thinking about the front side of your business," Star explains. "You're thinking about supporting your customers and getting new customers. A lot of times you don't even get around to the administrative side—paying the bills and thinking about payroll—until after five o'clock. And the less time it takes, the better."

The idea of creating an on-line service that would allow people to pay their bills whenever they wanted to struck a lot of people as a good idea, and Star was able to raise $800,000 in angel financing from his friends and family. But he could not convince any professional VCs to take him seriously. "I must have shown this thing to seventy-five different venture capitalists, mostly around Boston, but I could not get to the venture round," Star remembers. "They liked the idea, and everybody was interested, but nobody wanted to be first.

"I actually did get one venture firm to say, 'Yes, we'll do this, but we want to bring in another strong player to be number two.' What that means is that they really wanted to be the second investor and they wanted someone else to be the first investor. No one wants to be the lead investor, because that's a risky place—at least from a reputation perspective. If they come in at the end of the deal and the deal goes south, they can always say, 'Well, gee, look, the lead guys got snookered, too. It's not just me that got snookered.' If they're the first one in, it's their reputation on the line."

Star tried telling the VCs that he had found a lead investor and asking them whether they might be interested in rounding out the deal. But that didn't work, either. This time, the VCs said they didn't want to put any money into Star's business until they knew who the CEO was going to be.

Knowing that any CEO worth his salt would not agree to join his business until the money was already there, Star tried asking the VCs to invest in his company and then go to look for a CEO with him. But the VCs refused to budge, and Star was stuck in a classic Catch-22. "I said to the venture capitalists, 'Let me get this straight. You won't put money in unless there is a CEO here, but I can't get a CEO to come in unless there's money here.' How do you get out of this conundrum?

"Ultimately the answer was that we didn't get out of the conundrum, and we ended up having to shut down the business."

Star shut down his business on June 11, 1997, at about one-ten in the afternoon, and he remembers the event as being the worst experience of his life. "I had to let eighteen people go," Star reflects, pointing out that he had never failed to pay a bill. "I mean *never*. I'm one of those people. I don't have any credit-card balances. I always pay the bills when I get them.

"When I had to let all those people go, it was emotional as all hell. I hired each of these people at an emotional level, and I made a promise to all of them. I said, 'Look, I can't promise you that you are going to get rich. This is a start-up. It's the intent, but I can't promise you that. What I promise you is that you will learn a lot working with me. We, together, will learn a lot. You will walk out of this company eminently more marketable than you were walking in, and you will also have a good time doing it.' When you create that kind of emotional tie to employees, it's hard when your company goes under. I had to take apart that whole office by myself, and it was not fun."

Once he had shut down the business, Star went back to his friends—the ones who couldn't understand why he wanted to leave Fidelity in the first place—and told them what had happened. Predictably, these people told Star that they had been right: New businesses really were too risky. "People started saying, 'Well, gee, you ought to just walk away from it,'" Star recalls. And Star himself began to wonder whether he ought to walk away from the business. "I started drawing lines in the sand," Star remembers. "I kept saying to myself, *I don't want to get dragged into this thing too much, since I've already put maybe a year, year and a half, of effort into this thing. Maybe I should separate the emotional side from the rational decision-making that has to go on.*"

But whenever Star told people about his business idea, they told him that it sounded like a great concept. And right before Star reached one of his lines in the sand, "something would happen that would be interesting enough that I would say to myself, *I've got to follow this thing through. Otherwise I am not going to forgive myself. I am going to have to live with this thing for the rest of my life, and I am always going to be asking myself, Gee, would that have made a difference?*"

Although the business had been shut down, Star continued to talk to the VCs about the possibility of giving him money so that he could start things up again. And the VCs maintained their stance that if Star was able to solve the problem of finding a CEO, they might be inclined to make an investment.

One of the VC firms even went so far as to refer Star to a possible CEO candidate. "So I met the guy, and I really liked him," Star remembers. "This was a really good, hard-charging, successful guy with a tremendous track record. I said, *This is a guy I can work with. This is a guy who would make this business phenomenally successful.* I started talking to this person, and the person said, 'This is a great business, but there is a problem. The problem is that I just sold my last business for umpteen hundreds of millions of dollars two weeks ago, and I'm going to take the whole summer off.' But it was a positive conversation, because I said, 'You know something? I'm going to wait for this guy, and I'm going to try to find others.'

"I spent the summer running around looking for money, staving off creditors, and writing checks to keep things going. I had the servers, and I had all this equipment that I was trying to keep around, and I was trying to keep this thing afloat. I didn't have the employees anymore, but I had the source code and the development environments, and I was trying to keep them going. I was getting deeper and deeper and deeper into it.

"Creditors would call and say, 'Well, do you have your bankruptcy papers?' I would say, 'I can't pay, you know; the company's out of business.'"

But Star would eventually turn things around.

"So the business just kind of sat there," Star recalls. "When the fall came, the CEO candidate said, 'All right, let's talk. I'm back; let's talk.' Within twenty-four hours of when he said, 'Hey, this is great, I want to do this,' all of a sudden these venture capitalists (who wouldn't even talk to me before) came in and said, 'All right, we'll do this deal.' One in particular had said to me previously, 'You know, we never invest in these kinds of businesses. N-E-V-E-R.' But as soon as the CEO said, 'Yes, I'll do this business,' bam! That venture capitalist was right in the deal.

"So the deal started progressing, but it wasn't my deal anymore. It was the CEO's deal. I pretty much lost control over everything.

"At one point I was willing to sell the whole concept and all the business just to get my money out, but as the negotiation went on, there were a couple of things I demanded. One of my demands was to pay off all the creditors, and the second thing was to pay off the management team, since during the last three months of the company the management team had all deferred salary. And the third thing was for the original shareholders to own something." After all, the people who had put up the original $800,000 were Star's own family and friends. "It was a high-risk endeavor, and they all knew that there was a real good chance that the thing wouldn't work and they wouldn't get their money," Star explains, "but if this thing was going to take off and start all over again, I wanted anyone who invested in the original business to own a little something, even if it was a token amount of this new business."

Unfortunately, Star's new business partners didn't see things the same way he did.

"It turned into a very arduous negotiation," Star recalls. "I got about 98 percent of the shareholders to approve the new deal, and then we were down to the last six bondholders. I got five of the six to approve it, but when I got down to the last bondholder, he said, 'No, I'm not going to do this. I wanted it to go a different way.'"

At this point the CEO who was going to run the business and the final bondholder got into what Star refers to as a "pissing match," and the CEO imposed a "drop-dead date." When the drop-dead date passed and the final bondholder still had not given in, the CEO decided he had done everything he could. Since the impasse could not be bridged, the CEO chose to walk away from the troubled company, leaving Star to sort out the rest.

"I was devastated," Star remembers. "Earlier in this whole mess I had come home to my wife and said, 'Heidi, you know I don't drink.' She said, 'Yeah, I know.' I said, 'You know something, Heidi. If I did drink, this would be a particularly opportune time to do so, because the pressures are enormous.'

"This was November, and I had stopped taking a salary in March. By the time the whole ordeal was over, I hadn't taken a salary for thirteen months. Okay? And I've got two kids; I've got a wife, a house, and a fence. There was a lot of pressure. A *lot* of pressure.

"To be fair, my wife and I had saved up a significant reserve, a rainy-day fund for this type of thing, and we had talked about it. Heidi was very supportive of this whole episode. We had the rainy-day fund, but it was raining. I mean, it was pouring outside.

"At that time I called my wife on a cell phone, and I said, 'Heidi, I understand why people jump out of buildings.' You can't believe the amount of pressure I was under. I didn't sleep.

"You'd think I'd walk away then.

"I did walk away from it, actually. I wrote a bunch of letters to people, thanking them for trying to make it happen. I gave mementos. I gave gifts. I gave these things with a little message at the bottom: 'With greatest appreciation, thanks for trying.' I gave a whole bunch of these things to the venture-capital guys, hoping that someday they'd let me come in and tell them about another business.

"I made peace with it.

"So it was dead. Gone. I wrote a letter to all the shareholders that said, 'Sorry, it's gone. Here's how you should take the tax consequence. Go call your tax adviser, but the tax treatment is a total loss. Sorry. We tried. Gonzo. Whsshhhtttt!'"

One of the last people Star called was a VC named Mike Block, who works for Holden Capital Associates. And it turned out that by the sheerest of coincidences, Block had invested in the former CEO's last business alongside a number of the VCs who had been involved with Star's deal.

"Barry approached me because a mutual friend suggested that I might be able to help him in his dealings with the VCs and their CEO candidate," Block recalls. "When I found out I knew this candidate reasonably well, having backed him previously, I offered to act as a go-between and see if I could help get the deal done between them. At that point, I had never even looked at Barry's plan."

Unfortunately, Block's efforts were not enough: "I failed in my efforts to put Barry's deal back together," Block recalls.

After the deal had died, Star made another phone call to Mike Block, saying, "'Mike, thanks so much for trying, but I've dug a hole in my backyard, and I'm about to throw a million dollars of source code into it. I appreciate your help, but I am going to go sell hot dogs at Fenway Park for a while, and maybe I'll call you again.' I was trying to be gracious about the whole thing—keep my connections. The deal didn't happen for a variety of reasons, but I'm a networking kind of person, and I like to keep track of people. You never know when you need to talk to somebody again."

"When Barry called to thank me for trying, I told him he shouldn't give up, asked for the plan, and invited him to Chicago," Block recalls.

Star himself tells the story a little differently.

"Mike's words back to me were 'Barry, don't be an idiot! You can't stop now! You just had your deal vetted by the finest venture-capital guys in Boston. And the fact that you could get your CEO to like your deal and say that he was going to do it and run all that way means that the deal has excellent potential.'

"Mike said, 'Just because ego got in the way of being able to close the deal, that doesn't mean that it isn't a good deal. Why don't you come to Chicago and talk to us? We'll do it.'"

After such a prolonged period of uncertainty, Mike Block's words should have been music to Star's ears. But by this time, Star had enough experience under his belt to greet the investors' assurances with a healthy dose of skepticism. Although Star really did want to keep trying to start his business, he knew that by all standards of rational behavior, he should really let the matter rest.

"I said, 'You know, Mike, I'm not sure that I can go to Chicago,'" Star recalls. "It was December now, and I hadn't taken any salary since March.

I said, 'I don't know if I can do this anymore, because I need a job. I've depleted a big chunk of my savings, and I don't know if I can do this anymore.'

"Mike said, 'Why don't you think about this for a couple of days and then give me a call?' So I thought about it for a day, and I talked to my wife. I was exhausted from this whole episode, and I hadn't even gotten to the starting line. I was just trying to get the damn thing off the ground.

"I sat down and looked at my desk, and it turned out that I had a frequent-flier ticket. So I said, 'You know, what the hell.'

"The deal was dead, in my opinion. I mean, I had sent out all these letters; I had made peace with it. But I had a frequent-flier ticket. So I said, 'All right, Mike, I'll come talk to you.' I was thinking to myself, *I'll give it one more swoop.*"

So Barry Star flew to Chicago and talked to Mike Block. And when Block heard Star tell his story, he was intrigued. Block realized that Star had reached that stage of frustration that VCs refer to as being "singed"—having been slightly roasted by the pressure cooker of entrepreneurship but not entirely burned out. And if Block's instincts were right and Star was not completely burned out by his entrepreneurial experience, perhaps Block could help Star bring his company back to life.

They Have to Feel Like They're Getting a Bargain

Although some VCs are only willing to invest in companies where all of the elements are already in place and all their VC friends are also talking about how much they want to invest in the company, too, other VCs prefer to hold out for those instances where they do not have to go through a bidding war to get a piece of the action. This is the same principle that drives some people to scour outlet malls for "slightly irregular" brand-name suits or to seek out "slightly used" year-old automobiles with a couple of scratches on the fender. If a new high-tech company has all of its ducks in a row, it is likely to be the subject of an all-out bidding war among rival VC firms. And if a VC wants to win such a bidding war, he will have to pay far more for his shares in the company than the company is actually worth. This phenomenon—of winning bidding wars by paying through the nose for the privilege—is referred to among VCs as "winner's curse." And the tendency among VCs to avoid both bidding wars and the resulting winner's curse is one of the main reasons why VCs are so wary of business plans that look as if they have been mass-mailed to every VC firm listed in *Pratt's Guide*.

When Mike Block heard Barry Star mourning for his dead company, he must have realized that although Star's company had once been highly sought after by some of the best VCs in Boston, it was not presently the subject of a bidding war. Therefore, if Block decided to invest in Star's company, he might be able to do so at a reduced rate.

"Mike had the vision and the foresight and the wisdom to see that this was a business that was going to go," Star remembers. "He also had the wisdom to see that we didn't need a CEO at the beginning. I said, 'Hey, Mike, I don't need a CEO for nine months. Why should we pay somebody a lot of money to build a product? That's what I'm good at.' So we agreed that we didn't have to hire a CEO at the beginning. What we needed to do was start the business, and as soon as we started the business, we would retain a search firm, and we'd jointly agree on a CEO.

"How do you like that for a concept? You don't need a CEO on day one."

Instead of paying top dollar for a company with a CEO already in place, Block was willing to use the money he saved to retain an executive-search firm that would help Star find an appropriate CEO.

When Star came back home from Chicago, he felt much more confident about the future of his business. But then trouble struck: Mike Block moved from Chicago to Denver and "got distracted by a bunch of things," and Star found himself in a sort of entrepreneurial limbo. Whenever Star spoke with the investor, Block assured Star that his VC firm, Holden Capital, really was going to make an investment. But as winter turned to spring, Star began to have some serious concerns about his family's financial situation. During February and March, Star began to interview for jobs at financial-service Internet companies. But whenever it looked as if he might be on the verge of getting a job offer, he would call Block, and Block would assure him that the investment was imminent.

As it turned out, Block was telling Star the truth: In April 1998, Star closed on $1.5 million in VC financing from Holden Capital and an additional $1.5 million from a company called the Crown Venture Fund. And with the $3 million in the bank, Star was able to restart his conversations with one of the VCs that he had wanted to work with all along: Guy Bradley of CMGI. "I wanted to get an investment from CMGI not because I needed their money but because I wanted their money," Star recalls. "I'm a very stubborn type of person, and I basically said that I was going to keep coming back to them until they said yes."

Fortunately for Star, extreme stubbornness happens to be one of the character traits that Bradley looks for in the entrepreneurs that he decides to invest in. "Keep asking," Bradley said, to all the "poor entrepreneurs" who mail him their business plans. "If you don't hear back in a week's time, feel free to send it again or send a reminder. It will just bring it to the top of the stack again."

Of course, a stubborn founder isn't the only thing Bradley looks for when he is trying to decide which companies to invest in. With so many business plans crossing his desk, Bradley can afford to hold out for "companies which are IPOable" and businesses that appear to have a few well-defined competitive advantages. When Bradley is evaluating a given business, he tries to figure out how easy it would be for a rival firm to set up a comparable business. If Bradley does not see any "real barriers to competition, then my inclination is to invest at a later stage rather than at an earlier stage, because then it basically boils down to first-mover advantage," he explains.

"If it's prelaunch, the day after I invest, somebody else could launch a similar company, and these guys could still be three months away from launching." However, if the entrepreneur has managed to erect some substantial barriers to the competition, Bradley might be convinced to invest sooner rather than later. "In the case of OneCore," Bradley explains, "there were a lot of moving pieces that they had managed to pull together to build a bulletproof, high-throughput transaction system— which it would have to be, for a financial system like this is a nontrivial thing." Because Star had succeeded in building this kind of system and had managed to put together a "good and appropriate" team, Bradley "felt comfortable investing well ahead of when they were going to be launching.

"And frankly, that bet turned out to be right."

Getting to the First Customer

After Star had secured his VC financing, things began to get a lot easier. "I always knew that there was value in this company if we could get it to the first customer," Star says. "The trick was to get it to the first customer." The VCs were able to hook Star up with an executive-search firm, which was able to find him a suitable CEO. And with the new CEO and the VC financing, Star says that "this place has just taken off. We've got clients who are just blowing in the door—we're signing them up as fast as we can. I always knew that the whole concept of 'Gee, does your banker provide you with the level of support that you need?' would strike a nerve in people, but I had no idea how much dissatisfaction there was out there in the marketplace."

It appears that OneCore Financial Network could not have been started at a better time. As more and more new companies are starting, more and more high-tech entrepreneurs are seeing a need to have a payroll service provider who truly understands their needs. And if a financial institution is not specifically geared toward the needs of entrepreneurs, they could easily wind up being ignored. "I had lunch the other day with a guy who has a balance of $750,000," Star says, "and his banker basically said, 'We don't have time for you.' The guy was floored.

"I can't tell you how many people call us up wanting to do merchant card processing, and generally banks say that you need to be in business for three years in order to accept credit cards. This misses out on ninety percent of the Web boom."

OneCore Financial Network, on the other hand, is not encumbered by the traditional thought processes that prevent large banks from doing business with born-yesterday start-up companies and that prevented conservative VCs from providing the start-up financing that Star himself needed to start his own company.

Whereas more traditional banks shy away from providing credit-card processing devices to start-up businesses, OneCore goes out of its way to make it easy for small businesses to obtain the services they need. "We can't guarantee that they'll get a loan," Star admits, "but we pre–fill out the applications, and it's as easy as pie." He acknowledges that there are some inherent risks associated with providing credit-card accounts to new businesses, just as there are some risks associated with small businesses themselves. But Star says that it's all in how you look at it. "A lot of people, when they think about risk, they think in terms of black and white. But risk management is not black or white; it's shades of gray.

"You should wear a helmet when you ride a bike. Should you wear a helmet when you ski? Should you wear a helmet when you drive a car? At some point it gets to the point where the amount of effort isn't worth the amount of safety that you're adding. Risk in business is the same way. It's never 'Yes, there's a risk' or 'No, there's not a risk.' There are always degrees of risk. And how do you manage that risk?"

OneCore manages the risk of providing credit-card services to born-yesterday start-up companies through an elaborate system of risk-based pricing. "You may get a higher rate in the first couple of years," Star says, "and then as you get a track record and build it up, you move it down. Or, we may say that instead of six different alternatives, there may be only two alternatives. But we're trying to get to the point where we never say no."

Everybody Loves a Winner

Seventeen months after Star received his first round of VC financing, I'm sitting in his office in Bedford, Massachusetts, waiting for him to get off the phone.

Star motions that it will take just one more minute.

He is trying to get rid of a VC, but the VC won't let him be. This is one of those same VCs who was not willing to acknowledge Star's existence back when Star was first struggling to raise capital. But now the VC is saying that he'd really like to get in on the deal.

He's going to have to get in line.

Now that Star has been asked to speak at a national conference of the American Bankers Association, now that articles about his company have appeared in publications ranging from *USA Today* to the *New York Times,* and now that Star has been named one of the Top 10 Entrepreneurs of 1999 by the *Massachusetts Investor's Digest,* his phone is ringing off the hook.

Every investor who put money in the first round has expressed an interest in investing in subsequent rounds, and Star tells me that OneCore has also received financing from "strategic investors" like Merrill Lynch and Paine Webber. "We're opening up a round in the next couple of weeks," Star explains after he has finally gotten rid of the VC. "We haven't even started talking to anybody, and we're already oversubscribed. People are knocking on our doors, saying, 'We want to do this.'"

Success has made Star a great deal less willing to waste time with those members of the VC community who turned their backs on him when he most needed their help. But he tries very hard to make himself available to his fellow entrepreneurs. "When I was getting this thing started," Star says, "I talked to one of the CEOs who had advised me, and I said, 'You've been pretty helpful. How can I repay you?' He said, 'Barry, when I got started, people gave me a lot of advice, and now I'm giving you advice. You're asking how you can repay me? Keep your door open and keep your telephone open for the next time somebody comes to you and says, 'Gee, can you give me some advice?'"

Although Star does not spend much time at networking events like the ones at the Muddy Charles Pub, he tries to make himself accessible in other ways. "If you're an entrepreneur and you need advice and you don't know who to go to, don't be bashful; pick up the phone. If you're not asking for money—you're just asking for some feedback—there is almost no reason why someone wouldn't call you back.

"Entrepreneurs love to help other entrepreneurs—it's a club thing. I don't mean that in a negative way, but it's shared experiences and shared pain. It's not an exclusive club, and anybody can be a member. This past year I've probably gotten requests for advice from fifty or sixty companies."

Although Star is always willing to help those entrepreneurs who are serious about what they are doing, he says that all too often he discovers that people simply are not willing to put in the necessary effort to turn their business ideas into successful companies. And to preserve his reputation in the entrepreneurial community, it is necessary for Star to save his referrals for those people who truly deserve them. "I usually don't say no and shut the door," Star says. "I try to give people direction. I'll say, 'Gee, you're really better off going and raising angel money.' Or, 'Go to a second-tier firm.' Or, 'Go to a firm that really wants to invest in genome or biotechnology stuff, because CMGI isn't going to invest in biotechnology.'

"In some cases I'll say, 'Your business plan isn't really ready to show to a venture capitalist, and here's why.'"

Although Star goes out of his way to provide help for those people who ask, he is amazed by the number of people who do not bother to take his advice. "About a month ago someone sent me a business plan," Star remembers, "and I said, 'You really need to do A, B, C, D, and E before any venture firm will see it.' They came back and said, 'Aahh, never mind. It's not worth doing, so we're not going to pursue it.'

"Think of that. Look at the hell that I went through versus 'make some changes to your business plan to make it more presentable and make this clearer.'

"People say, 'Gee, it's not worth it.'"

Chapter Eight

Entrepreneur or Rock Star?

L ike many high-tech start-ups, ArsDigita's Cambridge office has a decidedly playful air. The building features an exercise room with a video game–equipped stationary bicycle, a game room with foosball and a DVD player, and a music room with a $60,000 Steinway grand piano that, although jointly owned by two ArsDigita employees who clearly intend to stick around for a while, is available to anyone who wants to play it.

Visitors to the office at 80 Prospect Street are first greeted by a vast collection of large framed color photographs taken by the company's founder, Philip Greenspun, and an enthusiastic sniff from Emma, the Labrador retriever. Those who venture to the second floor will come face-to-face with a deluxe two-compartment rodent apartment that serves as a combination nap room, restaurant, and gymnasium for the three wild mice who inhabited the building before the company began its recent renovations.

But when computer programmer Mark Dettinger was trying to decide what to do with himself after he finished his Ph.D. research at the University of Ulm, Germany, he didn't know about these things, since he was unable to visit the Cambridge office. All Dettinger knew about ArsDigita was what he could read on their Web site.

Luckily, the Web site contained more than enough information for Dettinger to decide to join the company.

Having been heavily recruited for a job at IBM's Poughkeepsie location, Dettinger recalls that when he first received an E-mail letting him know about the job opportunities at ArsDigita, he was unmoved. Although he was flattered that someone would invite him to fill out an application, Dettinger had already set things up to work at IBM, and he had already gone to the trouble of reserving an apartment in Poughkeepsie. But the more time he spent on the ArsDigita Web site, the more intrigued Dettinger became. "I read a book by Philip Greenspun, and his ideas sounded pretty good," Dettinger recalls. "In all the chapters, I thought, *Yes, this guy is right. This will be a success.*"

When Dettinger was trying to decide between working for IBM and working for ArsDigita, he considered the assignments he would have, the amount he would be paid, and the vacation time he would receive. But he also considered the way he would interact with his fellow employees. Speaking of ArsDigita, Dettinger says, "It just sounded fun to work there. At IBM, the atmosphere is more reserved, and the people are your colleagues. Here, everybody is writing funny things about themselves and putting them up on the Intranet module."

But the main reason why Dettinger chose ArsDigita over IBM was the extent to which the different companies were willing to reveal their true identities. "The ArsDigita Web site contains a lot of information," Dettinger says. "I had more information about ArsDigita than about any other company, including IBM."

Compared with ArsDigita.com, the IBM Web site was "just a big advertisement," Dettinger says. "There are a lot of phrases like 'Join the winning team' or 'Come to the place where you can make a difference,' but there is no real information. If you go to the ArsDigita Web site, they mention everything about the company—even about compensation. What other company does that on the Web site?"

The ArsDigita Web site clearly states how much a programmer is going to earn at each of the company's different levels—as the book goes to press, salaries range from $70,000 to $125,000 per year, plus stock options—and what is required to move up the corporate ladder. In contrast, the "job seeker's" portion of the IBM Web site states that the company's programmers will receive "attractive compensation," "educational reimbursement plans," and a menu of "childcare options," but it does not explain what is required to get to the next level or how much a person will receive once she gets there.

What's the Point of Sharing So Much Information?

The reason for ArsDigita's unorthodox approach to sharing information stems from the fact that the company began not as a business at all but as a sort of virtual photo album cobbled together by the company's founder, Philip Greenspun, upon returning from an automobile trip from Boston to Alaska and back. The photographs that Greenspun took during his journey were first-rate, and Greenspun was eager to share them with his friends. To help his friends understand the photos better, Greenspun narrated them with an extensive diary he had prepared on the trip, which included comments about the people he had met and the conversations he had had.

In addition to the travelogue, Greenspun used his Web site to share information about the laptop computer he had used to keep his diary, the camera he had used to take the pictures, and the Web servers he was using to maintain the site itself.

The resulting site, photo.net, was so candid and so informative that it quickly became an on-line mecca both for photograph aficionados and cubicle-bound Web surfers. As more and more people flocked to his site and Greenspun learned firsthand about the difficulty of managing the flow of traffic at a high-volume Web site, he began to dispense information about building and maintaining database-backed Web sites. This information eventually became *Philip and Alex's Guide to Web Publishing*, which is available both electronically—on the site—and in paper form. (The putative coauthor, Alex Samoyed, is actually a large white dog.)

Greenspun's book served as a calling card, letting people know about Greenspun's ability to create robust Web sites. And as more people learned about Greenspun's programming abilities, he was deluged with requests from people who wanted him to build robust database-backed Web sites for them.

The requests were so numerous that Greenspun hired a number of other programmers to come and work with him. But it seemed that no matter how many people he hired, there was always too much work to do, and Greenspun found it difficult to hire programmers fast enough to keep up with the demand.

To encourage his present employees to recruit their friends, Greenspun decided to present a new Ferrari to any person (employee or non-employee) who could bring ten new workers to ArsDigita. "I heard of some companies giving away cars, but they were always sort of lame cars," Greenspun says. "And I thought, *Okay, what would be extreme?* For a young male at least, there is no better car than a Ferrari. So I put it on the Web and spammed everybody, and the programmers at ArsDigita stayed up until four calling their friends and digging back through their old alumni contacts."

A Higher Purpose

When folksingers come to the realization that their songs about economic injustice have brought them wealth beyond their wildest dreams, they often try to set things right by announcing their support for idealistic causes. For example, when Joan Baez was at the height of her popularity, she joined the civil-rights movement, provided entertainment after the March on Washington, and founded a fifteen-student school known as the Institute for the Study of Nonviolence.

In the same spirit, Philip Greenspun, who wrote most of his travel vignettes from the perspective of an impoverished graduate student with an annual stipend of only $12,000, has begun to use his company's new wealth to create on-line resources for animal shelters, provide cash incentives for outstanding teenage programmers, and establish a tuition-free "university" that will transform a select group of gifted individuals into an elite corps of computer programmers.

Whereas Ms. Baez's school encouraged its students to discuss the writings of Mahatma Gandhi and Henry David Thoreau, ArsDigita University will encourage its students to establish new standards of professionalism in software engineering.

While Ms. Baez's school had no admission requirements save that the applicants be at least eighteen years of age, ArsDigita University demands that its applicants present "a minimum combined SAT score of either 1,400 (new scale) or 1,300 (old scale), a bachelor's degree in any major from a four-year college, a confidence-inspiring transcript from that four-year college, and an essay describing their professional goals."

Additionally, both institutions have received their fair share of criticism. For example, the writer Joan Didion reported in her essay "Where the Kissing Never Stops" that shortly before Christmas, 1965, Ms. Baez's Institute for the Study of Nonviolence was deemed so offensive to the residents of California's Carmel Valley that the Monterey County Board of Supervisors was asked to decide, at a public meeting, whether the school should be allowed to continue operating. Speaking for the community at large, a neighbor of the school announced, "We wonder what kind of people would go to a school like this . . . why they aren't out working and making money."

None of the residents of Cambridge, Massachusetts, who learn about the existence of ArsDigita University would ask what kind of people would be attracted to Philip Greenspun's school, since it is obvious that the school was designed to churn out computer programmers. But a handful of pessimists have complained that the operation is little more than an elaborate job fair. "People have different theories about why we started the university," Greenspun says. "If they are charitably minded, they think that we started it because we are philanthropists and we love our fellow man. If they are not charitably minded, they think it's a scam and we're doing it to recruit people. The real reason is that it gives our Ph.D. computer scientists a place to teach. It is actually about keeping our own employees happy."

It is certainly true that the educational opportunities being offered by ArsDigita are doing a great job to promote the company's reputation among computer programmers. Computer-science aficionados of all ages have been flocking to ArsDigita University, ArsDigita's free one-day intensive courses in Web programming, and the free three-week Web programming "boot camps" that are held in cities like Cambridge, Berkeley, Palo Alto, London, Munich, and Washington, D.C. But if Greenspun's detractors imagine that the main benefit of these educational efforts is the opportunity to recruit new programmers, they are missing the point. In Greenspun's estimation, the greater good that has come out of his free educational endeavors has been increased morale among the company's existing employees. "People like to teach," he explains. "And if you work at most companies, you don't have an opportunity to get paid to teach."

Teaching a portion of a three-week "boot camp" forces ArsDigita employees to remember what they themselves have learned, to organize their ideas in a coherent framework, and to communicate their innovations with fellow employees. Still, it would be wrong to pretend that Greenspun's motivations are entirely philanthropic. Having recently turned down a $450 million buyout offer, Greenspun is well aware of the value that his company is creating. And although he has pledged to use some fraction of his wealth to educate his fellow men, Greenspun is also determined to enjoy the fruits of his labors.

The other day, for example, Greenspun "took the Ferrari, drove it down to Cape Cod, and bought a multimillion-dollar house, on the beach, for use by the company as a place to do projects."

Hearing about Greenspun's great delight in taking the Ferrari out for a spin seems a bit odd, since it is out of line with the image Greenspun projected in one of the travel vignettes that helped make him so popular in the first place. "Speaking of cars," Greenspun writes in the travelogue *Berlin and Prague,* "I was shocked by the number of brand-new Mercedes on the streets of Prague. It was sickening enough in America to see a doctor drive by in a hunk of sheet metal worth four years' salary to the average worker. I wondered how Czechs feel when they see a businessman get so fat from just a few years of the free market that he can afford the same car, worth about fifty times the average annual salary here."

When I asked about this apparent discrepancy, Greenspun seems a bit flustered. "Did I say that?" Greenspun asks. "And now I've got the Ferrari? Oh, my God. That does show how much I've betrayed my roots." He continues: "It did occur to me at the time that there was something repulsive about it all. But on the other hand, there aren't too many companies that would start a foundation and dump a million dollars a year into a university while they were also trying to grow a thousand percent."

Indeed, the fact that Greenspun can devote precious time, energy, and resources toward the development of a free university while also trying to grow his company a 1,000 percent, is evidence that his unusual style is working. Although Greenspun encourages employees to stay late sending out E-mails to all of their friends and although many programmers, like Mark Dettinger, are drawn into the company via E-mails sent during these late-night recruiting sessions, many more new employees come to the company through the Internet grapevine.

Computer programmer Sam Klein first heard about Philip Greenspun and ArsDigita when he and his buddy were having a discussion about communities and the buddy directed him to chapter 3 of *Philip and Alex's Guide to Web Publishing*. After reading the chapter, Klein delved deeper into photo.net in an attempt to absorb more of Greenspun's personality. Intrigued by the amusing anecdotes and desiring still more contact with the site's creator, Klein applied for a job at ArsDigita. And he says that his experience is not unusual. "A lot of people come because of his writing," Klein says. "People who appreciate the message he delivers really appreciate the chance to work with someone who shares their opinions. I'm willing to be guided by this person because he has a very good sense about what matters. I have faith that his guidance can be trusted about other matters that I do not have experience in."

A Cohesive Multimedia Experience

The pages of ArsDigita.com, photo.net, and greenspun.com transfer fluidly to the real-world experience of ArsDigita's Cambridge office. Because the walls of ArsDigita are covered with much larger versions of the same photographs that adorn the pages of photo.net, anyone who walks into the office at 80 Prospect Street is immediately surrounded by the familiar. Here is the photograph of Alex Samoyed, the large white canine mascot. There is an arresting panoramic image of a series of scarecrows, one of whom appears to be caught in a spider's web.

Walking around 80 Prospect Street is like walking around in a life-size photo album. But instead of being narrated by Philip Greenspun and the folks who have sent him E-mails, the narration comes from the employees of ArsDigita.

"The pages ended up having a lot to do with the company," Klein tells me. "It was hard to separate the philosophies that are important to ArsDigita from the philosophies that were important to Philip." And be-

cause the comprehensive Web site allows candidates to screen themselves out if they do not agree with Greenspun's philosophy, the folks
who do choose to work there are more or less content with Greenspun's
worldview.

Of course, this is not all that unusual. To get along in a community,
it is necessary to have some kind of thread holding the group together.
The thread that is holding ArsDigita together is the set of goals articu-
lated in the company's rather frank, unorthodox on-line mission statement. "Our first principle is that we do not lie to customers," the Web
site states. "If a service goes down because of something we did wrong
and should have known not to do, we tell the customer exactly what we
did wrong in as clear language as possible. Even if the customer might
not know that this was a stupid thing to do under Unix or Oracle, we explicitly tell them, 'This was a stupid thing to do.' If we slacked off and
partied all weekend and didn't finish some work that we promised, we
admit it rather than conjuring up mythical technical dragons to slay. We
do not take advantage of customer ignorance to hide our mistakes, a
practice that is depressingly widespread in our industry."

Managing Growth

Now that his Web site has grown into a robust corporation, Greenspun has been spending more of his time on the road conducting seminars off-site and meeting with customers in distant lands. But he still tries
to keep in touch with the home office. He sends home souvenirs, such
as the gigantic wooden giraffe on display in the lobby, and he keeps in
touch via long E-mail vignettes describing how various customers reacted
to his sales pitch.

The E-mail messages that Greenspun sends provide an intimate look
at how the company's products are being received, and this helps programmers tweak the programs to meet the clients' various needs. For
Sam Klein, this is one of the perks of working at ArsDigita. "People want
to know what's going on," Klein explains. "Half of the E-mail will be
about the people he met and the places he went to. He doesn't pass up
the opportunity to talk about cool things."

The other benefit to sending extensive trip reports to every member of one's organization is that it allows employees to develop close virtual relationships with their company's leader. "It's great for people to think that the company is enough a part of their life that they want to share what's going on," Klein says. "These are important things about how we're really getting along with customers."

But not all employees agree that the lavish souvenirs and overly detailed road-trip E-mails are entirely a good thing. For example, there is some disagreement about whether the "privacy screen" made out of a combination of steel and Fla*vor*ice™ packets that Greenspun picked up on one of his shopping expeditions was worth what he probably paid for it. And some of the employees wonder whether the recent increase in E-mails and care packages means that Greenspun is feeling "disconnected."

"He didn't send them before," one dissenter muses aloud. "I think he's losing control."

To Share or Not to Share: That Is the Question

Some employees are concerned that it might not be such a good thing for Greenspun to say absolutely everything that is on his mind when he is trying to grow a company. But rock stars like Philip Greenspun don't usually spend much time worrying whether their words might end up hurting someone's feelings.

"I take risks that horrify my MBA Bain consultant executive team members," Greenspun says during an interview. "If we've had a bad idea or if we've screwed something up, I'll admit it. If I think that something is instructive and/or funny and I have to hold an audience's attention for six and a half hours through a one-day course, I'll say it."

Greenspun tells me about a time when he was giving a course in Web programming to some of his clients and partners and was inspired to tell what he considered to be an amusing anecdote about one of the companies with which he had established a strategic partnership. "I told it in a way that got a laugh, which I think is always good," Greenspun says. The comment "was not meant to be dissing" the partner, Greenspun insists; instead, he was just trying to amuse the audience. However, after the lecture, Greenspun's partner told him, "You never say anything bad about a partner; you just don't do that!"

Unmoved, Greenspun responded by saying that the individual in question "shouldn't have had such a thin skin."

Greenspun's Web-based travelogue about his trip to Berlin and Prague has also generated some controversy, for although Greenspun claims that he really does like doing business in Germany, the travelogue reflects a somewhat negative view of the German people. "I was in a bad mood when I wrote my Berlin/Prague travelogue," Greenspun explains. As one would expect, the existence of this rather pejorative piece of writing has had some adverse consequences for Greenspun's public-relations efforts in that country. When Greenspun was negotiating a major contract with Siemens Corporation, Greenspun remembers that "one of the senior executives at Siemens read that travelogue, and he was needling me. I think he thought that some of the feelings were genuine and fair, but it still bothered him a bit. He didn't cancel the contract, but he read [the travelogue] before he signed."

It is, after all, a big risk to publish stories on the World Wide Web that contain sweeping generalizations about the countries and peoples one has encountered during one's travels around the world. But Greenspun's ability to take risks is one of the key things that has made him what he is. He is not, after all, a politician trying to win the approval of more than 50 percent of the voters in a particular district. And he is not the stodgy head of a public corporation that needs to cater to the whims of a set of conservative industry analysts or the demands of a capricious public. Instead, Greenspun is an entrepreneur/rock star with a devoted following of people who truly appreciate his candor.

Programmer Sam Klein is one of Greenspun's biggest fans. But even Klein acknowledges that when it comes to running a business, it is important to establish certain limits. "The programmers want him to be idealistic," Klein explains. "But the businessmen want him not to be naive."

To manage his company's amazing growth, Greenspun was obliged to hire professional business managers to look after the financial side of his business. This has meant accepting money from blue-chip VC firms like Greylock and General Atlantic Partners, hiring an executive search firm, and locating a new CEO. But this has also meant learning how to get along with a bunch of extremely conservative people.

Referring to his new VCs, Greenspun says, "The way they see it, we are a first-round company, and all the money is theirs. So, at a board meeting, when we talk about spending some money on the Cape house or whatever, they say, 'Hey, you shouldn't be spending our money on that. That's too luxurious for programmers.' And the way I see it: 'Hey, we would have bought this, anyway, it was in the plan for two years, we still had money in the bank when we took the venture capital money, so we haven't even begun to spend one dollar of their money.'

"Where do they get off telling us that we can't spend money? We had two million dollars in profit last year. Why shouldn't we buy stuff that costs two million dollars?"

With every board meeting, Greenspun is learning that signing a deal with VCs means having boundaries placed on one's artistic freedom.

But then, it's always been that way.

The goal of an entrepreneur/rock star is to push the limits and to get attention for pushing these limits, while the goal of a corporate executive/ VC is to make sure that the restrictions are there.

It is amazing that the rock star Philip Greenspun was able to get as far as he did without falling under the iron thumb of conservative businesspeople.

It will be interesting to see how long this freedom lasts.

Chapter Nine

PARADISE LOST

I t's 10:45 on a Saturday morning some months later, and I'm gearing up for another interview with Philip Greenspun.

The last time Greenspun invited me to come by his condo on a Saturday, one of his famous brunches was in full swing, and I had to elbow my way past a gaggle of MIT professors, computer programmers, and a reporter for the *New York Times* to get Greenspun's attention.

This morning, however, the stairway to Greenspun's condo seems strangely quiet.

"I thought you would call first," Greenspun says when I reach the top of the stairway.

He's standing in the entrance to his condo, holding the door open.

He's wearing a white terry-cloth bathrobe.

Still wearing the bathrobe, Greenspun motions for me to take a seat on a powder blue chair in the living room.

"This is all that remains of the beach house," Greenspun says, gesturing to the new furniture. The chairs are large and extremely soft, but they look a little too big for Greenspun's living room.

As I fumble with my tape recorder, Greenspun says, "I assume you heard about the Ferrari."

I shake my head.

"The VCs decided that they couldn't afford the Ferrari, so they sold it."

The thought of losing both the beach house *and* the Ferrari does not sit well with Greenspun's large white dog, Alex Samoyed, and he starts to vomit on the hardwood floor.

Greenspun goes to the kitchen for some paper towels. "Okay, so this is not how Martha Stewart would entertain," he says, cleaning up the mess.

When the floor is clean, the dog goes to sleep beside the overstuffed chairs, and Greenspun and I settle into the interview.

I start by asking Greenspun whether he still thinks it was a good idea for ArsDigita to accept VC financing from Greylock and General Atlantic Partners.

Greenspun thinks for a minute.

"If you're profitable and you're growing ten times per year, you're going to have problems, and a deal with venture capitalists won't get you out of those problems," Greenspun says. "I think that it was naive to think that we could get all this money and continue the growth on that curve because of the magic of professional management and venture capitalists. What you discover is that there is no magic.

"When you spend millions of dollars quickly, most of it gets wasted. I think that's the ultimate lesson of the dot-com, dot-bomb phenomenon: You can't build a large organization really quickly because most of the people that you hire don't even know where the bathroom is, much less what would be productive activity on behalf of the organization.

"You expect the venture capitalists or the managers to have some insight into this because they've seen it before. But it turned out that they didn't really have any ideas. And it actually fell to me, in the end, to come up with the idea of having workshops around dinnertime, where people from different teams would meet each other and solve problems together.

"I guess there are a few companies that have succeeded, spending that much money and growing that fast. But you'd have to have very unusual luck or very unusual management talent, which you're not going to get from the VCs."

Greenspun's original plan involved developing software that would allow users to create their own database-backed Web site in about an hour, without having to write their own code. He planned to develop the software, or "computer-supported collaboration environment," over a fifteen-year period.

To finance the research project, Greenspun planned to deliver some progress toward his goal every few months. Then, during the chaos of the late 1990s, Greenspun somehow developed the idea that he could achieve his goal in fewer than fifteen years.

Now, in early 2001, Greenspun realizes how foolish that notion was.

"There was no reason to believe that you can shortcut that process from fifteen years down to two years," Greenspun says. "No matter how much money you have."

During the height of the stock-market boom, Greenspun became increasingly disturbed by the fact that ArsDigita had considerably less money than its competitors. Two of Greenspun's most outspoken competitors had recently begun selling their stock on the public markets, and this made Greenspun nervous. "We thought, *How can we compete against them if we have one one-hundredth as much capital?*" Greenspun recalls. "We had a million or two in the bank, and they had hundreds of millions in the bank. But they turned out to be paper tigers. They never built any interesting software with all that money."

When Greenspun and I last spoke, Greenspun told me that he needed to raise VC financing so that he would be able to attract a top-notch executive team. "We were having trouble recruiting managers," Greenspun explained. "We really wanted to hire great managers in Europe and other places. And frankly, people just wouldn't listen to us. When we said we had $20 million in profits and rapid growth, that was totally uninteresting to candidates."

The managerial candidates that Greenspun spoke with were not interested in evaluating ArsDigita on its own merits. "But if they hear that Greylock bought in, they assume that it must be a good company," Greenspun says.

"The same thing with headhunters. We couldn't even get headhunters to work for us. They laughed at me when I called them and asked them to help us recruit some top management. I said, 'We have ten million in revenue, and we're profitable!' They said, 'Hey, we just recruited the CTO for [a company that has] five hundred million in revenue. You guys are nothing.'

"But a company like Greylock—they have a big, long list of connections, so they got us a CEO."

Last April, Greenspun told me that the CEO his VC financiers had recommended was "a really good guy, and a lot better than anyone that the headhunter had found." A year later, I get the feeling that Greenspun's feelings have changed significantly.

"The kind of people who want a CEO job are the kind of people who want absolute power," Greenspun says. "So, within a couple weeks of arriving, he began to push me out of the company."

It isn't hard for a CEO to push a founder out of the company, Greenspun says, when "one of the people looking for the power is sort of naturally focused on making the venture capitalists like him and the other person is really indifferent to the venture capitalists' opinions."

Another thing that made it easy to push Greenspun out of ArsDigita was Greenspun's tendency to tell people "exactly what your opinion is—which is the way you make engineering progress."

New Management

Mark Dettinger, a Ph.D. computer scientist from Germany, left ArsDigita's Cambridge office in the summer of 2000 to take a job in the company's Philadelphia location. But he returned to the Cambridge headquarters six months later to teach a class at ArsDigita University.

This gave Dettinger the opportunity to observe how the company had changed during the time he was away.

During Dettinger's earliest days with ArsDigita, he lived with his colleagues in a house on Franklin Street. He recalls getting up in the morning, going jogging with his colleagues, and getting to the office around ten A.M.

After working all day, Dettinger recalls that he and his colleagues would often go out for dinner and then treat themselves to an 8 o'clock movie. Afterwards, the programmers would come back to the office to put in a couple of more hours of work.

"Basically, your whole life was cycling around ArsDigita," Dettinger recalls. "We not only worked together, but we lived together all the time. Our whole life was ArsDigita."

After the VCs were brought in, the environment at ArsDigita changed significantly. "They killed all the extras that you don't really need in setting up a company," Dettinger says. "And by doing that they also changed the happiness of the employees: It went down."

For example, "Last summer the refrigerators were always full," Dettinger recalls. "So if people got hungry in the evening, they just went to the kitchen, grabbed something, and got back to their desks. Now the refrigerators are empty. So people go home in the evening, and they don't come back after that."

Last August, some of the programmers worked until 3:00 A.M. and kept sleeping bags beneath their desks. "Now people leave at five or six P.M.," Dettinger says.

A More Traditional Approach

Philip Greenspun is also annoyed by the cultural changes that have been made by ArsDigita's new managers. "Now they have a marketing department, so the programmers don't worry about writing [journal articles about their latest discoveries]," Greenspun alleges. "They have client services, so the programmers don't have to worry about what they say to the customer. They have systems administrators, so [individual employees] don't have to worry about managing the box." Finally, Greenspun tells me, "they have project managers, in a lot of cases, who relieve [employees] of the responsibility of staying on schedule."

Greenspun believes that the quality of the work being done at ArsDigita now is "fairly comparable" to the work that was done at ArsDigita under his leadership. "But the cost to us is probably three or four times as high," he alleges.

"I had eighty people mostly on base salaries under $100,000 and was bringing in revenue at the rate of $20 million annually," Greenspun wrote a couple of months after we spoke. "The [newly restructured ArsDigita] had nearly two hundred [employees], with lots of new executive positions at $200,000 or over, programmers at base salaries of $125,000, etc. Contributing to the high-cost structure was the new culture of working nine to five Monday through Friday."

It is Greenspun's view that, unlike in the past, neither managers nor employees bother to come in on weekends.

The Next Generation

There have been a lot of changes around ArsDigita during the past year, but some things remain the same. One of Greenspun's cofounders, Eve Andersson, still celebrates "Pi Day" on the fourteenth day of March by throwing a large party. But the people who are attending this year's Pi Day party are nowhere near as jovial as they were in the past.

Andersson prepared for this year's party by purchasing pizza pies of all varieties and by decorating a hundred chocolate cupcakes with the first hundred digits of pi. But Andersson's preparations for the Pi Day party are nowhere near as elaborate as they were last year, when the market was strong and Philip Greenspun was being wooed by legions of top-tier VC firms.

Last year, Andersson led the team of ArsDigita employees who strung five thousand numbered beads on an extremely long string, creating a visual tribute to their favorite infinite number. But this year, with the Ferrari sold, the beach house liquidated, and the food budget cut in half, Andersson could only muster the enthusiasm to string up one hundred additional digits.

There was a time when Eve Andersson was so taken by the number pi that she used her "Garden of Eden" Web page to lure casual Web surfers to various pi trivia pages located throughout the Internet.

Some visitors, like programmer Mark Dettinger, wound up memorizing fifteen hundred digits of pi in the hopes of beating Andersson in the Pi Recitation Competition.

But those days seem distant now.

Once upon a time, Eve Andersson could recite six hundred digits of pi from memory.

These days, Andersson can only remember about two hundred digits. "I think that every time a cell dies, it dies from the pi area of my brain," Andersson says.

But while Andersson's infatuation with the number pi may be waning, eight-year-old Amos's love affair has just begun.

Amos's invitation to the Pi Day party came through his parents, both of whom have jobs at ArsDigita. And although Amos is too young to work here, he's doing his best to fit in.

"I like Pi Day parties better than birthday parties," Amos announces, dipping his hand into a jar of M&Ms. "Because you get cupcakes, and you get to recite pi!"

Around and around the lobby Amos goes, asking everyone present whether they want to hear him recite his eleven digits.

When he doesn't get any takers, he recites into the thin air. "Three point one four one five nine!" Amos shouts. "Two six five, three five eight!"

He points to Alex Samoyed. "You are the pi dog!"

Turning to an adult, he asks, "Do you know who the Pi King is?"

The adult does not know who the Pi King is or what Amos means by a "Pi King." But Eve Andersson does. "He had a crown last year," she explains. "The people who bought decorations last year got some crown at the party store. They gave it to me, but I didn't want to wear it. So I gave it to Amos, and he was the Pi King.

"This year I didn't get down to the party-supply store, so there was no Pi King. Not very deep."

Still, the coronation mattered to Amos.

"I can be the Pi King," Amos says. "I know eleven digits!"

Unfortunately, no one is in the mood to witness another Pi Day coronation. Ever since Philip Greenspun was locked out, the morale among those employees who celebrate Pi Day has been at an all-time low.

Frustrated, Amos walks over to the large stuffed gorilla that Greenspun brought back from one of his numerous road trips and begins to punch it in the stomach.

(Note: Amos's parents, both MIT graduates, quit ArsDigita in March 2001.)

A Venture Capitalist's Opinion

None of the VCs who have made investments in ArsDigita are willing to speak with me about the company, although I made several attempts to get in touch with them. So I arrange to have a drink at the Muddy Charles Pub with Jonathan Goldstein, a VC with the firm TA Associates.

"I had the privilege of looking at Philip's company when he was raising money," Goldstein says. "We bid aggressively for it, but we did not win the bidding.

"Philip raised money at what—if it was not the peak of the market, it was within weeks of it. The timing was perfect for entrepreneurs. The investment environment was like the Palo Alto real-estate market was a year ago: No one bid at or below the asking price. People started bidding at 20 percent above the asking price."

Goldstein has invested in normal, traditional companies before, but he has also invested in a company called Andover.net, which is run by open-source programmers—individuals who may not be driven by capitalist business principles. I ask Goldstein to tell me how investing in a company run by open-source programmers is different from investing in a company run by programmers who are more private about their source code.

"It's not really all that different," Goldstein says. "You probably always have idealists in every situation. And whenever you've got a board meeting or a management meeting, you've got different people who want to see different outcomes.

"To some people, the value of the share price is all that matters. To some people, having a happy, pleasant work environment is all that matters." For others, stability is most important. "Some people just want to see their technical vision carried out, because they may become famous in their industry for doing that, as opposed to just being the wealthiest," Goldstein says. "Nobody is going to be perfectly happy with everything, but you try and create a little bit of the greatest good."

One of Goldstein's strategies for creating the greatest good overall is by acting "tough" during executive-board meetings in an effort to help the company make progress toward its goals. "I like to describe our behavior as 'tough and fair,'" He says. "People bring us on to be tough. They want their organization to get to the next level. They want a partner with experience in helping companies get there."

Bringing in a group of outside investors, Goldstein says, forces an entrepreneur to "start behaving like this is no longer some sort of personal fiefdom" but rather a real, official company that has accountability to a greater constituency of shareholders.

Goldstein tells me that one of the ways an outside investor can help a company "get to the next level" is by making "the tough decisions on hiring and firing." For example, Goldstein and his colleagues might find themselves deciding "whether an individual will lead" or whether the individual is more likely to "detain a company's growth prospects."

Goldstein recalls that he once had to fire a founder of a company who was working as the company's chief financial officer. "It wasn't a fun conversation to have at the time," Goldstein says, "but that's what we're brought in to do: make the tough call and recommend what is best for the growth of the business."

Making a Video

A month or so after I interviewed Philip Greenspun, programmer Sam Klein invites me to stop by ArsDigita University's "Ivory Basement" to see Greenspun teach a class on database-backed Web sites.

Klein has told me that Greenspun's class is scheduled to start at 9:30 A.M., but when I arrive at 9:35, the class has not yet begun.

As I wait for Greenspun to arrive, two student programmers separate themselves from the maze of Herman Miller cubicles and pour themselves cups of coffee.

"Philip's not here yet, right, John?" a student asks.

"I don't think so," John replies. "We haven't heard from him."

By 9:57 A.M., there is still no word from Greenspun, and the students are growing restless.

"He was going to lecture at nine-thirty," someone grumbles.

No one responds.

Around 10:10, Greenspun walks in, and the university springs to life. Students who had been pacing the floor or even staring off into space suddenly begin tapping excitedly at their keyboards.

Greenspun strides through the rows of cubicles, surveying the student body.

A woman named Sofia goes ahead to prepare the video equipment that will be used to broadcast Greenspun's lecture over the World Wide Web. The rest of the class follows shortly thereafter, taking seats in nearly every one of the available chairs.

Greenspun comes in last, carrying a can of Diet Coke. He takes his place at the front of the classroom and begins lecturing.

Standing in front of the class filled with students, with the video cameras trained on his face, Greenspun is in his element. He invites the class to criticize one of the pages that he wrote on photo.net, and he tells them about one of the foolish things he used to do before he realized that there was a better way to program. "This is truly horrible," Greenspun says, referring to a student who used a particular development tool. "I just can't say enough bad things about this style of developing [web pages]."

He thinks for a moment. "Well, maybe I can, but I haven't yet."

The students stare straight ahead, their attention focused completely on Philip Greenspun. One woman puts her head down on her desk, but only for a minute.

"When you're building a database—" a student begins.

"Not just a database," Greenspun corrects. "The World's Best Database!"

The class laughs.

At the end of class, one of the students asks when a project is due.

"I said Thursday," Greenspun replies. "If you guys aren't in line for that, you better start stealing code."

After the students have filed out, Greenspun walks to the back of the classroom and sits down. He tells me of his recent moves at ArsDigita: holding a shareholders' meeting to rewrite the company's bylaws, giving his VCs' chosen CEO the role of president, and appointing himself CEO. He tells me that he hopes the VCs won't sue him, and he mentions that he does not believe it would be in their best interests to do so. "A company won't make much money if they spend all their time in Delaware courts," Greenspun says.

Although Greenspun does not seem concerned about the possibility of being sued by his VCs, he is aware of the fact that his actions—calling a shareholders' meeting to rewrite the company's bylaws, for example, and then shifting the VCs' chosen CEO to the position of president—are probably not going to sit well with the VC community.

"I definitely have to lie low in the VC world for a while, because this has got to be a VC's worst nightmare," Greenspun says. "They're used to having everyone so locked up that they *do* have absolute power. Shareholder accountability is not something they look forward to."

"Stockholders are sheep to be carefully herded," Greenspun's cofounder, Jin S. Choi, agrees.

Sure enough, five days later, a lawsuit was filed in the Delaware court system, pitting ArsDigita's CEO, the company's chief operating officer, and the VC firms General Atlantic Partners and Greylock Limited Partnership against three members of the ArsDigita founding team, including Philip Greenspun.

The VCs' View

When I found out that the VCs had filed a lawsuit against Greenspun and two of his cofounders, I invited them to tell me their side of the story. But the VC from Greylock did not respond to any of my messages.

The VC from General Atlantic sent me an E-mail saying that since ArsDigita was in the midst of litigation and since he was both a director of the company and a plaintiff in the suit, he was "prohibited from making any comments at all about the company or the legal proceedings."

The VCs said, in court papers, that ArsDigita was a highly successful start-up company that grew very rapidly in part because of the explosion in e-commerce during 1999 and the dot-com craze. "Given the Company's high growth rate, and the fact that the Company not only had revenue, but was also profitable (a rarity in a 'new economy' start-up in 1999), it attracted substantial attention from the venture capital community, including some of the best known venture firms in the U.S.," the VCs said in court papers.

As part of ArsDigita's bid to attract the attention of "first-tier venture firms," the company represented to its potential venture partners that it would hire a CEO, the lawsuit states. To support this claim, the lawsuit references a "business plan summary" that reportedly stated that "Philip will assume the position of Chairman and focus on education and technology strategy . . . when we bring in a new CEO."

The VCs claimed that an integral part of the "business deal" was that Greenspun would be replaced as CEO and that the governance scheme set forth in the bylaws of the company at the time that the stockholders agreement was put in place clearly anticipated that the board and only the board would have the power to hire and fire the chief executive.

The VCs say that between March 2000 and early March 2001, their relationship with Philip Greenspun deteriorated significantly. They say Greenspun then removed the board's ability to hire and fire the CEO, demoted the outside professional CEO who had been brought in when the funding was received, and named himself CEO. The VCs argued to the court that this was all contrary to the intention that the parties expressed in their contract.

Philip Greenspun's Web site indicates that the dispute between Greenspun and ArsDigita has been settled amicably. In the end, Greenspun resigned from ArsDigita's board of directors and gave up the right to exercise control over the corporation either as a manager or a stockholder. Details of the settlement are being kept confidential.

One of the people who followed the Greenspun saga very closely was a would-be ArsDigita employee named Ben Ballard.

Ben Ballard first heard about ArsDigita when he was working as an assistant readiness officer in the U.S. Navy. In the navy, Ballard recalls that he was "discouraged from mentioning to people that I found some area of inefficiency."

But at ArsDigita, noticing inefficiencies is the name of the game.

When Philip Greenspun chooses to use a piece of software, Ballard says, "he goes through all the reasons why he chose the thing he chose and why other methods weren't going to be as stable or reliable. That really appealed to me: someone who just tells it like it is."

If, for example, Greenspun does not like a competitor's software, he might label the product "junkware." "And he'll tell you why," Ballard says. "He's not just saying it because it's competition. He'll spell out twenty reasons why their software is inefficient, bloated, unreliable, unstable, unusable, whatever. He'll have it all figured out. There aren't many companies with CEOs who are like that."

In his previous position, there weren't many opportunities for Ballard to call bloated, inefficient, and unreliable pieces of software "junkware." In the navy, Ballard says, "you are very careful not to offend certain people, regardless of whether you feel like they are right or wrong."

Ben Ballard was so enamored with the idea of working for ArsDigita that he went out of his way to prepare himself for the company's boot camp. He bought and read Greenspun's book, *Philip and Alex's Guide to Web Publishing*, and he bought and read a desk-high stack of books about Oracle databases. In his spare time, Ballard began teaching himself a programming language called Tcl, which he knew would be used at the camp.

Ballard hoped that the hundred or so hours he spent preparing for the ArsDigita boot camp would increase his chances of getting a job at ArsDigita. But during the second week of camp, Ballard learned that the company would not be able to hire anyone, regardless of how well they had performed.

This made Ballard upset. "It was a significant sacrifice of time to take off two weeks of work" to attend the ArsDigita boot camp, Ballard says. "I think most of the people who go to it are students on summer break or people who aren't working full-time. There aren't too many people who use their vacation to do this."

If Ballard hadn't been spending the two weeks auditioning for a job at ArsDigita, he would have spent the time flying to other places for interviews. But Ballard did not really want to fly anywhere else for a job interview: "ArsDigita was at the top of my list, and everything else was at the bottom."

Even though Ballard understands that Philip Greenspun is no longer at ArsDigita, he hopes that one day he will be able to spend time with the entrepreneur. "I tell you what I'd love more than anything else," Ballard confesses. "Just to have an opportunity for him to be a mentor. I think that would be extremely beneficial and fun.

"I don't know if he'd have the time for that, because it sounds like he's pretty busy right now, and it sounds like he's got all these other people in the company that he knows a lot better. We'd probably all want him to be our mentor. So I doubt that would fly."

A Chance to Vent

There are, of course, plenty of additional opinions. Rumor has it that some of the people who work at ArsDigita are pleased that Greenspun will no longer exert control over the company either as a manager or as a stockholder. And there are plenty of anonymous postings on the Internet site called *Slashdot: News for Nerds* that say that while Greenspun definitely has a knack for public relations, he is a terrible manager and a loose cannon.

Some postings allege that Greenspun's admirers are "brain-dead" and that ArsDigita under Greenspun resembled a cult.

Shortly after these messages were posted, Greenspun sent me an E-mail in which he referenced the chain of postings: ". . . (haven't checked all the comments but assume that it will give all the employees that I ever told were pinheads a good chance to vent :-)))," he quipped.

Back at ArsDigita University, Greenspun told me that he was aware that some of his employees were disillusioned with his managerial techniques. But he says that at least when he was running the company, employees were never subjected to mass layoffs. "I guess losing your job isn't as painful as losing your self-esteem," Greenspun reflects. "If you cherish the belief that you are brilliant, being told something you're doing is crap is more painful than being told you're not going to get paid anymore."

Going Forward

In December 2000, Greenspun accepted a position as lab director for a new research center being started up in Cambridge, Massachusetts, by France Telecom/Orange. His "Software Engineering for Internet Applications" course was recently adopted by MIT faculty as part of the core curriculum. Greenspun still teaches the class, known as 6.171, every spring.

At this point, it is unclear how the resolution of the ArsDigita court case will affect Philip Greenspun. But one thing is certain: No matter what happens, the story of Philip Greenspun, ArsDigita, the VCs, and the large white dog will continue to fascinate Web surfers for quite some time.

Chapter Ten

GETTING THE PEOPLE IN PLACE:

Executive Headhunters and the Right CEO

After NBX Corporation had been sold to 3Com Corporation, seed-stage investor Charles Harris commented, "It is kind of amusing to think that two students from MIT could come up with an idea that these companies, with their hundreds of millions of dollars of research and development, couldn't come up with. It reaffirms one's faith in youth and creativity and the sorts of educational opportunities that young people have."

But when he was making the decision to invest in the tiny Ethernet telephone corporation, Harris was nowhere near as optimistic.

When Harris first learned about the proposition to build a device that would transmit voice and data over a single line, the investor thought, *My goodness, they must be working on similar schemes at Lucent and Nortel and all these places, and that is scary!*

Although Harris's VC firm ultimately decided to ignore its fears and make an investment in NBX Corporation, the firm was "never comfortable that there wasn't competition lurking that we couldn't identify." Looking back on the early days of NBX Corporation, Harris reflects, "It was like trying to sail a little sailboat between glaciers."

To do a good job steering that little boat through glaciers, it is helpful to bring someone on board who has spent some time on one of the glaciers. In the case of NBX Corporation, the secret to steering the tiny sailboat around the glacier known as Lucent Technologies was convincing Dan Massiello, then general manager of Lucent's small-business division, to quit his job and help run NBX.

"That was the most critical thing of the whole company," NBX cofounder Alex Laats reflects. "That we were able to hire Dan Massiello, who absolutely had the skills that we needed, and that he and I were able to mesh. We got so lucky there: Dan's strengths were almost an exact match for my weaknesses, and my strengths were almost an exact match for his weaknesses."

A self-proclaimed detail-driven, anal-retentive Type A personality, Laats served as an excellent foil for Massiello, whom Laats describes as being "more big picture driven." With Laats's fastidiousness and Massiello's ability to take a broader view, the two formed a team that was able to operate extremely well under all sorts of adverse circumstances.

Looking back on the NBX story, it seems incredibly fortunate that the original three-man team of Alex Laats, Chris Gadda, and Pehr Anderson was able to convince the general manager of the small-business division within Lucent Technologies to serve as their CEO. But it was not luck that brought Massiello to NBX Corporation; it was an executive headhunter from the search firm known as Ramsey Beirne.

In asking Ramsey Beirne to find a CEO for NBX, Laats used the same strategy that E*Trade, Netscape, and Healtheon used when they needed to find CEOs. With Ramsey Beirne, Laats knew that he would be paying top dollar for the company's services, but he felt confident that the work would be first-rate.

What Laats did *not* know when he asked Chuck Ramsey to find him a CEO was how Ramsey was going to do the job.

The work of an executive headhunter is shrouded in mystery and speculation. For example, few people who are not involved in the executive-search industry would be able to figure out how to convince Jim Barksdale to quit his job at AT&T and join the start-up Netscape, and fewer still would know how to convince Dan Massiello to quit his job at Lucent Technologies and move to the unheard-of NBX. If asked, the average reader might guess, as I did, that before it is possible to perform these manipulations, it is necessary to accumulate a vast collection of leather chairs, mahogany desks, and other objects that would signify to the person being recruited that the recruiter is himself a member of the upper class.

But assuming these things would be a mistake. For when I met Chuck Ramsey in the Boston office of the executive-search firm Ramsey Beirne, I discovered that this "Boston office" was not an office at all, but rather a set of two upholstered chairs located on the second floor of the Boston Harbor Hotel.

It should be noted that the Boston Harbor Hotel is a gorgeous facility and that its rooms are not cheap. But although the hotel is stuffed full of evidence that its overnight guests are well-to-do, it is not necessary to part with large sums of cash to make use of the aforementioned upholstered chairs.

Prior to our interview, Ramsey informed me that, throughout the course of his long career, he had conducted more than 1,240 executive interviews at various locations inside the Boston Harbor Hotel. But when our interview was completed, Ramsey revealed that he had taken a room there on only two occasions.

Instead of booking a room, Ramsey would simply show up in the hotel's lobby at the appointed hour, greet his candidate with a firm handshake, and usher him to his favorite set of chairs. And then, "after you've gotten through all the schmoozing about how you got here on a little boat from the airport and what a great location it is, you say, 'We've got a few minutes. Tell me a little bit about yourself.'" Ramsey believes that if one pays close attention to the way the candidate answers, a good executive headhunter can learn a great deal about the person with whom he has just shaken hands.

To do a good job as an executive headhunter—to convince people with huge salaries and prominent positions in well-established industries to leave the glaciers and throw their weight behind the uncertain sail of a struggling high-tech start-up—it is necessary to build a reputation for making good matches. And the most important component in making good matches is knowing how to identify outstanding individuals.

Of course, this is not an easy thing, since most people sound pretty good during an interview. But if an executive headhunter is skilled enough, he can figure out whether a candidate is truly exceptional at what he does or whether he is simply skilled at making himself appear acceptable during an interview. To separate the doers from the pretenders, Ramsey instructs, "You just listen with your ears wide open, and you ask yourself: 'Do the stories make sense? Are there great accomplishments there?'

"When the person says, 'And that's how we made Lotus 1-2-3 the number one spreadsheet in the world,' you say, 'That's a wonderful story. Help me understand exactly what your role was in that.' Because you have to define whether or not the person happened to be in the room when a whole bunch of smart people did something or whether this was the smart person who told everyone else in the room what he had. There are probably a thousand people who could put down on their résumés that they had developed Lotus 1-2-3, because it's a big company. The question is, what was this person's role there?"

After establishing what a candidate was able to do in the past, Ramsey asks the candidate what he is hoping to do next. And to make sure that the candidate is being honest and forthright in describing his ideal business opportunity, Ramsey repeats this question, or "a piece of verbiage that gets at the same question," time and time again.

Although it might seem that a CEO candidate would get a little annoyed if a headhunter asked him to state his managerial philosophy six or seven times during a single interview, Ramsey claims that this habit has been the key to his considerable success. Being a good headhunter, Ramsey says, means "having the ability to ask the exact same question seven times and not have the person recognize that they've answered it before."

Ramsey might start a conversation by saying, "'Describe to me what you think your best opportunity would look like.' And you remember what was said, and you put that in your pocket. Fifteen or twenty minutes later, you say, 'Well, let's change topics a little bit. If there were an ad in the newspaper that really made you say, 'I want to dust off my résumé and get it over there,' what would that ad say?'

"Now you've got two pieces of information, and you compare one to the other. Are they the same?

"Number three, say, 'Can I ask you a question? If a friend called you from the Cisco location here in town and told you a story about an opening down here that really made you think this might be the time to cash in the chips at the place where you're currently working, what would that opportunity look like?' And you wait for the response. Now, you see that it's really the same question, but it's phrased entirely differently."

The candidate's ability to articulate a goal and to stick to that goal throughout the course of the interview shows Ramsey whether or not the person really knows what he wants and, by extension, whether he is truly ready to move to a new position. But locating qualified candidates who are able to state their objectives clearly and consistently is only half the battle. Before Ramsey can reach into his database and select a candidate who would meet a company's requirements, he must make sure that the position the company is asking him to fill is the position that actually needs to be filled. This means going into a company and second-guessing the instructions that were given to him by the most powerful decision makers in the building.

All too often, when Ramsey goes into a company, he discovers that the people in charge do not want to hear what he has to say, because they are afraid he might interfere with the status quo.

To determine whether or not he will have the chance to solve a company's problems, Ramsey will ask the person in charge a variety of questions before he will agree to perform the search. If a CEO tells Ramsey that he needs to hire a vice president of marketing, Ramsey might say, "Okay, you say you need a V.P. of marketing. But share with me—why do you think you need a V.P. of marketing? 'Oh, because our sales are down.' Okay, why don't you get a V.P. of sales? 'Because ours is perfectly good.' Well, then, why are sales down? 'Because the marketing is no good.' Who told you that? 'The sales guy.'

"After looking at this thing, you come to the conclusion that the marketing is fine; the sales guy is no good. A large percentage of the industry would have gone out and gotten a marketing person, and somebody who was following the company would have noticed that nine months later the marketing person was fired. Why? 'She didn't perform.' What do you mean? 'Sales didn't go up.' So it's her fault? 'Sure, we need a good marketing person to get those sales up.' What about the sales guy? 'Oh, he's still here.'"

Because Ramsey and his colleagues rely more heavily on their own intuition than what the company's chief decision makers say they need, they are quite often able to locate candidates who appear, on paper at least, as though they might not be qualified for the position in question.

For example, when David Beirne came up with the idea of moving Jim Barksdale from AT&T to Netscape, Ramsey remembers that some people said, "Well, wait a minute. What does somebody from Federal Express know about Internet browsers? I don't get it." But the shipping company and the Internet browser company had more in common than most people realized. "You may think that Federal Express is in the business of moving parcels from coast to coast," Ramsey says. "They aren't. That is a by-product of what they do: They keep you very happy by getting your stuff there on time. So that's where the parallel is when you're doing a search."

Ramsey Beirne's unusual "pattern recognition" approach to figuring out how to best fulfill a company's hiring needs is a result of exploring new frontiers: When they were first starting to find executives for new high-tech companies, there simply weren't any people with the experience necessary to fill the new high-tech positions. "When we got into the new worlds of shrink-wrapped software, there was no model, because there was no other shrink-wrapped software company," Ramsey remembers. "You couldn't unplug and replug; you had to do this pattern-recognition thing. Saying, 'Okay, what is the company actually doing? What else, someplace else in the U.S., looks like that? Is it a distribution model, is it a sales and marketing model, is it an engineering model, is it a production model?' And figuring it out."

If a company's management team expressed concern about the fact that some of Ramsey's CEOs didn't have much experience in the industries in which they would be working, Ramsey reminded them that the success or failure of a high-tech start-up is rarely dependent on a single individual. "If you can come up with the *perfect* CEO, then you're doing probably a better job than I can," he said. "Because by the time you finally get done with the description of the ideal CEO, you realize that if you run that through anybody's database, he or she doesn't exist."

Before Ramsey will begin searching for a new chief executive officer, he sits down with the company's board of directors and tries to figure out what the group is looking for. But more often than not, he discovers that each member of the board of directors is looking for a different set of characteristics.

"The first member says, 'Well, guys, you all know that we have a really technical product, so I want to see someone with both an under-graduate and advanced degree in a technical field,'" Ramsey hypothe-sizes. "The second member says, 'Although I couldn't agree more, I feel that sales has been the boondoggle of this company forever, so I want a guy with a strong sales background.'

"The third member chimes in, 'You guys are right on track, but I think that the sales issue is also one of not being able to position our product in the right way, so I want a guy who has a marketing back-ground that can give us the direction that we need.'

"The fourth member is nodding enthusiastically. 'But don't forget the VC and Wall Street. They always look for a CEO with a strong financial background. We need a guy who knows his way around Wall Street, in-vestment bankers, the venture capital committee.'

"They all look at each other with a smile of agreement and say to the search guy at the end of the table, 'Well, Chuck, I guess you've got your marching orders!'"

A CEO Is Like a Lead Singer

Believing in successful mid-career changes isn't difficult for Ramsey. He himself went through a substantial career change. Before getting into the business of figuring out how to satisfy the demands of big-time cor-porate executives, Ramsey spent his days figuring out how to satisfy the requirements of big-time rock-and-roll stars. "My first trips to Boston were to all the folk rooms along Boylston Street," Ramsey remembers. "I was a road manager, a manager, an agent, and I eventually worked my way up to [a top-flight talent agency called] International Creative Man-agement.

"Just on the other side of forty, I decided that it was a silly business, so I took a year of outplacement counseling—which is just basically a lot of testing and discussions of what you like to do and what you don't like to do—and in the process of networking, a fellow whose name I have forgotten said, 'Have you ever thought about being a headhunter?' So I said, 'What's a headhunter?' Having not the faintest idea."

Ramsey soon found out that being a headhunter for high-tech companies was remarkably similar to being an agent for star musicians, with one principal difference: As a headhunter, he could do some of his work over the telephone. For example, when Ramsey was working as an agent in the music industry, he used to spend his days following people like Chuck Mangione. When Mangione came to the greater New York area, Ramsey "would be at his shows every single night, hanging out against the dressing-room wall just in case he wanted something, or wanted to complain about something, or whatever."

After Ramsey moved over to the high-tech headhunting business, he still needed to make himself available to the high-flying VCs and CEOs, but at least he could do it from the comfort of his own living room.

"One of us answered that phone Christmas Eve, Christmas Day, Yom Kippur, Sunday afternoon," Ramsey remembers. "We didn't have an answering service, we transferred the call to one of the partners' homes. You sat there all evening with your wife answering the phone." If one of the Ramsey Beirne partners was out for the evening, the designated answering person would take each of the messages one by one and then relay the information to their partners' answering machines.

"Once when I was winding down my career with Ramsey Beirne, I was in the engine room of my boat when one of the venture capitalists called," Ramsey remembers. "I had to go out and lie on the front deck with the phone so that he couldn't hear the sound of the engines and know that I wasn't in the office.

"It's that kind of instant response, wherever you are. If you're unhappy, tell me what you want me to do and we'll stop everything else and make you happy. Partners would get us into problems, and we'd simply say to the president, 'What do you want us to do for you that will turn you into somebody who will say wonderful things about Ramsey Beirne?'

"Never walk away and never fail. Never have somebody out there saying, 'I think that their reputation is a lot better than they are.' Whatever it takes to make you happy, we will do. Period. End of discussion."

Give Yourself a Big Break

Turning struggling folk musicians into overnight sensations required more than simply making one's clients *feel* like stars. The other part of being an agent was figuring out how to introduce new talent to the kind of audience that would appreciate their music. This meant, for example, putting together so-called package tours that would allow unknown artists to piggyback on the success of a more established musician by serving as his opening act.

One of the struggling artists that Ramsey helped in this way was Billy Joel. "Fourteen thousand kids who had come to see Loggins and Messina were exposed to Billy Joel," Ramsey remembers.

But rock-and-roll singers are not the only ones who understood the importance of hitting the road and reaching out to their fans. At the same time that Chuck Ramsey was working to raise Billy Joel's recordings from the obscurity of record-store discount racks to the top of *Billboard*'s charts, Teradyne cofounder Alex d'Arbeloff was crisscrossing the nation with a similar goal in mind.

Although d'Arbeloff did not throw autograph parties, plaster his likeness across billboards, or conduct extensive rap sessions with the nation's deejays, he did spend time talking to the people who used Teradyne's testing equipment and asking them what they thought. "I believe strongly that if I really wanted to know how the company was doing, the thing to do was to go on a plant tour and ask the technician on the floor what he likes and dislikes," d'Arbeloff says, although he notes that this practice was often looked upon with suspicion by the company's regular field representatives. "Sometimes salespeople don't even want you to go out into the account because they are worried that you are going to stir things up and put them in trouble," d'Arbeloff says. But d'Arbeloff insisted because he believed that these interviews allowed him to observe the company's troubles firsthand.

D'Arbeloff believes that if a CEO is not willing to go out into the field and conduct his own customer-satisfaction surveys, he is unlikely to find out about his company's real problems, because salespeople don't want their bosses to think of them as complainers. "They're worried about the shooting-the-messenger problem," d'Arbeloff explains. The shooting-the-messenger problem refers to a scenario where a subordinate employee tells his superior that something is wrong and the superior responds by saying, "The trouble is that you have a bad attitude. You're negative." "Meanwhile," d'Arbeloff exclaims, "aahhh!!! People worry about that, and they have a tendency not to want to give you bad news. And yet it is the bad news that you need in order to fix things."

When he was not out on the road, collecting information firsthand, d'Arbeloff spent a great deal of time writing letters. "I would be writing to potential customers, writing to people that I was trying to recruit," d'Arbeloff says. By making a habit out of writing letters to both customers and employees, d'Arbeloff forced himself to come up with answers to the questions he encountered during his travels. And he claims that this practice—making himself available to both customers and employees (and then actually thinking about the problems that were brought up)—has been one of the key reasons why Teradyne was able to transform itself from a two-man operation into a proud member of the S & P 500.

"A lot of the young guys who are starting companies today—you ask them a question, and they haven't thought about it," d'Arbeloff says. "I would work on the idea until I could answer all the questions. And then, if I didn't know some answer, I would seek advice."

Is Your Career Based on Family Rooms?

One of the hardest things about making oneself accessible to one's customers and employees is that it gives people an opportunity to change their minds. If, for example, a customer knows that he will always be treated with respect and courtesy, he will not hesitate to bring a piece of unwanted merchandise back to the store. And if, in the case of an executive-search agency, the company's stock-in-trade is human beings, it becomes necessary to worry not only about whether the customer is satisfied with the purchase but whether the piece of human inventory will feel comfortable inside his new corporate package or change his mind and walk away from the deal.

"The last fifteen minutes of the deal—getting the deal closed—is what makes your mettle in search," Ramsey says. "You prove your quality at this juncture because there are so many competitive influences that affect a candidate. 'Gee, Chuck, if I'm doing this, I'm leaving N million dollars on the table.' Or, 'I can't relocate to California. My kid is here, my grandmother is there, I'm the chairman of this committee, my roots are here.'" To be successful as an executive headhunter, Ramsey says, the headhunter must remind candidates that they really are acting in their own best interests.

Of course, before an executive headhunter can encourage someone to act in his own best interests, he needs to understand all of the different factors that will have an impact on a person's ability to succeed at a given job.

"It's the hidden objection that stands up and bites you," Ramsey says. "'I finally talked to my wife about it last night, and she just is not all that excited about moving to Los Gatos, California.' Or, 'I talked to my son about it last night, and he said that if we leave X-Y-Z high school, he'll lock himself up in his bathroom and never come out for the rest of his life.' I remember once, for example, where a brand-new family room in a home in Acton was something that was causing somebody to say no to an opportunity. The family had finally added on to their home, and they had this great new family room, and that was affecting the decision. That's when you get involved in saying, 'Well, when you look at the opportunity we're talking about here, if we do everything the right way, you can have a family room in Los Gatos that's ten times what you've got now. Is your career based on family rooms?' And a high number of times, the candidate goes away and comes back within twenty-four or forty-eight hours, usually after hiding out, and says, 'Okay, I've talked it over, and you're right.'

"In the real world, people make decisions based on emotion and back them up with logic, not the other way around. People will decide to buy the second Jaguar and then will sit there and very logically explain it to you, while you say, 'My God, isn't that conspicuous consumption?' It's the same thing in leaving a company and going to another company or saying no to a partner and starting your own firm. It's emotional to begin with and then backed up by logic. So you have to get in step with them emotionally and understand what they are concerned about.

"You might say to a second in command, 'Do you want to live in the shadow of X for the rest of your career? Is that what you want history to talk about, that you were the number-two guy?' And a certain number of people will say, 'Hey. I really like this. This is really neat. He has to worry all night. He's the one who has the sweats on Thursdays. I like being number two.' But the people we're looking for are saying, 'No. You're right. I want to be number one and have history say that I was capable or I was not capable. It's a test for me.'"

This is why it is so important to make sure that candidates are able to state their goals clearly and consistently during the initial meeting: because if a person does not know what he wants or is not entirely sure about what he wants, it will be extremely difficult to hold him to his words at a later date.

"If search is practiced the right way, all you're doing is offering an opportunity to someone who has previously told you that they were interested in that type of opportunity," Ramsey says. "The recruiter has no way of forcing somebody or threatening somebody. All you're doing is saying, 'You told me you were looking for 1, 2, 3, 4, 5. Here is 1, 2, 3, 4, 5. Is this what you're looking for?'

"You have to keep pointing out to them that they said they were looking for a start-up that was backed by first-tier venture-capital firms, where they could get at least 9 percent of the equity and where the cutting-edge technology is perceived by everybody as important. The candidate keeps saying, 'Yes, I agree,' to all of this."

When Ramsey feels confident that the search candidate is ready to accept the offer that he has presented, he goes back to the person who paid him to do the search and asks, "'Did you tell me you wanted somebody who was able to think in terms of global rather than small, who would make our technology not just a technology but a necessity in order to do business?' And they keep going, 'Yes, yes, yes,' as you waltz them up the aisle to say, 'Will you take me?' 'Yes, I will.'"

Abandoned at the Altar

"The harder you hammer and the more you talk instead of listen, the higher the degree of probability that it won't happen," Ramsey says. "So let's say, for argument's sake, the issue is that the guy doesn't want to relocate because of a sick grandmother. And what you're trying to do is build up the logic of all the other positive things and sweep this under the rug. You can get the person to say yes to all these other things, and out of a hundred points, ninety-nine are yeses. But what is going to bite you in the ass is the sick grandmother, because you can't sweep her under the rug. So it's got to be a two-way street between what the client is looking for and what the candidate is looking for, with the search person just being that effective conduit."

Another major consideration is the feelings of the candidate's spouse. "I can't tell you how many times people have said to me, 'I appreciate it, Chuck, we've been through all this, and I know I am making your life miserable, but I am not going to lose my marriage for XYZ corporation.' That kind of reasoning is absolutely, totally fair, because it is right and propitious. If you shove somebody to Checkpoint Software and their marriage goes out the door, then what have you got? You don't have a brand-new executive; you have some guy who's on the phone fourteen hours a day talking to the kids and the attorneys and whatever."

But regardless of what people say, Ramsey believes it is relatively uncommon for executive matches to fall through because of sick grandmothers and wives who do not want to move. Most of the time, people are simply trying to figure out whether they could get a better deal somewhere else. "People weigh their decisions," Ramsey says. "People who have told you that they are looking for this are, in fact, weighing that decision against other decisions."

Assuming the Close

Knowing that his executive-search candidates are probably using the same set of techniques to shop for a new position that they would use to shop for a new Rolex, Ramsey feels free to borrow liberally from the art of sales. "When you get down to the end, it's just like in basic table selling," he explains. "You're assuming the close. It's all played out in white shirts and blue suits and rep ties and high-powered cafés, but it's no different than that."

Basic table selling involves certain ritualistic behaviors that allow a person to perceive, on both a conscious and unconscious level, that the long and protracted sales cycle is about to end. And here Chuck Ramsey goes into work mode. "The first thing you do when you get to the table," Ramsey says, drawing himself up to his full height while seated, "is you get your pen out, and you get your paperwork out, and you put your pen right there."

Ramsey puts his pen down on the table halfway between us so that it would be easy for me to reach out and grab if the spirit moved me. Then he folds his hands and rests his forearms on the table. "Okay," Ramsey says. "I've got an offer on the table, we've gotten the number of options to a reasonable number, and we've straightened out these three things you were talking about." He pauses for dramatic emphasis. "Is there anything else we should be talking about?" Pause. "Are there any concerns that you have about doing this?" Pause. "Is there anything that you want to share with me before we call up and accept?"

At this point, Ramsey stops and waits yet again and looks at me as though I should say something. But I don't know what to say. In fact, as I am sitting there in front of Ramsey, the only thing I can think about is the fact that he's sitting there in front of me, looking straight at me, and neither of us is saying anything.

It's the moment of truth. And to be honest, it feels a little awkward.

Wanting the moment of truth to be over, I pick up the pen and pretend like I am signing a contract.

This causes Ramsey to relax and finish the interview.

"If you and your customer are doing the job right," he says, "there is no heavy-handed close. You've met with the board, and the client has met with the board. The client has spent time with the hiring authority, whether it's the president of the company or the founder or whatever. It's not like a slam-bam-thank-you-ma'am kind of thing; it's working in that direction. 'Is there anything else we should be talking about? Are there any concerns that you have about doing this?'

"And then, if you want to check your work, you could say things like: 'Do you want to start on the first or the fifteenth?' Always close on a minor point."

Chapter Eleven

THE DARK CORNER

It's hard to work at a high-tech start-up. The frenetic pace at which technology advances is far greater than the rate of human evolution. Sometimes the stress of running a young company can make a person do things he would never dream of doing if he were relaxed enough to see the bigger picture.

A Silicon Valley Story

Software engineer Christopher Cotton had heard a great deal about the huge fortunes being made in high-tech start-ups, often by twenty-something computer programmers just like himself. So when a friend suggested that Cotton quit his job at AT&T Labs and come work for Scout Electromedia, Cotton decided to jump. "Everyone was talking about start-ups, saying, 'Oh, it's the coolest thing,'" Cotton recalls. One of Cotton's friends had founded an electronic calendar company that had been sold for millions, and another friend had been an early employee in that company.

The stories that Cotton was hearing—about twenty-six-year-old multimillionaires, thirty-something billionaires, and lucky latecomers who somehow wound up with a couple of hundred grand—were always tempered with the admonition that one should not count one's chickens before they've hatched and one should definitely not bank on the possibility of being able to cash in one's stock options. Still, Cotton admits he was "definitely hoping to do well and actually get some money."

If Scout did well and Cotton was able to trade in his stock options for a substantial chunk of cash, he figured he might do a little traveling: to Central America, to Asia, or even Europe. "Not just to sightsee," he emphasizes, "but maybe even to live there for a while."

In addition to traveling, Cotton hoped to earn enough money to work on some "open source" software projects that would be freely available to anyone in the world and possibly even to put some money aside for his relatives. "I thought about setting up a trust fund for my sister's kids or for the entire family," Cotton says. "No one would ever have to pay to go to school. They would be able to go to whatever school they needed to."

These days Cotton refers to such thoughts as "fantasyland," but he admits that his far-fetched dreams were a large part of what kept him coming back to the start-up day after day as the situation went from bad to worse. "If I knew that it was going to end up like this, I would have quit sooner," Cotton says. But Cotton did not know what the future had in store for Scout Electromedia. All he knew was what he was reading in the Internet chat rooms, the business magazines, and the daily newspapers.

When Cotton was making the decision to quit AT&T and join Scout, the news media were nearly unanimous in proclaiming that since the stock market was at an all-time high and VC was flowing in record amounts, it had never been easier for engineers like Cotton to make themselves a fortune.

"You get so sucked in by looking at it," Cotton says. "There is a whole fantasy that you play along with. Like 'If we get this, it could be worth this.' If we did this well, there was potential to never have to work ever again."

Christopher Cotton's recollections about what he was hoping to get out of Scout Electromedia are quite different from what Scout's cofounder, Bill Cockayne, remembers. "No one I know focuses on the reward part of it," Cockayne says. Instead, "they're doing it because they love it. The reward just happens to be part of the way it's structured out here [in Silicon Valley]."

Instead of trying to get rich, Cockayne's goal in starting Scout Electromedia was to create a wireless handheld device that would allow users to obtain information about various forms of entertainment, including movies, restaurants, and the theater. "We wanted to build something cool," Cockayne says. "We wanted to deliver cool information to cool people whenever they wanted it. If we had just set out to be rich, there would have been much easier ways to do that."

Cockayne wanted his wireless handheld device, called a modo, to be so easy to use that customers would not have to think about the fact that it was wireless. He wanted the modo to be attractive enough that people would feel comfortable using them in bars, in coffee shops, and in front of their trendy friends. He wanted the modo to be cheap enough that most people would be able to afford to buy them. And he wanted the original purchase price to cover all of the costs associated with creating new content and delivering that content to consumers.

Nine months after Scout Electromedia went out of business, Bill Cockayne is proud to report that he did meet all of his goals. Scout *did* create a beautiful handheld device, and the device *was,* for a brief period of time, offered for sale in stylish boutiques. The modo was easy to use and trendy enough to become popular with movie stars. Finally, the product's $99 purchase price was the only fee that anyone ever had to pay to access Scout's wireless network.

From Café to Garage

The brainstorming sessions that developed into Scout Electromedia took place in a series of coffee shops in and around Silicon Valley. Cockayne recalls drinking lattes in Menlo Park, espressos in Cupertino, and "anything with caffeine" at a place called Printer's Ink Palo Alto.

The more coffee Cockayne drank, the more excited he got about starting a new high-tech company. But as Cockayne and his colleagues became more serious about developing their idea, they recognized the need to build their company in a more traditional environment.

Scout's first noncafé office was a closet-sized room located "some-where in Los Altos." But the cramped, windowless vault was not the kind of place where Bill Cockayne felt comfortable spending a lot of time. And so, while the other two founders labored away in the small office, prepar-ing the company's business plan and envisioning potential partnerships, Cockayne worked to define the company's technology and architecture wherever he could find a free seat. Cockayne recalls doing much of his work at Café Borrone in Menlo Park, drinking latte after latte and envi-sioning the future of wireless media. "I'd sit there all day and work on the thing," Cockayne remembers.

As time went on, it became clear that the café-plus-closet combina-tion was not going to meet the company's real-estate needs. And so the group moved: first to a second-floor space on Brannan Street and then to a former tire-and-radiator warehouse in the SOMA district of San Fran-cisco.

Although Silicon Valley garages have become legendary for nurturing generations of highly successful high-tech companies, Bill Cockayne tells me that the decision to move into a literal garage was made for purely practical reasons. The Internet boom had driven rents on class-A office space up to around $100 per square foot, and Scout wanted to keep its costs down. Because the tire-and-radiator warehouse had been zoned for heavy manufacturing, it was off-limits to the sort of dot-coms that were driving up prices. And since Scout was planning to deliver its content through a physical device, which would need to be physically manufac-tured, the company was able to classify itself as a manufacturing opera-tion for the purposes of obtaining the lease.

It would be hard to understate the romance that has attached itself to those start-ups that are lucky enough to begin in bona-fide Silicon Val-ley garages. But Cockayne assures me that there was nothing glamorous about the Scout warehouse. When the company moved to 580 Bryant Street, Cockayne says, there was nothing in the building except a few pil-lars.

"It was about half the size of a high school gym, with twenty-five or thirty-foot ceilings," Cockayne remembers.

Scout's employees spent a particularly grueling weekend laying down carpeting, cleaning the windows, and hanging up white boards. But their efforts at transforming the warehouse into a fully functional high-tech of-fice were only partially successful. The building's main lighting source was a series of ancient skylights, which Cockayne describes as being "pretty leaky." The roofing situation was so bad that the first time it rained, several Scout employees took it upon themselves to climb up on the roof of the building and throw tarps over the skylights in the hopes of reducing water damage.

As more and more skylights were covered and as the warehouse be-came darker and darker, Cotton began to marvel at his own ability to put up with the working conditions. "You have this idea of the kind of per-son you are, what your standards are," Cotton says. "Looking back at it, you say, 'Well, how did I stay so long when I really wasn't enjoying it?'

"It's almost like you're in a bad relationship. Looking back, you say, 'Why the hell did I stay so long?' You don't have a good answer. But you know, somehow, that you did."

Throughout most of his tenure at Scout Electromedia, Christopher Cotton had been motivated by the expectation that if everything went ac-cording to plan, he would wind up an extremely wealthy man. But after the stock market collapsed and the possibility of an initial public offering became increasingly remote, Cotton kept his job out of a sense of loyalty to his fellow engineers. "I couldn't leave," Cotton explains, "because I re-alized that if I left, there was no way we would finish the product, and it would pretty much screw everybody else."

A Very Ambitious Task

Before Scout could get its entertainment reviews into its signature handheld devices, it needed to hire journalists to prepare the reviews in the first place. Next, the company needed to build a special wireless-enabled Web site that could receive the data and store it until it was re-quested.

After they had built an appropriate Web site, Scout's engineers needed to develop a working relationship with a company that knew how to transmit wireless messages. And then there was the task of build-ing the devices themselves and getting them into stores.

Taken singly, none of the things Scout was trying to do were particularly challenging. But since the company was not trying to do any one thing, but rather to put together an entire chain of semidifficult processes, there were a number of places where mistakes could be made. "The complexity of the product from end to end was more than most people could understand," an engineer named Steve Orens recalls.

To make matters worse, Christopher Cotton recalls that the company was running into several troublesome areas. "The device was having some reception problems," Cotton recalls. "We weren't sure what the problem was, but we were only getting 40 or 50 percent of the stuff we were sending through, and sometimes we wouldn't get anything."

Cotton identified his various concerns at a company meeting, but he felt that the managers had unrealistic expectations. One thing that Cotton says made it difficult for him to meet his deadlines was that there simply weren't enough engineers to do the work. "We hadn't been able to hire people as easily as we had wanted, so we didn't have the people working on this stuff, and it was taking us longer than we had thought." Cotton recalls that when the company lured bright-eyed recruits into the building, Cotton sometimes had difficulty holding up his end of the interview. "Some of it felt like, 'Yeah, it's really great to work here. I absolutely hate it, but you ought to come and work here, anyway.'"

Bill Cockayne remembers things a little differently. "We ended up getting great people, and more of them than I had planned," he says, noting that he had personally hired about fifteen of the company's eighty employees.

It Can't Happen to Me

As time went on, Cotton became increasingly aware of the wide variety of high-flying Internet companies that were starting to declare bankruptcy. But it never occurred to him that *his* company might go out of business. "It didn't really register that that could happen to us," Cotton says. "It was like, 'Oh, those guys didn't have a good idea.' If you let it register, then you wouldn't be working on it at all. You have to have an optimistic outlook to be able to attempt something."

As frustrated as Cotton was during the company's final days—about the unrealistic deadlines, the debris raining down from the ceiling, and the lack of light—he still retained a flicker of hope that he would at least be able to see the product through to completion.

That is, until he received an E-mail informing him about the Meeting.

"Normally we had this Monday meeting at one o'clock," Cotton remembers. "And we got this E-mail saying that the Monday meeting was being postponed until Tuesday morning at ten o'clock and it was mandatory for all employees, including remote offices.

"None of the meetings had ever been mandatory for remote offices, so I knew something was happening. And then, the next morning at ten o'clock, the meeting got postponed until eleven o'clock, and then it got postponed until twelve o'clock and one o'clock.

"Around one o'clock we had the meeting. They said, 'Sorry to say we're closing our door today at five o'clock. So you'll have half of your owed vacation time, and you get paid up until today, but no severance. Sign and turn in all your keys and everything at five o'clock.'

"Then the H.R. person talked, telling us to go through and clean out our desks, and they had recruiters there to try to get all of our résumés together to help us find other jobs.

"And then that was it.

"People were asking, 'What happened?'"

What happened was that Scout's managers decided that since they would not be able to raise future rounds of VC, it was necessary to shut down the business. "I found out later that it [the reason they kept postponing the meeting] was because they were on the phones with various investors and people, trying to get money from somewhere," Cotton recalls.

Perhaps the management team decided that there was no longer any possibility of being acquired by one of the big-name technology companies with whom they had been having conversations.

Perhaps the management team was disheartened by the dot-com downturn articles they kept seeing in the very same glossy business magazines that had once sung their praises.

Perhaps the company's managers got sick and tired of trying to enforce deadlines that were not enforceable.

Or perhaps, when the last plywood board was finally placed above the last remaining skylight, the managers simply lost the will to continue.

The Explanation

There was, of course, some logic behind what happened at Scout Electromedia. According to Bill Cockayne, the explanation is "pretty simple."

Like other manufacturing companies, Scout Electromedia was obliged to run up high manufacturing costs to create its stylish handheld devices. And also like other manufacturing companies, Scout Electromedia was obliged to use its capital to pay for the manufacturing of these devices.

Cockayne recalls that Scout's managers had been expecting to receive a bridge loan that would allow the company to pay its employees through January, at which point the company would be able to use its strong Christmas sales receipts to raise another round of venture financing.

Confident that they would be able to obtain that bridge loan, Cockayne recalls that the company's managers "took $2 million in cash and sent it to Malaysia to have the devices built."

Scout Electromedia did not squander its money on high salaries and complementary back rubs. Instead, Scout's management team made the completely rational decision to spend their remaining dollars buying parts.

"The problem wasn't really us," Cockayne tells me. "We got caught on some financing issues that weren't really our fault." When the stock market collapsed, Cockayne says, it rendered the company's current investors either unable or unwilling to put any more money into Scout.

And with the newspapers filled with tales of dot-com doom, Cockayne and his colleagues developed the idea that even if they were able to obtain a bridge loan, "the stock market probably wasn't going to be any better in January."

In the end, Cockayne says, he and his colleagues were obliged "to put the company to sleep."

"There were no evil intentions on anyone's part," Cockayne says.

Looking back on the situation, Cockayne can think of about a thousand things that he would have done differently if he had the chance to do it all over again. "But none of them really have to do with the things that took us down," Cockayne says. "People just aren't paying for technology companies now." As a result, "We're just losing technology."

The company named Scout Electromedia does not have anything in common with the dot-bombs that attracted so much negative publicity. "The product was real," Cockayne emphasizes. "It did all of the things that we set out to do, from a conceptual and tactical standpoint." And besides that, "it looked cool."

That Scout Electromedia ultimately went out of business does not diminish Cockayne's pride in having built a beautiful and easy-to-use wireless handheld device. "In Silicon Valley there is no onus for failing as long as you didn't fail for stupid reasons," Cockayne says. "You're not going to be tainted by the failure. If you're not failing quickly and failing often, then you're not really trying."

The loss of Scout Electromedia, or of any other individual high-tech corporation, is unlikely to have an effect on the reputation of an entrepreneur like Bill Cockayne. "You work for the Valley," Cockayne says. "You don't work for any of the companies inside the Valley."

What Cotton and Orens Learned

"One of the big things I learned was being able to trust myself more when I don't think we can do something," Christopher Cotton tells me. "And even if people don't agree, to stand up and say, 'No, it's not going to work this way,' as opposed to just going along with the masses." Cotton now understands the value of setting modest but achievable goals rather than banking on the notion that one's company will eventually become publicly traded. "A much better thing is to take something and try to develop it and sell it for double or triple the amount of time and energy that you put into it," Cotton says. "I'm amazed at any company that can go from five people to a hundred people and have the infrastructure, because it's really hard. There is just so much to do there in order to have a well-run company."

Engineer Steve Orens agrees. "We would all like to be rich million-aires one day, but you have to be realistic," Orens says. "It's much better if you can do less and actually get your product out the door."

There was a time when Steve Orens believed that it was necessary to solve all of a company's technical problems before a product could be shipped to customers. But he now believes that it is better to ship a product that is imperfect—and to earn some money from that imperfect product—than to wait until all the kinks are worked out. "Don't try to hit a home run at the first shot," Orens warns. "It's much better to get on base and to get another turn at bat."

The Trouble with Customers

In my travels through the high-tech community, I learned a great deal about the dangers of working for a start-up. The following stories are based on real events, but some names and identifying details have been changed or presented in composite form.

"Steven" is a young man with jet black hair and extremely attentive eyes. I interview Steven at a tiny café in Harvard Square, which has carved out a niche for itself by refusing to serve coffee. We pour ourselves glasses of iced tea, and Steven makes fun of me when I try to sweeten mine with honey. "Honey gets crystalline when it's iced, doesn't it?" Steven asks. "It doesn't dissolve like sugar."

He's right. As I sip my tea, I keep crunching on chunks of the newly crystallized honey.

A few years ago, Steven founded an Internet consulting company that helped people design strategies for the World Wide Web. When Steven was first starting out, he became excited whenever he received queries from foreign lands. "We had customers in Japan and Russia and Saudi Arabia," Steven brags. "But after a while, we started to specialize on customers closer to home."

Steven's decision to focus on domestic accounts resulted from a problem he had with a customer overseas. The customer was a prominent insurance salesman who wanted help with the development of his Web site. Steven was happy to have the man's business, since it seemed likely that the site would attract a great deal of traffic. But as Steven worked on the site, he began to notice a number of news articles about fraud allegations against insurance companies in the man's country.

"So I sent the guy an E-mail," Steven says. "I said, 'Hey, I've got a great idea. Why don't we build some antifraud mechanisms into the Web site? That way the site won't be able to be used by any computer hackers.'"

The insurance salesman responded in an extremely defensive manner, saying that in thirty years of doing business he had never heard of a single instance of insurance fraud. This response didn't make sense to Steven, since the newspaper articles had appeared only the week before. But he tried not to think about it. The insurance agent was one of Steven's most dependable customers, since he always paid his bills on time. Although Steven's intuition told him that there might be something fishy about the account, he was able to rationalize the business relationship by focusing on the bottom line. "When you're a small business, you can't always pick and choose who to work with," Steven explains.

A week after Steven received the defensive E-mail, tragedy struck. The same newspapers that carried the stories about insurance fraud reported that Steven's customer, the prominent insurance salesman, had been forced into a bathroom and shot dead. "The whole thing was really weird," Steven says. "I completely didn't know what to do about it. This guy was our client, and suddenly he got shot. And it definitely had to do with the business. It's not like he was fighting over a woman or something."

The newspaper articles made a number of allegations about the man's possible involvement with an international drug circle, which may or may not have committed the crime. Steven had no way of knowing whether any of these allegations were true, but they made him extremely nervous. "What if he had been part of an international drug ring?" Steven wondered. "I'd heard he had been making a number of trips to Malaysia."

The more Steven thought about the possibility that his client may have been associated with the international underworld, the more nervous he became. "I didn't want to have anything to do with a drug ring, but we found ourselves in a Catch-22 situation," Steven recalls. "If we kept on working with this company, we might be doing business with the mafia. But if we dropped them as a client, we'd piss them off."

As an Internet consulting company, Steven had a serious relationship with his clients. If he were to suddenly walk away from an account, the client would have an extremely difficult time recovering. "If you spend four months working with a company to design a Web site and then you run away from the project, the customer is pretty screwed," Steven says. "You can't just hand the code to someone else and expect them to know what to do with it. Besides, this is the Internet we're talking about. You lose six months of effort in Internet space and you're dead. You know what I'm saying?"

After carefully considering his options, Steven decided to keep on working on the account. "We didn't want to take the chance of pissing off somebody who was going around shooting people," he explains.

But it was much easier to decide to keep the account than to sit down at the computer and actually build the man's Web site. Whenever Steven would try to work on the site, he would become extremely agitated. And it didn't do any good for Steven to take long walks to calm his nerves, since the more he walked, the more he became convinced that someone was following him. "I wanted to walk away from the whole situation as fast as I could, but I kept wondering about the repercussions," Steven says. "I mean, what was happening on the other side of the world that I didn't know about?"

Steven eventually decided to minimize his risk by finishing the Web site as quickly as possible. "We ignored our other clients and spent all our time on this one project," Steven remembers. In the end, he didn't even bother to send out an invoice for the final portion. "We ate $25,000 so we could get out of there quickly," Steven says.

Looking back, Steven feels that the experience taught him an important lesson about doing business in an environment where face-to-face meetings are rare. "It's important to know who you are doing business with even if they do pay their bills on time," Steven emphasizes. These days, Steven and his coworkers go to great lengths to screen new clients before committing themselves to an extended relationship.

The Importance of Vesting Schedules

"Rob" and "Jake" had been working on their video-game company for about nine months, but they hadn't been able to convince any VCs to provide them with seed-stage financing. The problem, the VCs kept saying, was that the engineers didn't have anyone on their management team with enough experience to properly manage a growing company.

When "Pete" expressed interest in serving as CEO for their high-tech start-up, the engineers were delighted. Pete had an MBA from a top-tier business school and an extremely impressive résumé. Pete said he would have no problem lining up financing, since the VCs would be blown away by his amazing track record. And the boys wouldn't have to waste their time shopping around for a corporate lawyer, since Pete had a lawyer friend who had been helping him out for years. While Rob and Jake were putting the finishing touches on the company's special video game, Pete would ask his lawyer to draw up the company's official legal documents.

This arrangement seemed fine with Rob and Jake, since they didn't know a thing about raising VC. Up until this point, the engineers had been financing the company with their combined life savings, which they had already deposited into their corporate bank account. The engineers estimated that the money they had in their corporate bank account would keep the company solvent for a few more months, but no one wanted to wait for the money to run out before they started to look for financing. If Pete thought he would be able to use his connections to raise VC financing right away, the engineers were happy to let him do it.

The incorporation document that Pete's lawyer came up with said that the company's stock would be divided into three equal pieces, with Pete, Rob, and Jake each taking one-third. Each team member would receive full ownership of all his stock, or become "fully vested," on the day he signed the letter of agreement. Rob and Jake were happy to sign the document, since they thought this meant they would all be equally committed to the new company. Unfortunately, that's not how things worked out. While Rob and Jake were grinding away on the video game, Pete continued to work at his day job.

Pete was drawing a huge salary at his large and well-respected workplace, and he told the boys he just needed to stay there "a little bit longer" to build up his rainy-day fund. It was hard, Pete said, for a person as prominent as himself to sever his ties with his large and impressive employer. Besides, Pete said, if he made his phone calls from inside his impressive workplace, the financial folks would see him as an "insider." As an insider, it would be that much easier for him to raise money.

As time went on and Pete remained with his original employer, Rob and Jake became increasingly uncomfortable with the equity arrangement that Pete's lawyer had set up. Pete had full access to one-third of the video-game company, but he didn't seem to care about the company's future. Whenever Rob asked Pete when he would be able to join the company full-time, Pete reminded him how difficult it was to find a CEO with such an unbelievable track record. When Rob asked how things were going with the fund-raising process, Pete said, "Great!" But he never talked about the details.

After a while, Pete stopped returning Rob's phone messages. And then, one day, he told Rob that he didn't want to be part of the company anymore. After taking some time to think things over, Pete had come to the conclusion that he just wasn't cut out for life at a high-tech start-up. He said he would feel much more comfortable holding on to his job at the big corporation.

In retrospect, Rob said that he should have been able to see this coming, since Pete had never done any work for the company in the first place. But while Rob and Jake were slaving away on the video game, they didn't have time to worry about Pete's behavior. They were so relieved to have a top-notch guy on board that they never bothered to ask themselves whether or not he was committed to running the company. Instead of confronting Pete about not quitting his day job and not bothering to do any of the things he said he would do, Rob chose to focus on Pete's track record.

The most surprising thing about Pete's decision to leave the tiny company was his insistence that when he left, he would take "his third" with him. Rob and Jake were a bit confused about what Pete thought his third was, since as far as they could see, the company didn't have any appreciable assets. At the time of Pete's departure, the boys hadn't managed to raise any VC financing, and they hadn't sold a single copy of their video game. When they looked around their tiny, cramped office, the only things they saw were their trusty computers, their extensive collection of medieval-theme playing cards, and a few cans of Coca-Cola.

But Pete's lawyer pointed out that the company *did* have three important assets, regardless of whether or not the engineers could see them. They had the video game that Rob and Jake had created, the goodwill that they had managed to establish with other members of the video gaming community, and the money in their corporate bank account.

Pete didn't want to have anything to do with the company's embryonic video game, since he didn't know a thing about computers. And he wasn't able to walk away with the company's goodwill, since that only existed inside people's minds. But Pete *could* take the money in the corporate bank account. By Pete's lawyer's calculations, that money, the engineers' combined life savings, represented exactly one-third of the company's total assets.

Pete's lawyer told Rob that if he didn't hand over his cash reserves, Pete would bring a lawsuit against their company. And nobody wanted that to happen. Rob and Jake had enough to worry about just getting their video game ready for market, and they had signed a legal document that entitled Pete to one-third of the corporation. Pete's lawyer told the engineers that he appreciated the fact that they were likely to have a difficult time recovering from the loss of their impressive CEO, but business was business. And as difficult as the breakup was going to be, a protracted legal battle would be even worse. The lawyer argued that it would be much better for everyone involved if they simply settled the matter out of court and promised never to talk about what happened. After all, the lawyer emphasized, Pete had a fantastic reputation to protect, and if the engineers got a reputation for being the kind of video-game developers who engage in lawsuits with their CEOs, no one in the financial community would want to have anything to do with them ever again.

Looking back on the situation, Rob wishes that he and Jake had threatened to bring a lawsuit against Pete instead of the other way around. "Suing him would have annihilated his reputation at his prestigious firm and completely destroyed his career," Rob reflects. "He would have realized that, and he would have backed down. We would never have had to go through with the lawsuit." But when the situation was actually occurring, the young engineers were reluctant to follow their instincts and challenge the advice of such an important and experienced businessperson. "We should have gotten a second opinion from someone we trusted," Rob reflects years later. "But we were naive and trusting and young."

In the end, the situation was resolved when Rob and Jake wrote Pete a check for the entire contents of their corporate bank account.

How to Avoid Getting Taken

The case of Rob and Jake is certainly appalling, but corporate divorces happen all the time. And whenever relationships break up, there are bound to be disagreements about how to divide the assets. I asked corporate lawyer Andrew Updegrove if he has ever heard about entrepreneurs disagreeing about equity arrangement.

Yes, Updegrove replies, he certainly has.

"A typical case starts out with four or five people who munge around for a while, and then two or three of them decide to go forward," Updegrove says. "Two people decide not to go forward, but they think they've already earned the right to something. Now, even if we assume that they were right, that they had participated enough to have a right to something, they often have totally unrealistic expectations about what a fair amount is. So you get into some ugly wrangling between people who used to be friends.

"Meanwhile, the company ends up with a diversion, an expense, and a cloud over its capitalization. In the extreme case, we've had clients who've spent over $100,000 on litigation before they had a product, and they almost killed their financing. The lesson is that founders should be very clear about who gets what and what they have to do to get it. And then they should put that on a piece of paper and sign it."

The legal phrase that means "deciding what you have to do to get your stock" is "setting up a stock-vesting schedule." In a typical stock-vesting schedule, the stock vests over a four-year period. During the first year, the company might utilize something known as "cliff vesting," where none of the stock vests for an entire year. At the end of the year, the founders might take full ownership of 25 percent of the stock that they are ultimately entitled to. The remaining 75 percent will vest over the next three years on a quarterly, or monthly, basis.

Some entrepreneurs believe that stock-vesting schedules were invented by VCs to ensure that entrepreneurs would receive as little of their own companies as possible. But Updegrove believes that vesting schedules will also serve an entrepreneur's own best interests. "Let's say that there are four people in the company," Updegrove hypothesizes. "The founder owns 20 percent, three other people each own 20 percent, and everyone else in the company owns 20 percent. Now, let's say the three other people were there for a total of six months before they decided to go their separate ways.

"Four years later, the company is completely different from the company that they started during the first six months. But because they didn't have vesting, the three people who effectively did nothing are getting a huge windfall. The person who really did all the work, sweating it out and living on nuts and berries that whole time, is getting horribly undercompensated. So, in my view, vesting is something which every founding group should have for their own protection."

A founding team wouldn't necessarily use the same vesting schedule that a VC would, because a VC's standard vesting schedule involves five years of labor with nothing vested up front. If they have already done a significant amount of work before they get around to setting up a vesting schedule, Updegrove recommends vesting 25 percent up front for work already performed and allocating an additional 25 percent for cliff vesting. The remaining 50 percent would vest gradually during the second and third years.

If entrepreneurs do find financing relatively quickly, the VCs might ask them to extend their vesting schedule. But not all companies wind up with VC financing. "Sometimes companies are acquired before they receive their venture capital, and sometimes they simply aren't able to find any willing investors. But they succeed, anyway," Updegrove says.

Another way to ensure that a company's stock will be distributed in a fair and equitable manner is to tie a person's vesting schedule to that person's performance rather than to the amount of time a person spends at a company. When Pehr Anderson, Alex Laats, and Chris Gadda were setting up NBX Corporation, Anderson and Gadda's vesting schedules were tied to their ability to achieve certain technical milestones by certain specific deadlines.

The underlying assumption in NBX's stock-vesting schedule was that if Anderson and Gadda could get their telephones to work on the days that Alex needed to show them to the investors, the investors would be more likely to give the company the financial resources it needed to continue to grow. If Anderson and Gadda were not able to get the phones to work in time for the investor meetings, the investors would lose faith in the company, and the stock would lose its value.

In this particular "results-based" stock-vesting schedule, Anderson and Gadda demonstrated their commitment not by remaining with the company for an extended period of time but by working extremely hard to develop the telephone prototypes by the deadlines that Laats had established.

One of the reasons why NBX Corporation grew into a $90 million business was that Anderson and Gadda knew exactly what they were supposed to be doing, when they had to be finished, and why this was important. This clear understanding of the what, when, and why of the equity-vesting schedules provided a solid basis of trust among the founders of NBX Corporation.

The following story illustrates what can happen when founders are unwilling to discuss the exact details of the way a corporation's equity will be distributed.

The Importance of Writing Things Down

"You have two choices in life," a high-tech entrepreneur named "Chang" tells me. "You can work for someone else, or you can start your own business. I would prefer to start a small company and build it up big rather than work for someone else in a large corporation." To earn the capital he would need to start his own business, Chang got a job as an independent consultant for a large Philadelphia-based company, helping the company create a software package that would streamline its preparations for the year 2000.

When Chang was finished with the consulting gig in the late spring of 1998, it occurred to him that many other large corporations would

also need to prepare themselves for Y2K. Since Chang already understood the sorts of procedures a company needed to go through to prepare itself for Y2K, he saw an opportunity to apply this knowledge to
other companies around the world. If Chang could develop a reputation
as the world's premier provider of large-scale Y2K solutions, he could
make a killing.

Chang estimated that the places that would most need his services
were places like hospitals and air-traffic-control towers, where the risk of
Y2K-related lawsuits was thought to be especially high. To achieve Y2K
compliance at a place like a hospital, Chang told me, it was necessary to
take inventory of every single piece of machinery that contained a computer chip and figure out which of these items would need to be replaced. Then, after the hospital had made a list of everything with a
computer chip in it, they would need to obtain written documentation
from each and every company that had manufactured these chips to determine whether or not the chips were Y2K compliant.

Chang's solution to this managerial headache involved hiring a team
of technical experts to go through a hospital, take inventory of every suspect item, and feed this information into a database. Once the database
had been created, Chang's software could compare the information
about the hospital's various chips against information that had already
been provided by the chips' individual manufacturers to determine
which chips were and were not Y2K compatible. Once the entire suite of
chips had been entered and checked, the software could compile an extremely targeted report detailing how much work the hospital would
need to do to achieve Y2K compliance. "Then you could play a game of
volleyball with the due diligence," Chang explains. "The liability was
being passed around like a hot potato."

Chang had no intention of stating conclusively whether a given chip
was or was not going to shut down on New Year's Eve. And because
Chang's database did not actually verify that the chips were Y2K compliant but instead simply reported what the chip's manufacturers had reported, Chang believed that he had found a relatively risk free way to
profit from a business niche that could potentially be worth hundreds of
millions of dollars.

To take full advantage of this unique business opportunity, Chang would have to build on his previous job experience and develop an entirely new database. But simply building the database was not enough. Chang would have to begin marketing his company's services as soon as possible or else risk missing the window of opportunity.

Building such a database would require the cooperation of a wide variety of individuals. And convincing them to help out was not going to be an easy task, since Chang didn't have the money to pay them.

Chang felt confident that he would be able to recruit enough programmers to finish the database long before December 31, 1999. But he worried that a larger software manufacturer might create a rival product and steal his market share.

To reduce the probability of having his idea stolen, Chang made the decision to classify all of the information related to his company as a trade secret and to make certain that everyone he talked to signed both nondisclosure and noncompetition agreements. To further protect the security of his idea, Chang went out of his way to avoid creating any sort of written agreements whatsoever, including agreements that specified how much stock each employee was going to have.

Chang's decision to avoid preparing these documents created a great deal of stress for an employee named "Jun," who had agreed to work for the company, sans pay, in the hopes that he would eventually receive a percentage of the company's equity. And the decision to avoid writing things down seems to have created some tension for Chang, too, since it prevented both Jun and Chang from coming to a complete understanding about how much stock Jun was eventually going to get. "Jun would agree that a certain amount of equity was okay and then change his mind," Chang remembers. "You can't agree and then keep changing the structure of the company just to please somebody. That's just not okay."

Jun remembers things a little differently. "I tried to cement my role in the company and talk about what my equity stake was, but Chang kept telling me I was being too greedy," Jun explains.

Jun thought that he and Chang had reached a verbal agreement about equity. According to Jun, 20 percent of the company's equity would be reserved for VCs. Of the remaining 80 percent, just over half would be reserved for Chang, in recognition of the fact that the company had originally been his idea. The rest of the stock would be divided among the company's various employees, with Jun receiving about 6 percent.

Once they had gotten the equity discussion out of the way, Chang thought that things were more or less settled. But in Jun's mind, things weren't settled until he had received a piece of paper with the equity agreement clearly laid out in black and white and with both their signatures. Half of Jun wanted to continue hounding Chang until he had produced something in writing that explained how much stock he was going to get, but the other half thought that would not be a good idea.

After all, Jun rationalized, if he truly trusted Chang, then he should trust Chang to come through with the agreed-upon amount of equity. And if Jun revealed that he did not trust Chang to do what he said—by continuing to nag Chang about the equity agreement—Chang might start to doubt Jun's loyalty to the organization.

Jun did not want Chang to doubt his loyalty, since he truly believed that his buddy's "bullheaded" tendencies would ultimately cause him to be extremely successful as a high-tech entrepreneur. "I thought that as long as I could stay on his good side, even if this company didn't work out, there would be other opportunities to work together in the future," Jun recalls. Therefore, to show Chang how much he valued their friendship, Jun chose to stop nagging Chang for a written equity agreement and instead focused his energies on building the best possible Y2K-preparedness database.

Those Crazy VCs

Chang's unwillingness to explicitly state how much equity each employee had in the business was regarded with some suspicion by the VC community. "Venture capitalists are picky," Chang explains. "They have a set notion of what they want to see in a company." One of the things that VCs wanted to see was a well-defined equity arrangement between the members of the founding team, which Chang's company most emphatically did not have. Another thing that VCs wanted to see was the potential for a well-defined liquidity event, where they could get their money back several times over. "They want to see a return on investment over a five-year period, with the potential for a buyout or an IPO," Chang explains. "This company didn't have time for either."

Chang had heard stories about VCs who took over boards of directors and replaced perfectly good twenty-something founders with more experienced management teams, and Chang had no intention of being replaced. ("It wasn't that he was a control freak," Jun explains. "He had an idea, and he saw the potential in it. What would happen if he gave control of the company to someone else and they screwed it up? He would never be able to forgive himself.")

Concerned that the VCs would likely take his company away from him or at the very least spend several months deciding whether or not to make an investment, Chang began to reconsider whether he wanted to strike a deal with VCs in the first place. Chang had connections to a number of extremely wealthy angel investors who lived in eastern California, several of whom appeared to be interested in backing his company. But the angel investors stipulated that before they would give Chang a red cent, he would have to relocate the company to California.

With only fifteen months to go before 2000, Chang wanted to close on his seed round of financing as quickly as possible, and he was more than willing to go through the trouble to move to California. But Jun wasn't sure he could afford to move. There was no longer any money in his bank account, and he was getting awfully close to the limit on his credit cards. Still, Jun recalls that when he mentioned this to Chang, Chang told him not to worry about a thing. Once the money came through from the angel investors, everyone would be able to start drawing a salary. In the meantime, Chang told Jun that the angel investors would cover Jun's moving expenses, and they would provide Jun with food and shelter once he arrived in California.

When Jun hesitated, Chang reminded him that they were talking about the opportunity of a lifetime and that if he passed it up he would never be able to forgive himself.

In the end, Jun decided to move to California.

Trouble in Paradise

Once Jun arrived in California, his feelings of insecurity about not having a piece of paper that told him how much equity he had in the company began to intensify. And Jun's uneasiness became even more pronounced once he got settled inside the communal house that was provided by the angel investors. "Chang gave himself the master suite and put me in the closet," Jun remembers. "I didn't even have a bed."

Because the house was over a mile and a half from the nearest town, it was necessary to have a car if one wanted to go anywhere. But since Jun didn't have a car, he found himself spending all of his time in the house. "I was the workhorse," Jun remembers. "My job was to sit in the corner and program."

The situation became worse when Chang cut Jun out of the company's tiny board of directors. "So now, in addition to not knowing how much of the company I owned, I also didn't have a say in the decisions," Jun recalls. "Putting his friend on the board and leaving me off was just saying to me, 'You're a piece of shit.'"

Jun recalls that when he complained about being excluded from the board of directors, Chang and his friend reminded Jun how lucky he was to be part of the company at all. And then they took it a step further. "They made it personal," Jun recalls. "They said I wasn't able to project a good social image for the company. They said the only reason I was still involved with the company was because I had these technical skills."

That hurt. After everything Jun had done to show his friend how dedicated he was and how much he wanted to be a part of the company, Jun couldn't believe Chang would say that Jun lacked social skills.

The more he thought about it, the more Jun began to wonder whether he had made a mistake by agreeing to come to California. "I felt like I betrayed myself," Jun recalls. "I kept asking myself, *How could I have allowed this to happen?* But then I thought, *If I make my millions off the company, it will all have been worth it.*"

Unsure about what to do next, Jun placed a long-distance phone call to his parents. And Jun's parents advised him to call a lawyer, which he did. Unfortunately, the lawyer that Jun happened to choose at random from the phone book on Chang's kitchen counter turned out to be working for Chang. "Chang found out about the call," Jun recalls. "I don't know how he found out about it, but he found out. He said that if I needed to call a lawyer, I should have gone to him."

When Jun realized that the lawyer he had called was working for Chang, he began to panic. "It looked really strange that I would call his lawyer," Jun says. "I thought he would see that as the ultimate act of betrayal."

Trying to remain rational, Jun placed another phone call to his parents. Then he put his cell phone in his pants pocket and went to talk to Chang. "I left the phone on so that my parents could contact the authorities if he became violent," Jun explains.

Jun recalls that as he went to confront Chang one final time, he was shaking. "I know what I said about being committed to the team," Jun said, "but I just can't handle this. I quit."

"You're fired," Chang reportedly shot back. Then: "You need to leave right now."

Jun had so little money that he could not afford to hire a cab to take him to the airport. And he no longer trusted Chang enough to ask him for a ride. Luckily, Jun's parents were willing to give him their credit-card number over the telephone. With his parents' help, Jun was able to find a taxi driver who accepted third-party credit cards. Then he went back to the closet, hurriedly packed his things, and carried them out to the driveway.

Jun recalls that as he waited for the taxi, Chang surprised him by offering to solidify their relationship. "He offered me one percent of the company if I would promise not to tell anyone else about the idea," Jun recalls. "And standing out there on the driveway, I still wanted to accept that one percent."

But as Jun looked around at the pile of suitcases, jackets, and sleeping bags, he made the decision to cut his losses and move on.

Accepting the equity agreement that Chang was offering him would have forced Jun to promise that he could never, ever, discuss the idea with anybody else. But even worse, it would ensure that at some point in the future, Jun would have to see Chang again. The last thing Jun wanted was to put his signature on a piece of paper that would bind them together in perpetuity.

At the final moment, Jun decided to put the past behind him and get as far away from Chang as he possibly could.

When the cab pulled up, Jun told Chang that he would think about his generous offer. Then he climbed in the cab and shut the door.

He left without signing the paperwork.

Dealing with the Fallout

It took Jun over a year to get to the point where he was able to talk about his start-up experience. But now that he's had a chance to think things over, he's determined to seek out new entrepreneurial opportunities. "If I allow this to kill my spirit, then I would have really lost," Jun says.

In the future, when Jun joins a new high-tech start-up, he plans to do a few things differently. Here are some of Jun's resolutions:

- Define roles early on and be explicit. "Communication is key, especially when they give you legal documents to sign and say, 'Trust me.'"
- Pay attention to, and follow, good advice. "I got a lot of help from people, but I didn't use any of it. I wish I had."
- There is a fine line between wanting to protect one's ideas and being completely paranoid. "It's hard to know who to trust, but trying to maintain control to that extent is not going to be healthy," Jun says.

A corporate lawyer added the following: "If it is such a touchy situation that the person has a problem with anything being memorialized, you should see that as a warning flag."

What Chang Learned

Not surprisingly, Jun's departure from the company did not make anywhere near as much of an impression on Chang as it did on Jun. "Jun did not stay on throughout the duration of the business," Chang said simply. "We had some differences, and he didn't end up staying on. He was just there in the very beginning."

What Chang does remember is how successful the company became after Jun left. "It was really a fast-moving start-up," Chang remembers. "The entire life span was less than four months. We found that it was in our best interests to sell it rather than to pursue the direct-market thing, although there was a potentially large sum of money to be made. We just ran up against a wall in terms of time.

"In the end, we sold the rights to the software to a competitor, which is good. I got out more than I put in, so that made it worth it to me."

Chang is proud of the success of his company, and he is glad to have had the opportunity to learn the things he did. One of the things Chang learned is how important it is to develop a solid business plan and to create explicit written agreements stating how much stock each individual is going to get. "Because when you think about it," Chang explains, "your initial team is basically working for free—those people aren't getting paid during that time.

"It's amazing when people do that much work without discussing what the equity arrangements are. So you should really define equity arrangements well in advance. But you shouldn't always say that every person that came on in the first stage gets the same amount of stock." Chang admits that it can be extremely challenging to determine how much equity each person will receive, for there is no preexisting formula. "It's almost like you're trying to assign a tangible value to people who have no tangible value," Chang reflects. "But the person who has ownership of the idea is worth more than anyone else."

The idea that the person who has "ownership" of an idea is worth more than the people who are brought in later to develop that idea is shared by many people in the high-tech community. But in cases like this one, where entrepreneurs refuse to leave a written record of who came up with what and when, it can be difficult to determine who has "ownership" of which ideas. For his part, Jun remarked that "Chang had the original idea, but the idea was developed during conversations with me. And we had been talking about this on an informal basis for a long time."

Chang suggests that entrepreneurs spend some time, at their company's earliest stages, figuring out how they are going to protect their intellectual property—by filing for patents, for example, and obtaining official copyright protection for one's software—if only to improve the chances of obtaining financing from professional VCs. "The people who are going to fund the idea will be very worried if they don't see protection," Chang warns.

Finally, Chang observes that in some instances, it may be better if technical founders allow professional business managers, with real business experience, to perform some of the company's key roles. "It could be worse for the company to have a technical founder running it," Chang reflects. "But really, it's just a matter of personality."

Getting Caught Up in the Details

When a VC decides to invest in a new corporation, he asks his lawyers to draw up a legal document known as a "term sheet." The term sheet provides the legal basis for the VC's future involvement in the company, and it contains clauses that are designed to protect the investor's interests.

Since the whole point of a term sheet is to protect an investor's best interests, it may seem to an entrepreneur that the term sheet is slanted in favor of the VCs.

It is.

Quite often, when entrepreneurs take the time to read the fine print on a VC's term sheet, they become annoyed. One entrepreneur, whom I'll call "Robert," became so annoyed with the fine print on a term sheet he was offered that he got into a fight with his VCs. "We were going back and forth on this horrible term sheet, and each time it came back it was worse," Robert remembers. "They would just throw in traps. Like, you know, 'We aim to approve all employment agreements.' They wanted us to sign this term sheet before we had any employment agreements. What does that mean? That means that the investors can do whatever the hell they want. They can say to me, 'Well, if you leave this company anytime within the first year, you lose all your equity.'"

Robert's obsession with convincing the VCs to alter their term sheet rendered him unable to consider his actions within the bigger picture. In hindsight, Robert can see that the terms he was fighting over were irrelevant. In hindsight, Robert wishes he had asked an expert to help him figure out whether or not it was worthwhile to press for better terms or to simply accept what was on the table. But Robert did not ask any dispassionate outsiders to help him with his negotiations, and in the end he was not able to reach an agreement with his VCs. Sadly, the term sheet that Robert was so vehemently opposed to wound up being the only term sheet that he ever received.

Looking back, Robert wishes he had been less idealistic, and more realistic, about the term-sheet negotiation process. "My experience tells me not to be too picky on terms, because it's all about bottom lines in the end," Robert says. "Either today I have five million dollars, or I don't have five million dollars and I'm still trying to raise money."

Andrew Updegrove has seen approximately seven hundred term sheets during his long career in corporate law, and he has developed strong opinions about which terms are, and are not, relevant. "There are a lot of terms in VC deals that look horrible," Updegrove admits, "and some of them may be horrible, but there has never been a VC deal without those terms in it. If you start trimming back on a lot of terms that really don't matter, you'll wind up looking amateurish. Second, you'll waste a lot of time and goodwill arguing about things that don't matter. Third, you'll delay the deal." To avoid wasting time on details that don't matter, it's a good idea to seek advice from people who are experts at negotiating term sheets.

A VC's View

Over beers at the Muddy Charles Pub, I ask Jonathan Goldstein of the VC firm TA Associates to explain why VCs insist on putting weird-looking terms in a term sheet. "Most terms in a term sheet exist because of the institutional history of the firm, where the firm has been burned before on a certain issue and wants to avoid making the same mistake twice," Goldstein explains. "In other words, they've learned, 'Hey, you know what? I don't want to be involved if a company is going to be like this. I only want to be involved if it's like that.' So they put that into the term sheet.

"We personally have had bad experiences in companies with CEOs that don't live in the same city where their companies are located. Now, I think it's unlikely that we will make an investment where a CEO does not live where the company is. We've tried it enough times, and you bang your head against a wall, and no matter how many times you think it's different, you find out that it's not different enough.

"There are a variety of terms that I like to use that are unconventional, but I like to use them because I think they help each party gain comfort. For example, I like to see selling shareholders [i.e., company founders] represent that they own the stock certificates that they are selling us. Okay? I don't think that's an unreasonable thing to ask. And in fact, if a selling shareholder won't sign that they own the stock certificates that they're selling us, it naturally makes me nervous, as I am not a big fan of buying property from a seller who does not own it.

"I once spent two weeks negotiating with a company because they would not, in what's called 'representations and warranties,' sign on that they owned their stock certificates. And I just said, 'Hey, guys, whether or not you own the stock certificates is something that you know and I will never know before closing this investment. And if you're not willing to bear the risk that you own your own stock certificates, how can I bear that risk?'

"I also like to make sure that the companies that I invest in have in fact paid their taxes. Okay? And if they haven't paid their taxes, there is a penalty to the seller, not the buyer. There is a representation and warranty, and if they violate it, there is something called indemnification, which means that they have to make good on it. The CEO of a company knows whether he or she has paid the corporate taxes."

[The Appendix contains a sample term sheet that was drafted by a corporate lawyer named Gordon R. Penman. The right-hand column contains the actual terms, and the left-hand column contains Penman's comments about which terms do, and do not, matter.]

"It's so sad," Robert admits, looking back on his failed term-sheet negotiation. "So many term sheets are abandoned because people can't agree on terms. After my deal fell through, I started to hear stories about how often it happens."

Being Broke

If an entrepreneur operates under the assumption that she will be able to close on a round of financing and then her deal falls through, she may find herself in an extremely uncomfortable situation. Shortly before Petra Krauledat was about to close on a round of financing for a biotech company called Sienna Biotech, her VCs went out of business. "We started talking, we got to the term-sheet level, and then the fund crashed," Krauledat remembers. "It was a very unpleasant experience. At that point we had broken off discussions with other people, so we had to reactivate everything."

While Krauledat was reactivating her relationships with the other VCs, she and her husband had to find some other way to pay the bills. "We had to sell one car because we didn't have enough money to live another month," Krauledat remembers. "I drove the car over to the dealership, took cash, and walked home."

In the end, Krauledat was able to obtain $4 million in VC from the plumbing-fixture company known as American Standard. And the biotech company that she founded was successful enough to be sold for a handsome profit. But Krauledat will always remember how difficult it was to convince VCs to invest in her tiny start-up. "We had given ourselves basically two more months until Peter would go back and look for a job and I would give up the idea," Krualedat said. "We went pretty far down the road and said if this doesn't work, we're just not going to start a company."

While it is extremely unlikely that an entrepreneur will find himself in Krualedat's position, negotiating a term sheet with a VC fund that is about to run out of cash, it is quite common to underestimate the amount of time necessary to close on a round of financing.

While I was researching this book, the business newspapers were filled with glowing stories about how easy it was to obtain VC financing. And the fund-raising process was easy, for some people. But for many more entrepreneurs, the fund-raising process was extremely long and arduous. For this reason, many of the people who have observed the entrepreneurial process over a period of years recommend that new entrepreneurs spend some time thinking about what they can and can not afford to put at risk. "Put the absolute minimum number of dollars of your own money into your start-up, particularly if you're going to go for venture capital," Updegrove advises. "Invest your time and your ideas; don't invest your money. It's bad enough to have it fail and to be replaced by the venture capitalists, but to have sunk your life savings in it as well isn't a good idea."

A long time ago, when entrepreneur George Emmanuel was trying to obtain financing for his first high-tech start-up, he spent every penny he had preparing a demonstration for a VC. The demonstration went well, and when it was finished, the VC invited Emmanuel to go out for a cup of coffee.

The VC's invitation to go out for a cup of coffee put Emmanuel in an awkward position, since he didn't have any money in his pocket. But Emmanuel didn't want to offend the VC, so he and his cofounders agreed to go along.

The awkwardness reached its peak when the group got to the cash register and Emmanuel made an exaggerated attempt to avoid reaching for his wallet. "After you," the VC said. "No, after *you*," Emmanuel replied. After a few rounds of increasingly desperate politeness, it occurred to the VC that Emmanuel was flat broke.

"It's like that poster with the frog in the bird's mouth," Emmanuel says, referring to his entrepreneurial experience. "The frog's head and his body are already gone, but he's still pressing against the beak with his arms and legs. The caption says, 'Never give up.' That's what it's like in a start-up. You just keep going and going. Something inside you makes you keep going."

In the end, George Emmanuel did succeed in raising the VC financing.

It's Like Sales

NBX cofounder Alex Laats never ran out of money, but he did come extremely close on several occasions. One of the things that Laats did to reduce the level of tension inherent in the fund-raising process was to keep a written record of every conversation he had. "I had a little binder, and in that binder I put sheets of paper for each venture capitalist I was going after," Laats recalls. "I put down their names, their addresses, and their phone numbers. Almost every day I would take the thing and go page by page and make the follow-up phone calls, set up the meetings, do the whole thing. If I had to add another page to that particular venture capitalist, I would add another page. And when the thing died, I would just say, 'Dead.' Or, you know, 'No.'

"It's like sales. You have to track it, follow up leads, send information. The process stays the same at each stage of raising money."

One of the people Laats talked to was a man named James Currier, who was at the time an associate with Battery Ventures. Currier was impressed enough by Laats's sales pitch to investigate the opportunity more thoroughly, but he was disappointed by what he found. "I knew of at least four other Ethernet telephone companies that had gone out of business," Currier remembers. One of the companies Currier uncovered as he was performing his due-diligence research had blown $8 million in VC financing before going out of business.

Wary of wasting another $8 million on yet another Ethernet telephone disaster, Currier opted to pass on the NBX opportunity. "It's just timing," Currier explains. It was an accident of chronology that Laats presented his business plan to Currier after the four other Ethernet telephone companies had already gone out of business, and it was equally accidental that the Ethernet telephony market happened to pick up when it did. "Back then, datacom and telecom didn't talk to each other," Currier recalls. "I just don't think the market was buying. And maybe the record will show that NBX wasn't actually selling much when they sold the company. That just proves once again that it's 70 percent luck."

Chapter Twelve

ENTREPRENEURS AND THE MEDIA

Back in the 1960s, when Alex d'Arbeloff and Nick DeWolf were founding Teradyne, it was possible to start a new high-tech company without much help from the media. "I don't think that we thought that a lot of advertising was going to make the difference," d'Arbeloff says. "We've done advertising, but our main method of distribution was direct sales. And we spent a lot of time on direct sales."

Instead of spending his time building his company's brand, d'Arbeloff recalls spending time building new products, distributing those products, and recruiting people to join his company. "We expected that we would sell the equipment, but we didn't think anybody would buy it unless somebody came and talked to them," d'Arbeloff explains. "The equipment was expensive, and it needed a human face to represent the company. I spent a tremendous amount of time on that issue."

When I ask d'Arbeloff how important it was for a young entrepreneur to obtain positive press coverage, he says, "It depends what business you are in. If you are in the movie business, then it's probably vital. If you are in the capital-equipment business, it's in the 'it would be nice' category. Not vital."

I was intrigued by d'Arbeloff's nonchalant attitude toward the

media, because it was so different from the attitudes of the other entrepreneurs I had interviewed. Most of the entrepreneurs I had interviewed
understood that a well-crafted advertisement or a favorable mention in a
prominent business newspaper could mean the difference between obtaining a much-needed round of VC financing and watching one's company fade into obscurity.

"The dirty little secret of the whole Internet craze is that most of
these companies are based solely on marketing," Mike Bloomberg, the
founder of Bloomberg Markets, told *Business 2.0.* "The problem is, if you
stop the marketing, if you run out of advertising dollars, a lot of these
businesses will go away."

What Publicity Did for Gregg Favalora

Before Actuality Systems became the subject of an extremely favorable article in
the *Wall Street Journal,* it had been having a hard time making ends meet. Having
used up most of the money that founder Gregg Favalora had been able to raise from
his own family and the $10,000 that Favalora won in MIT's $50,000 business-plan
competition, the company was operating out of the basement of Favalora's shared
apartment and paying its employees largely with chunks of stock.

But during the week after the article appeared, traffic on Actuality System's Web
site increased by 2,000 percent, and Favalora began to be deluged with calls from
prospective investors.

At the time that the article appeared, Favalora had already convinced a professional investment banker that his company warranted a $115,000 investment. But
the banker's offer was contingent on Favalora's ability to raise an additional $400,000
from other sources.

Thankfully, Favalora didn't have to wait very long to close his round. Slowly but
surely, the buzz that was generated by the article in the *Wall Street Journal* was translated into a round of angel investments from sixteen different individuals totaling approximately $1.5 million.

"That initial offer, with the *WSJ* article coming out soon after, was the initial push
we needed to get the funding excitement going," Favalora recalls.

With cash in hand, Favalora was able to exchange his basement laboratory for a
garden-level suite of offices just outside Route 128.

The Effect of Publicity on High-Tech Start-ups

Matt Kelly, features editor for *Mass High Tech,* is well aware of the positive effect that good publicity can have on a high-tech start-up. Several months ago, *Mass High Tech* ran a story about a twenty-two-year-old who had come up with an idea for putting a computer chip inside a running shoe. Inside the shoe, the chip would measure the amount of pressure on the foot and help make jogging more comfortable. "We had a great little picture, and we put him on page one," Kelly recalls. Today, a news producer from an Italian television network expressed interest in featuring the shoe on Italian television. "That could be the critical mass this guy needs to start selling these shoes in Italy, then in Europe, then in America," Kelly says. "He could be the next Nike. But who knows? Had he not had that great photo, we might have put it on page twelve."

Quite often, Kelly's decisions about what to put on his newspaper's front page and what to put in the back are influenced by what he happens to have on his desk at the moment he is putting the paper together. If a glossy color photograph originates from one of *Mass High Tech*'s photojournalists, fine. If a photograph is taken by a commercial photographer who has been retained by an entrepreneur and the photograph is on Kelly's desk on the day that he is putting the paper together, that's fine, too. As news editor, Matt Kelly is always more interested in the newsworthiness and quality of a photograph than in how the image comes to him.

A good news photo, Kelly says, "could be something as simple as a head shot of the CEO. Or it could be the CEO of a shoe company, sitting in a pile of sneakers. That's good, it's eye-catching, it tells you what the company is." But all too often entrepreneurs are unable to tell the difference between a good news photo and a run-of-the-mill brochure photograph. "If it's just you sitting at a desk with a big corporate logo behind you, that's not really a good photo," Kelly says. "If my photographers did it, I would scream at them. If you do it, I'll look at it. If I need something to fill space, I'll run it. But if I have the choice, I'll spike it."

A Newsworthy Photograph

Entrepreneurs are encouraged to page through a traditional photojournalism textbook to find out what makes a photograph newsworthy. A good place to start is the *Associated Press Guide to Photojournalism* by Brian Horton.

If an entrepreneur is putting together a corporate brochure and he only has enough time to take one photo, he should consider making that photo as newsworthy as possible. That way, if he finds out that his company is going to be featured in a publication like *Mass High Tech,* he can send a copy of the already-existing photograph to the editor who does layout.

When spending money on corporate photography, always remember the following: Newsworthy photographs can be used for corporate brochures, but traditional brochure photographs are not front-page news.

The Importance of Being Flashy

"One of the things I feel bad about," Kelly tells me, "is that there are companies out there that legitimately are run by good, smart people. And just because nobody knows about them or nobody cares about them or they are not doing anything particularly interesting, they never get the critical mass to fly on their own.

"We cover a lot of start-ups, and a lot of start-ups fall into that category: They are doing important, yet boring, work. They never get written about, nobody knows about them, and they go out of business. You feel really bad that you see companies come and go."

When a company does get media coverage, it makes it easier for the company to obtain the resources it needs to grow. And as the features editor, Kelly is often responsible for deciding what stories will be presented more prominently to his readers. "I did it this afternoon," Kelly says. "I decided, 'I'm going to put this story on top with the big headline, and this one is going to go on page twelve.'

"Which one is going to get more interest from the people who have the money? From the lawyers who are going to pitch them services that they might need to go public or to sue a competitor? Who is going to get that attention? The guy on page one. Not the guy on page twelve." The guy on page 12 might have a better idea, but if Kelly can't find a color photograph to go along with the great idea, "that's going to go on page twelve, because it's just a block of gray text. That's life."

The Journalist's Dilemma

There is a difference between reporting the news and making the news. A person who reports the news is supposed to remain objective about the stories that he or she is covering, whereas a person who makes the news is free to derive as much benefit as he possibly can from the news articles that are written about him.

Most business newspapers have strict policies about whether or not their reporters are allowed to own stock in the companies they are covering. In many instances, reporters are prohibited from owning stock in the companies they are writing about. The idea behind these sorts of guidelines is that a journalist will find it easier to be objective about a given company if he or she does not have a financial stake in that company.

When the stock market is crashing, most journalists are happy to obey their publishers' guidelines about not buying stock in the companies that they are covering. But when the stock market is booming, it can be awfully difficult for an impoverished journalist to remain objective about the companies that he or she is writing about.

During the height of the dot-com frenzy, print publications were filled with stories about those individuals who seemed to exemplify the promise of dot-com wealth. Journalists were often asked to write about people who commissioned $300,000 automobiles, double-decker boats with two toilets, and $41 million airplanes that they bought, for cash, over the Internet. But the journalists who wrote these stories were not allowed to share in the wealth that they were helping to create.

Granted, no one was forcing the journalists to keep their jobs at the print publications. Journalists have always had the option of quitting their jobs at traditional newspapers and taking better-paying jobs at high-tech start-ups. As dot-com employees, journalists would probably not face the same rigid restrictions about buying stock in young companies that they faced as business journalists. But it's important to remember that those individuals who did choose to remain behind at the print publications and to write more and more stories about the huge amounts of wealth being generated by high-tech start-ups were able to write these stories because, and only because, they had decided *not* to take part in the Internet gold rush.

Of course, many writers did choose to go after the dot-com wealth. In February 2000, the *San Francisco Chronicle* reported that "journalists are jumping on-line, either to pure media ventures or to start-ups that desire some quasi-journalistic content."

India's *Business Today* agreed: "We were in the thick of a mass exodus, with journalists from the print media quitting at the drop of a hat, beckoned by . . . fat pay packets and the lure of the Internet."

The "mass exodus" from paper-based publications to quasi-journalistic Internet-content jobs had a profound impact on the people who stayed behind. After all, whenever a reporter left a newspaper, another reporter had to be brought in. This meant collecting résumés, conducting telephone interviews, checking references, flying candidates out for interviews, putting candidates up in hotels, and taking them out to expensive dinners—while simultaneously trying to put out a newspaper. It was therefore not surprising that as the Internet frenzy continued and journalists were confronted with more and more examples of former colleagues who had made their fortunes at Internet start-ups, some newspapers were forced to take drastic steps to retain their best writers. "In December [1999], the *New York Times* quietly surprised more than 140 newsroom staffers with stock options as one reward for sticking with the paper," the *American Journalism Review* reported.

Chris Jennewein, vice president of technology and operations at Knight Ridder New Media, told *Business 2.0* why such steps were needed. "The pay is often higher in new media, the upside potential is far higher, and the work is often more interesting," he explained. "Would a bright college graduate rather join a content-oriented on-line start-up or slog her way through covering suburban city-council meetings?"

Why Journalists Loved the Internet

When the Internet was new and therefore newsworthy, journalists loved to write stories about it. And for good reason: In addition to creating more jobs for journalists and increasing competition for journalists' services, the Internet promised to have a profound impact on how journalists performed their jobs.

"It boosts your reporting ability tremendously, and it interconnects news outlets far, far more than they were ten to fifteen years ago," Matt Kelly says of the Internet. "It's sort of like, once one of us reports it, in short order we all know about it and can report it."

The Internet also made it easier for journalists to conduct background research. "When you are gathering information, you can find any source on any topic at any time," Kelly says. "When I started this business in 1993, that was not possible. You can get a whole lot more detail, you can get much more information, and you can get it faster."

But newshounds weren't the only ones who stood to benefit from the coming of the Internet.

The Internet was supposed to be good for consumers: It would allow them to search for the lowest price on anything they wanted to buy.

The Internet was supposed to be good for the nation's youth: It would allow them to access any number of different encyclopedias without having to trek down to the local library.

The Internet would be good for the nation's elderly: It would allow them to buy groceries without leaving the house.

The Internet would be good for democracy: It would make it easier for voters to get information about political candidates.

Finally, the Internet would be good for authors: It would provide them with thousands of new opportunities to interact with their readers.

Before the Internet, there was not much that an author could do to improve the way that her book would be received. She could go on a book tour, of course, and she could take out advertisements in print newspapers, and she could ask her local bookstore to display the book in their front window.

But it was exhausting to go on a book tour, and it was expensive to take out space ads in prominent newspapers. And it was frustrating to compete with all the bookstore's other authors for the privilege of having one's book displayed in the front window.

Into this maelstrom of writerly angst stepped a company called Amazon.com, which promised to completely transform the way that books were marketed. Because Amazon.com was bent on becoming "The Earth's Largest Bookstore," it was only natural that the company would want to carry every single book that had ever been published.

Never again would authors have to beg bookstores to display their titles in prominent locations. With Amazon.com's referral system, readers who had purchased similar books would automatically receive information about new books in the same category.

Never again would authors have to deluge potential book reviewers with free "review" copies and other promotional materials in the vain hope that someone would say something nice about their work. With Amazon.com's reader-driven reviewing program, reviews could be written by anyone with an Internet connection: the author herself, the author's mother, or any number of the author's closest personal friends.

No longer would authors have to beg their editors to tell them how many people were buying their book and how their book's sales compared to the sales of rival titles. With Amazon.com, if an author wanted to know how her book was selling, she could go to her book's Amazon.com homepage and see for herself.

In her novel *4 Blondes,* Candace Bushnell described a writer who is so taken with Amazon that she visits the site every morning, as soon as she arrives at work, to see how a fellow journalist's book had fared the previous evening. "She checks his book's sales ranking, then she scrolls down over the reader reviews," Bushnell writes. "Her favorite one is this: Boring and Utterly Pointless."

The reviews vary from day to day, but their effect on the journalist is always the same: The journalist, Bushnell writes, "feels thrilled and terrified at the same time."

Thrilled and terrified at the same time. Clearly, Amazon.com had the power to addict writers. And once they were addicted, writers responded to their new favorite Web site by showering it with previously unheard of levels of adulatory press coverage.

"As you sit there reading, say, a literate and charming book review from Bangladesh, the real power of the Amazon brand comes home," *Time* proclaimed in the article that explained why it had named Amazon.com's founder, Jeff Bezos, its 1999 Person of the Year. "It is a site that is alive with uncounted species of insight, innovation, and intellect. No one predicted that electronic shopping could possibly feel this alive."

Amazon.com made writers feel more alive because it allowed writers to see what other people were saying about them behind their backs. And it is difficult to imagine any gift that would be valued more highly, and written about more obsequiously, by a group of individuals who make their living telling people what everyone else is saying about them behind their backs.

The more press Amazon.com got, the more people found out about the company.

The more people found out about the company, the more people used the site.

The more people used the site, the more reason there was to buy the company's stock.

And so Amazon's stock went up.

Way up.

As the stock rose, it became even more socially acceptable for journalists to write about Amazon.com. If the company was valued that highly, it had to be doing something important, right?

"Because publicity is the currency of our time," wrote journalist-turned-entrepreneur Michael Wolff, "it is not unreasonable to assume that there is a Darwinian capitalistic earning process to such riches. Even people who should know better (even those for whom manipulations of the press are a daily accomplishment) are almost always impressed, or rankled, by someone else's publicity."

The more publicity Amazon.com got and the more its stock went up, the more it deserved to get such publicity/currency, and the more people wanted to copy the company's success.

And so a rash of business-to-consumer Internet companies emerged, selling everything from cosmetics to outdoor barbecue sets.

For a while, this seemed like a good thing.

An increase in the number of Internet businesses meant an increase in the number of new jobs created and more money for those industries that were associated with them.

More Internet companies meant more computers sold, more coffee consumed, and more mouse pads given away.

But What About Everyone Else?

As the Internet boom continued and more and more journalists abandoned the paper-based publications in favor of more glamorous and higher-paying jobs at born-yesterday Internet companies, some of the writers who remained at those paper-based publications began to wonder what sort of an effect the so-called Internet revolution was going to have on the folks who did not have any stock options.

"Whatever the reason, in America today the skills that come with age and experience appear to count for less and less," *Fortune* announced in an article called "Finished at Forty." Because the New Economy was, after all, being driven by twenty-something workaholics who had both the physical stamina and the child-free lifestyles necessary to accommodate their eighty-hour workweeks, it seemed clear that if the dot-com revolution was allowed to achieve its alleged potential, *Fortune*'s readers would experience a rude awakening. "For those who have made it (status, money, fan mail, a title, a corner office), there's no problem; but for the millions who are just decent everyday performers, it's another story," *Fortune* warned. "These people are squeezed: They can't rise to the top (there's no room), and right behind, ready to overtake them, is another generation."

Tim Carrico, the owner of TCO Real Estate and Property Management Company, told the *San Francisco Chronicle* exactly what it meant to get squeezed out by the dot-com marauders. "The people we rent to make lots of money, and those who don't, the artists and writers, they just have to move out," Carrico was quoted as saying. "And I'm just sick about that. I hate the artists and writers being displaced, because that's part of the reason I'm here."

Tim Carrico wasn't the only person who resented the social restructuring that occurred when Silicon Valley real-estate prices went through the roof. "A growing number of Bay Area cities are closing ranks in a simmering battle against dot-coms that have swarmed into once-sleepy downtowns," the *San Francisco Chronicle* reported in another article. Apparently, a large number of Bay Area residents were coming to the realization that the "daily congestion, skyrocketing housing costs and dwindling parking spaces" associated with the encroachment of high-tech start-ups were too great a price to pay for the increased tax revenue and new jobs that such companies were creating.

Kill the Dot-Coms!

As the Internet frenzy began to wane, I attended an entrepreneurial networking event at a once-celebrated dot-com. A few months earlier, the company's founder had assured me that everyone he talked to was over-joyed to hear about his latest ideas. But now, as the entrepreneur stood on a raised stage before his circle of guests, it appeared that his fifteen minutes were up. "Some people are saying that the era of the dot-com is over," the entrepreneur began, his voice quavering. "But I think they're wrong."

As he prattled on, a VC from one of Boston's finest VC firms, who was standing between myself and the entrepreneur, raised the index fin-ger of his right hand to the soft, fleshy area below his left ear and drew his hand quickly across his throat. Glancing at his partner, he made a strange half-choking, half-gargling sound in the back of his throat and began to laugh softly.

His partner elbowed him in the ribs.

Up onstage, the entrepreneur directed his comments toward a mi-rage located somewhere above our heads.

The Revenge of the Print Media

"Two of my best reporters quit to form their own dot-com," says *Mass High Tech* features editor Matt Kelly. "They also happened to quit to open an on-line site that tried to compete directly with my newspaper.

"They were part of the dot-com bubble. They were paid far more than we will ever pay a reporter. They got stock options, which, at the time, seemed very lucrative.

"I didn't fault them for doing it. I mean, both of these guys want to buy a house. They want to have a family and whatnot. They could have done it much more quickly working for that dot-com had all the rules stayed true.

"Well, all the rules didn't stay true. Their stock options are now worthless. Do they still make money? I assume so. Their dot-com is still in business, but I don't know what their cash flow is. Could they lose their job at any point? Yes."

The task of trying to find, and retain, qualified technology writers has become one of Matt Kelly's biggest headaches. "It's a great problem to have, that we're doing so well we can't find the people, but nonetheless . . ." Kelly says. After going to all the trouble to find a qualified writer and train him to write for *Mass High Tech,* "it sort of stings to see somebody who I've hired for three months announce that he's going to quit, and he's got a 50 percent raise and stock options. Do I take a little glee in the dot-coms stumbling? Well, yeah, I do. Because the simple way for them to have avoided that was to have made money. And they weren't. They planned to conquer the world but didn't really figure out how to do it without a whole lot of red ink. So, I get some glee about that.

"On the other hand, if this reporter who left came back and said, 'Look, I need a job, I'm willing to work for you guys,' am I going to hire him? Of course I would. I have a reporting job to fill."

Frustrated news editors couldn't very well use their headlines to address their true feelings by printing "Hey, Dot-Coms! Quit Stealing Our Writers!" across their front pages. But they could emphasize how risky the young companies were, and they would write long, detailed articles about the dot-coms that went out of business.

"The sock puppet is roadkill," the *San Francisco Chronicle* announced.

An article in the *New York Times* said the following about Pseudo Programs: "Building a sort of on-line television network of video channels, its employees used to boast that they would destroy television as we knew it. Six years later, the networks are still here and Pseudo is nothing more than a memory of a brash company gone bad."

"These days, it's open season on the Web," the *Wall Street Journal* observed. "In fact, the pile-on deriding the tech sector sometimes is as over-the-top as the initial hyping was."

Michael J. Mandel, the economics editor at *Business Week,* wrote a book called *The Coming Internet Depression: Why the High-Tech Boom Will Go Bust, Why the Crash Will Be Worse Than You Think, and How to Prosper Afterwards.*

"When venture capital dries up, so will the multitude of jobs being funded by it," the editor predicted. "The young college and business-school graduates who joined the dot.com revolution hoping for a quick score will be back living with their parents. . . . The biggest cuts will happen among the people most intimately associated with the New Economy—the Web site designers, the marketers at dot.coms, the consultants and investment bankers who rode the boom, and the journalists who covered them."

And the journalists who covered them. In other words, *Business Week*'s economics editor was telling anyone who would listen that the seemingly glamorous Internet writing jobs were not any better than the good old-fashioned entry-level jobs at places like *Business Week.* Any journalist who thought he could do a better job delivering content than the editors who paid his salary had better think again, because any journalist who left his post to try his hand at Internet bingo was likely to find himself not only unemployed but back home living with his parents.

"In an increasingly inhospitable environment, many dot-com companies that seemed destined to rule the world only a few months ago are abruptly dying off," the *New York Times* announced. Later in the same article, the *Times* told its readers that "experts foresee an acceleration [of dot-com bankruptcies] in the months ahead, as hundreds of Internet companies simply run out of money."

It was a clear message to any reporters who were still harboring fantasies of leaving the paper and going off to pursue their own Web fantasies. "Spinning Web sites into gold, it seems, has become nearly impossible," the *New York Times* declared.

A reporter from the *San Francisco Chronicle* tracked down a man named Doug Levy, who left "a great gig" as a tech writer for *USA Today* to work at an on-line drugstore and health site called PlanetRx. Levy was laid off from his dot-com job a year after he started, the *Chronicle* reported, and now he was forced to make his living as a public-relations "flack." "Levy's experience shows what can happen when a writer goes to a Web company that does not run a pure 'content' site—such as Salon.com or TheStreet.com, where journalism is the main product," the *Chronicle* warned.

But as the Internet euphoria began to wane, some of the journalists who had taken jobs at Web sites with high editorial standards were also affected by the dot-com downturn. In December 2000, twenty-five people were laid off at Salon.com, which the *San Francisco Chronicle* called "one of the most well-written sites on the Internet." And another content site, TheStreet.com, was also affected by the dot-com chaos. Having replaced its chief executive, changed its business model, and lost a string of key writers and editors, TheStreet.com of November 2000 had a little in common with the Internet "high flier" that it once was. Advertising revenues had failed to meet the company's lofty expectations, "and the explosive growth of magazines such as the *Industry Standard* and *Red Herring* created tremendous demand for financial journalists—leading to higher salaries," the *Chronicle* reported.

Having had their own businesses disrupted by the dot-coms, newspapers like the *New York Times* could sympathize with other old, established companies that had also been disturbed. It would, of course, have been somewhat awkward for the *Times* to interview its own newly laid-off ex-employees about the various ways that the company's own reduction in its workforce had transformed their lives. But the *Times* could direct readers' attention to the plight of a man named Larry C. Canoy, whose comfortable North Carolina lifestyle was turned upside down when a Web site called Living.com acquired the Shaw Furniture Gallery.

The "dot-com revolution" that swept through High Point, North Carolina, resulted in the closure of Mr. Canoy's former employer, "leaving Mr. Canoy and some coworkers in perilous financial straits," the *New York Times* reported. Mr. Canoy himself was ill prepared for either the dot-com transformation or the bankruptcy that followed, but the "perilous financial straits" in which he ultimately found himself provided the *New York Times* with excellent copy. "They tried to high-tech us rednecks," Mr. Canoy reportedly said. "But they ruined us."

New York Times Digital's coverage of its own Internet layoffs was far less theatrical. On January 8, 2001, *New York Times*–owned Boston.com told readers that its parent company, the New York Times Co., would be laying off sixty-nine employees in its Internet division. The article revealed that the job cuts would reduce the Internet unit's staff of about 400 by 17 percent.

I Told You So, I Told You So

"Only months ago, corporate America seethed with envy at all the money lavished on the dot-coms, and the workers' up-yours attitude toward the cubicle drones who just didn't get the revolution," the *San Francisco Chronicle* observed. But the times had finally changed, and perhaps the dot-commers would finally learn humility. Shortly before Christmas Day, 2000, a reporter from the *San Francisco Chronicle* watched a recently laid off dot-com employee scrambling to fill his duffel bag with logo-enhanced corporate giveaways so that he would have something to put under the Christmas tree. "In many ways, these risk takers are now embarrassed that they were so thoroughly drawn into the outrageous promises of the New Economy," the *Chronicle* observed.

It made sense that print journalists would aim their literary harpoons at the great white whales of the New Economy. After all, their own newspapers had been thoroughly battered by the bursts of hot air that had come out of the dot-coms' various blowholes. But few writers were able to hook their prey as skillfully as *eCompany Now*'s Ralph King. In an article called "Do You Believe in Jim Clark," King persuaded the mighty Clark, once heralded as a sort of King Midas of dot-com corporations, to confess that reports of his superhumanity had been somewhat exaggerated. "I don't think I can live up to the reputation," Clark admitted. "I can't fill the New New shoes."

With the Internet bubble now officially punctured, the wizard of dot-com Oz could be exposed as an ordinary man who had figured out how to work the levers on a tremendous media machine. "I don't think I'm that fucking great," Clark reportedly said. "I am proud of what I've done . . . but I'm no fucking genius."

Scandal Sells

"That's an interviewing talent I would aspire to," Internet columnist Julia Lipman tells me in reference to the above quote from Jim Clark. "Just to get an interview where you have somebody that prominent saying something they've never said before."

When I ask Lipman to explain why she is impressed by King's ability to document Jim Clark's admission that his alleged mythical qualities might not really exist, she says: "If you're going to write a story that makes your career, it's going to be something that hasn't been written about before. And it's going to be something that's harder to derive and research and investigate."

Lipman and I are sitting in the back of a funky café in Central Square, and Lipman is trying to figure out what she is going to do next, now that her "Internet Culture" column in the *New York Times*–owned *digitalMass* has been canceled. Lipman is intrigued by all the attention that is being given to once-celebrated technology companies that are now experiencing huge layoffs, and she is considering doing a freelance article about the dot-com layoff Web site known as FuckedCompany.com.

The Web site, which has become extremely popular with the former employees of now-defunct Internet companies, is awash with disparaging commentary. The site's "Happy Fun Slander Corner" provides disgruntled netizens with a place to complain about anything that makes them angry, and an interactive video game called Pinkslip Panic encourages players to fire bullet-shaped job-termination notices at an assortment of cartoon employees, who smile facetiously and hide behind their desks.

"It represents so much unbridled bitterness and hatred," Lipman says of FuckedCompany.com. "And you have to think about this: Why are all these people posting this stuff to a dot-com-failure message board?"

It does seem rather odd that those individuals who have just been laid off from highly publicized Internet businesses would choose to process their frustrations by patronizing yet another highly publicized Web site. But it's possible that the new breed of newly laid off former dot-com employees don't have any other way to make themselves heard.

Consider Lipman herself, who fulfilled her duties as "Internet Culture" columnist by surfing the Internet, writing her column, and E-mailing the finished column to her editor. During the ten-month period that she wrote for *digitalMass*, Lipman met only one of her fellow columnists, and she never once had the opportunity to meet either her editor or the people who signed her paychecks.

Now that Lipman's column has been canceled, she felt compelled to send her colleagues an E-mail, asking whether they would like to get together and meet one another before they all go their separate ways.

"When I'd go to tech-type parties, I'd always feel out of place, because to most people I'm just this voice on-line," Lipman reflects. "I'd go to these parties, and I wouldn't introduce myself to people, because I'd always feel nervous. And I thought, *If I were a print journalist, I would feel less so, because I'd be working with journalists all the time, so I'd know more people.*"

Although Lipman does not have any experience working in a physical newsroom, she imagines that the experience of spending time in the company of other journalists would provide her with more opportunities for socializing. "You're more on your own as an on-line journalist," Lipman says. If Lipman were required to spend her time in a physical newsroom, she imagines that "we'd probably all go to these things as a group, and people would introduce you to people."

The Season of Gloom and Doom

On Halloween Day, 2000, I interviewed Jack Pascal, president of an Internet company called BEAM: Bankruptcy Exchange and Auction Market. Since it was Halloween, I was hoping that Pascal would give me some really scary statistics about how the so-called recent market downturn was pushing the rate of bankruptcy filings to previously unheard of levels and how we should all prepare ourselves for an extended period of Internet-related devastation. But even though such a prediction would be very good for Pascal's business and very good for my Halloween story, Pascal was unable to provide any support for my hypothesis.

"If you look at bankruptcies, they're not at an all-time low, but they are at a historical low," Pascal says. "So what we're doing is, we're building our database.

"There is a lot of talk about bankruptcies, but my personal feeling of why everybody is talking about it is that the dot-coms got so much good publicity for so long. This is kind of like, 'Wow. I told you. I was right.' And people are really excited about writing about it.

"I talked to one reporter from the *Washington Post,* and he said, 'Why is everybody so interested in this stuff?' And that's my theory: There is not as much bankruptcy as everybody thinks there is, but it's a trendy thing."

According to Pascal, the dot-com phenomenon "got totally out of control, and this is just the process to get everybody back in. I think you get a process where newspapers pick up on it, it becomes trendy." Eventually, Pascal says, things will settle down, and "everybody will forget about it."

In other words, according to the president of the Internet company called Bankruptcy Exchange and Auction Market, while many, many writers are absolutely convinced that the dot-com bankruptcies are getting out of hand, society at large is not likely to be affected.

"If you look at the total economy, what the dot-coms are worth, it's really kind of insignificant," Pascal says. "I don't know what the real statistics are, but common sense tells me that it's small in dollars compared to real companies.

"That's the other thing about bankruptcy: Almost no research has been done. There are a lot of statistics on individual bankruptcies, and the reason is because American Express and Mastercard and Visa and all those people spent a lot of money, because they are involved with it. But there are no statistics on the non–publicly held companies."

How to Manipulate the Media

Many entrepreneurs hope that the material they put out in their press releases will cause journalists to think favorably about their companies. But not every press release is successful. "At least twice I got press releases where I just had to mock the thing that was being hyped," Julia Lipman recalls. For this reason, entrepreneurs "have to be prepared" to take the bad publicity along with the good. "If they send me something ridiculous, I might just write a column that says it's ridiculous," Lipman warns.

With that said, Lipman does look favorably upon public-relations professionals who seem to have a sense of humor. And her favorite public-relations pitches are from "people who acknowledge that they are from a PR agency, and you might not want to hear from them."

The best pitch Lipman ever received was from a man who said, "Yes,

I'm with this PR agency. If you've gotten other pitches from this agency, disregard them unless you associate our agency with cuddly bunnies and stuff.' It was a really well-done E-mail, and I ended up writing favorably about the thing after I looked at it," Lipman recalls.

In other words, if an entrepreneur is going to act like a public-relations professional and pitch his company to a jaded journalist, he needs to understand that the journalist has most likely already been pitched to by every single one of his competitors—and possibly by someone else in his own organization. An entrepreneur cannot invent the public-relations pitch, since the public-relations pitch has already been done to death. But if an entrepreneur acts as if he knows his place as a "person who wants publicity," rather than a "person who deserves to be written about all the time," he *might* be able to convince a journalist that his cause is worth supporting.

"In general news, there are more reporters chasing fewer stories and fewer subjects," Matt Kelly tells me. "In high-tech, there are more subjects and not enough reporters. I think a lot of high-tech PR people don't understand that dynamic as much as they should."

Do Your Homework

When contacting a journalist, it is very important to understand what sorts of things that particular journalist likes to write about. For example, because Julia Lipman's column at *digitalMass* was supposed to cover the Internet as it related to Boston, she was unlikely to write about a company unless the news event in question was of interest to Internet users and the company in question had some connection to the Boston area. She recalls several occasions when entrepreneurs would send her E-mails asking if she wanted to set up an interview with their company's CEO during the week that the CEO was planning to be in Boston. "I would think, *Well, if he's in town for the week, it's not a Boston company, and therefore I can't really cover it,*" Lipman recalls.

Lipman especially enjoyed writing about a start-up company called Spindle Top, which was trying to put together a new social organization that would bargain with hardware manufacturers on behalf of GNU/Linux users. In the process of writing about the collective-bargaining project, Lipman happened to mention that the company also manufactured a kind of server called a Blackbird. But if Spindle Top had not launched their collective-bargaining program, Lipman says she probably would not have written about the company.

If a story has some greater social resonance, "then I'm definitely more likely to write about it," Lipman says. On the other hand, "if you've got data mining software and you can't describe in twenty-five words or less why it's better than all the other data-mining software, then I'm probably not going to write a column about it."

Matt Kelly agrees that it is important for an entrepreneur to tailor his public-relations pitch to the individual journalist with whom he is speaking. In his role as features editor, Matt Kelly takes phone calls from as many as ten public-relations professionals each day. And Kelly says that he can sense right away whether a person has taken the time to become familiar with *Mass High Tech* or whether he has simply plucked Kelly's phone number out of a database.

Kelly is far more impressed when a person takes the time to read his newspaper and figure out which reporters cover stories in each of the different high-tech fields than when the person simply dials the newspaper's main number and asks Kelly to direct him to the appropriate reporter. "It is fairly easy to find that out through other channels without intruding on my time," Kelly says. "And we don't have enough time for anything.

"I feel bad that I hang up on people a lot, but I pretty much don't have the time to talk to them. I have to get off the phone."

Once an entrepreneur has ascertained that his company really does fit into the category of companies that a particular newspaper writes stories about and after he has read the newspaper enough to figure out which reporter handles which field, an entrepreneur should make sure that the message he is trying to deliver is newsworthy. "Plenty of them [the entrepreneurs who contact *Mass High Tech*] just call up and say, 'I have a software company,' and they expect news to exist in a vacuum," Kelly says. "It doesn't work that way."

Winning a multimillion-dollar contract with the U.S. Navy is newsworthy. Establishing a strategic partnership with an industry competitor is newsworthy. Settling a class-action lawsuit that was pending in a U.S. District Court is newsworthy.

Signing a multimillion-dollar purchase order might be newsworthy, provided that the customer in question has given you permission to use his or her name in a public announcement.

Raising a round of venture-capital financing might be newsworthy, provided that your financiers say it's okay to use their name.

Simply sitting in your office and thinking about how great it would be to release a new product, if you could get the darn thing built, is not newsworthy.

"There are some companies who have pitched to us, saying, 'We want you to write about a product,' but they don't have it," Kelly says. "It isn't in development, or they're not willing to talk about it, or they're not willing to talk about the technology behind it. They just want us to say, 'Company X is working on XYZ software version 2.0, and it will come out in March.'"

Before *Mass High Tech* can convince itself that a product really does exist, "we would want to actually see it, we'd want to see the administration of it, and we'd want to see who the customers are," Kelly says.

If an entrepreneur is trying to obtain media coverage for an upcoming news event but the event has not been formally announced, the entrepreneur might consider delivering the news under cover of a news embargo. A news embargo is a special agreement made between public-relations professionals and journalists during instances when companies know they are going to make an important announcement in a few days but the announcement has not been made yet. If, for example, a company knows that it will make a certain announcement the following Monday and they discover that *Mass High Tech* only publishes on Mondays, they can call Kelly at any point during the previous week and ask him to put a reporter on the story.

This sort of additional lead time is useful for reporters because it gives them an opportunity to fully understand the complicated technical issues that they are writing about. And the additional lead time is also beneficial for companies because it increases the chance that papers like *Mass High Tech* will run their stories at all.

Many companies shy away from speaking to the press about matters that are not yet public for fear that reporters will break the news embargo and print the story early. But if a company waits too long to spill the beans, Kelly says, the event might stop being news. If, for example, a telephone company waited until Monday to tell Kelly about a new long-distance service offering that was going to be announced that day, "I couldn't print it for another week, because my print deadline is already past," Kelly says. "And by then, it's next Monday, and everybody already knows that they can get long-distance service, so I probably wouldn't print it at all."

Do-It-Yourself Public Relations

Many high-tech start-ups spend $10,000 or more each month to retain the services of a big-name public-relations firm in the hopes that retaining such a firm will increase their company's profile. But all too frequently, cash-strapped entrepreneurs report that they are unable to see any difference between the amount of press coverage they received with a public-relations firm and the amount of press coverage they were able to obtain when they handled their own publicity.

After all, the thing that newspaper reporters value most is being able to get some quality time on the telephone or in person with an honest individual who really does have a good story to tell.

"Our readers are looking for companies that will succeed and that they might wind up doing business with either as investors or business partners or whatnot," Kelly says. "They want to see who is here to stay and what they are doing." To convince Kelly that an entrepreneur is operating a business that is likely to be around over the long haul, Kelly says, "all you have to do is make money.

"You do not have to get $100 million and go into debt and expand nationwide. That is a lot of flash. We'll give you coverage then, sure. But we will also cover you when you go out of business. And we do that an awful lot right now.

"If you've got two employees and you're paying their salaries, you pay your expenses, and you have five dollars a year left at the end, you know what? You are ahead of the game for nine out of every ten other competitors.

"If we don't find out about it right away, someone else will find out about it because they will want that money you're making. Venture capitalists will show up, customers will show up. We'll notice that they're going somewhere, and we'll follow them. We'll get to the bottom of it, and we'll find you. You're making money. That's all you need to do."

Instead of shelling out hundreds of thousands of dollars to a public-relations firm in the hopes that this will increase a company's chances of getting attention from jaded journalists, Matt Kelly recommends simply calling him directly.

"I'll always talk to an entrepreneur," Kelly says. "PR people, I'll put them on hold, I'll tell them to E-mail me, I'll tell them to call me back. Entrepreneurs, I will let them get through. I don't think one call out of twenty is from an entrepreneur. But when it is, that's the best call.

"One of the greatest calls I ever got was from a graduate student from MIT. He was twenty-four, and he called me up on a Thursday morning. He said, 'Hi, I just sold my company to a firm out in Chicago for like $9 million. Do you guys want to hear about it?'

"My very first question was 'How old are you?' He said, 'I'm twenty-four.' I said, 'Who is in charge over there?' He said, 'I am.' I said, 'All right, fine. We're happy to hear from you.' And I explained that he was talking to the wrong guy but there was a reporter next to me and he would talk him through this.

"That's really what it was. It was this reporter who had been in the business for years dealing with an entrepreneur who obviously was very young. He had sold his company for $9 million, and it was talking him through how to give out the news.

"This kid didn't know anything about how to say what the deal was, how long he had been in, or anything like that. He didn't have a press release. The deal had closed the afternoon before, and he happened to read *Mass High Tech,* so he called us up to tell us about it.

"I loved that call. That was the best call I've had. And I'll always remember the line I told him just before I transferred him. 'We'll put a reporter on, and he'll talk you through this.' That's the way it works."

Chapter Thirteen

SUCCESS

Because entrepreneurs set such lofty goals when they start their high-tech endeavors—putting an end to unnecessary bank charges, say, or changing the way that telephone signals are transmitted—it's often hard to tell when they cash out of their corporations whether or not they have achieved their objectives. Of course, if an entrepreneur has trouble measuring the impact he has had on the world, he can always borrow the yardstick used by mainstream society.

More than a year after NBX Corporation had gone through a significant liquidity event, I ask co-founder Alex Laats how he gauges the impact of NBX Corporation. "There is no question that money is a measure of success," Laats says, "but a bigger measure of success is the long-standing value of the product or service that is actually being put out on the marketplace." In Laats's opinion, a truly successful business is one in which the company's employees feel so satisfied with the work experience that they are able to say to their next employer, "I did well by that company, and that company did well by me."

"If that happens, we've achieved value in every way," Laats tells me. "We've achieved value in having a useful product, we've achieved value by gaining money or realizing return on investment of our blood, sweat, tears, and investors' money, and we've also increased the value of the humans involved.

"You'll be able to see these people, and they will have grown up. Part of their evolution as a person and as a productive member of society will have happened with you, as part of the company that you're at.

"I won't be there when that person is talking to somebody else and says that. I will measure it simply by whether or not they feel, regardless of whether or not they ever enunciate that feeling, that 'I did well by the company, and the company did well by me.'

"Pehr [Anderson] and Chris [Gadda] and I and everybody else made money, but in the long run what I care more about is the fact that this is a product on this earth being used by people and growing in revenue and being useful."

For his part, Anderson believes that success means having your ideas realized and changing the world so that it can't be changed back by anyone, ever. He believes that he was successful "because the companies that we were competing against are scrambling to build products like ours" and because he believes his Ethernet telephone has caused the entire telephony industry to shift in the direction of higher compatibility with computers. "The thing I take most pride in is that I accelerated the move in the industry toward a more open system that puts computers in the loop in a way that they weren't before," Anderson says. "What I like most is when people say, 'I want a computer in that loop.' I was looking for a phone system that had a computer in the loop, and I wasn't able to find one.

"My real goal in doing this was to create pressure to change the giants to make them improve their own offerings. There was always the possibility that we would be bought by one of these giants and that they would incorporate our products directly into their systems, so we would become a tool for one giant to beat another giant over the head with. But it was all good—there was no way to take the power away from people. There was no way that the genie could be put back in the bottle after NBX."

How to Cash Out and Move On

The phrase "after NBX" is somewhat misleading, since NBX is still going on, although now it is located inside 3Com Corporation. And as part of being acquired by this larger competitor, the value that NBX had created was translated into U.S. dollars, and the people who had built the company were compensated for their various contributions.

But the sale of NBX to 3Com—the event that told the world how much value the NBX team had created—didn't happen by accident. Like many liquidity events, the acquisition included a variety of difficult managerial decisions and complex legal maneuvers that occurred over a period of months.

By the fall of 1998, NBX had already developed a number of sales relationships with a variety of small telephone resellers. Confident about his company's ability to meet the demands of its various small customers, cofounder Alex Laats tried to expand the company's reach by establishing relationships with some of the industry's larger players. In October 1998, Laats placed a call to "a very big cheese at 3Com," the executive vice president in charge of 3Com's equipment line of business. Laats hoped to establish a business relationship in which 3Com would sell NBX telephones under the 3Com brand. If this occurred, we would say that NBX was an original equipment manufacturer (OEM) for 3Com.

Laats's phone call was a success, and within a month of the call, 3Com had assigned a team of people to figure out whether NBX phones could be sold through 3Com's channels. After an evaluation period, 3Com indicated that it was interested in setting up an OEM relationship, and the negotiations began in earnest.

3Com started the talks by asking Laats how many telephones he expected his company to produce and how much it would cost NBX to produce these phones. But NBX's CEO, Dan Massiello, was wary of sharing this information. Laats recalls Massiello saying, "No, you have to tell us what you think the demand will be from your customers, through your channels—in what volume and at what price."

3Com responded by giving NBX a figure that was greater than the sum total of all of the other reseller relationships that NBX had established to date. And although Laats was delighted that his phone call had yielded so much business, he recalls that Massiello was concerned about the ramifications of selling so much of the company's output to a single player. "Once you have relationships with one of these guys," Laats explains, "the others kind of treat you as beholden to that one player." And once a company is perceived as being the pawn of a larger competitor, it would be extremely difficult for the little company to conduct an IPO.

Careful to double-check Massiello's assumptions, Laats asked a few investment bankers about the way that such a relationship would be perceived by the financial community. The investment bankers told Laats, "Wall Street can stomach having one customer that represents fifteen percent of your business, but get above that and forget about it."

Having confirmed Massiello's initial suspicions, Laats and Massiello decided that they could not agree to the reseller relationship, and they decided to give 3Com an ultimatum. "We said, 'Look, at this stage we're building our reseller channel, and you're going to overwhelm our reseller channel,'" Laats recalls. "'This original equipment-manufacturer thing is not going to work out, so the only conversation that makes any sense is if you just buy us outright.'"

Apparently, the company's assertive stance had the required effect, for "by Christmastime, the conversation had turned completely to a conversation about an acquisition." On March 5, 1999, 3Com acquired NBX Corporation for approximately $90 million in cash and stock options.

Play Hard to Get

Just like in human relationships, when a company is independent and self-sufficient, it becomes much more desirable to other companies. An example of this phenomenon can be seen in the case of Direct Hit.

According to entrepreneur Gary Culliss, when a company begins to talk to investment bankers about filing to go public, it generates a certain buzz within the investment-banking community, since investment bankers are always talking about the hot new companies they are working with. Going public also forces the company to tie up all of its financial loose ends in preparation for the intense public scrutiny it will receive from the Securities and Exchange Commission. "So the company is all packaged up, and investment bankers start talking about it to the companies that they work with, and they say things like 'Direct Hit's filing to go public. This is going to be your last chance to buy them before they go out and have a market cap of a billion dollars after five months or so,'" Culliss says. As a result, potential competitors "come in, start kicking the tires, and start finding out how we might work together. If they see real value, they might take it to the next level."

One of the consequences of being closely scrutinized by a cadre of investment banks is that a company begins to develop a sense of its own worth. This means that when another company talks to them about a possible acquisition, the debutante is able to drive a hard bargain.

When rival search engine Ask Jeeves followed up on the investment bankers' suggestions and approached Direct Hit about a possible acquisition, Culliss and his cofounder, Mike Cassidy, were able to compare the amount that Ask Jeeves was offering with the investment bankers' predictions about how much the company might be worth in an IPO. Seeing that the two numbers were very similar, Culliss and Cassidy decided to accept the offer from Ask Jeeves.

Direct Hit was acquired by Ask Jeeves for some $500 million in Ask Jeeves stock, calculated at the price of $100 per share. And Gary Culliss says that although he was happy about what this would mean for his bank account, he was even more excited about having the opportunity to work at Ask Jeeves. "This new position, V.P. of new-business development, will allow me to create new products and expand into areas beyond the Direct Hit technology," Culliss says. "I'm quite excited about that." Culliss is also excited about the fact that "the Ask Jeeves brand is more extensible than the Direct Hit brand.

"The Direct Hit brand was centered around people and popularity, as a mode of finding better information. The Ask Jeeves brand is centered around service. A butler is going to give you answers, as well as bring you things, or help you do things that you wouldn't be able to do on your own."

But handing his company over to a larger competitor has a price: Culliss worries that in a year or so, no one will remember the name Direct Hit.

Alex Laats experienced a similar twinge of sadness when NBX was sold to 3Com. "We kept the business in Andover, and we tried to keep control of our distribution to a certain degree," Laats says, "but the acquisition meant that the team, as we had been building it, was no longer going to exist.

"It's almost like when you do a musical in high school; you build this bond of how to work together. You do the shows, and then the show's over, and you have this big cast party." But at least with a high school musical, Laats says, everyone knows that the show will eventually end. With a start-up, some people might be thinking that the company will eventually go public or stay private and pay its shareholders with its own earnings. In the case of a sudden acquisition, Laats says, "you kind of don't expect it to be over, so you're not planning for it to be over psychologically. And that's a bummer."

Big Success Means Big Responsibility

When I ask Gary Culliss how the acquisition of Direct Hit has affected his life, he says, "I now feel a tremendous amount of responsibility to take care of what has been created." Referring to the stock he received from the Ask Jeeves acquisition, Culliss says that he feels obliged "to manage it, to protect it, and to give some of it away.

"By protect, I mean not lose it," Culliss explains. "It's a very concentrated position in a highly volatile stock, and as any investment adviser will tell you, that is not a safe place to be."

If a public company uses a huge chunk of its stock to purchase a new company and the founders of the new company decide to sell their stock immediately, this massive sale of stock might cause all of the rest of the shares of stock in the public company to experience a significant drop in price. To prevent this from happening, companies usually set up something called a "lockup period," during which time founders and other large shareholders are prevented from selling their stock.

When the lockup period is over, the large shareholders—including the VCs and angel investors who bought stock when the company was still private—must make a decision about whether to sell their shares of stock or hold on to them for a while longer. And this is not an easy decision to make, since the stock prices of new high-tech companies are notorious for going up and down without warning.

In many instances, stock agreements are set up so that the people who found companies do not receive shares of their company outright but instead receive legal documents guaranteeing them the right to buy shares of stock in their company at a certain price. And quite often these legal documents specify that if the entrepreneur does not exercise his right to purchase shares by a certain date, say, three months after he leaves the company, he will lose the right to buy the shares at the specially reduced price.

Stock options allow founders to pay a very small amount of money (maybe $1 per share) for a quantity of stock that is worth much more (maybe $40 per share). And the idea behind stock options—allowing founders to get a really good deal on the stock of their own companies—is hard to find fault with. But once the founder exercises his options and actually buys the stock, the IRS says that he has experienced a large financial gain—say, $39 per share. And once the founder has experienced this significant financial gain, he is faced with the difficult task of deciding what to do next. Should the founder hold on to his shares and hope that they go up? Or should he sell the shares and put his money into something a little safer?

Regardless of whether the entrepreneur chooses to sell or hold, he will have to pay taxes on the gain he received. And if the gain is large, the entrepreneur might not have enough money in his bank account to pay these taxes. It seems obvious that if the entrepreneur needs money to pay his taxes, the thing to do would be to sell some shares of stock. But it is difficult to predict how much the shares will be worth when April 15 rolls around.

One entrepreneur, who was confident about the future of his company, chose to exercise his option to buy shares of stock for $1 each when the shares were trading at $40 per share. Then he chose to hold on to his stock. Unfortunately, when the time came for the entrepreneur to pay his taxes, the stock price had fallen to $7 per share. To raise the money he needed to pay taxes on the gain of $39 per share, the entrepreneur was forced to sell every single share of stock he had—but that still wasn't enough. To make up the difference, the entrepreneur was forced to take out a loan from the bank.

And so, after working for many years to get his company off the ground, the entrepreneur found himself emotionally burned out and deeply in debt. He told a friend that he would have been better off if he had collected welfare for the entire period.

A Liquidity Event Changes the Way Employees Think About Their Jobs

In addition to providing entrepreneurs and employees with the opportunity to exercise their stock options, the transformation from a private to a public company causes a number of other subtle challenges as well.

Wes Davis has served as the head of both private and public corporations and has noticed a number of differences between the two types of organizations. "Once you're a public company," Davis says, "every day you get a report card on how you're doing. You go from having stock options in a company that is private, and thus effectively impossible to evaluate," to a situation where an employee can see for himself exactly how much his shares are worth at all times. And Davis reports that this has a significant effect on the way that employees think about their jobs. Instead of speculating about whether or not the company will eventually succeed, employees ask one another, "Are we getting wealthier *today?*"

The cognitive shifts associated with going from a private to a public company also occur when private companies are acquired by publicly held competitors. For example, when 3Com bought NBX, Alex Laats noticed a subtle change in the way that his employees regarded their jobs. "It is very hard to make the reality of a start-up post acquisition compete with the hope of a start-up before they have any money," Laats explains. At a public company, "technical people have a bunch of money which vests every month. They can take this money and compare it with equity in another start-up, and they can make their decision to stay or go based on comparing the reality that we have now with the hope of a start-up. Even though you get money—cash money—the people that tend to go to start-ups like the hope. They like to be driven by the hope that [their stock options] might wind up being worth much, much more than that."

As a result, when a start-up company experiences a liquidity event, it often loses some percentage of its employees. "Somewhere between five and ten of our technical people have made that decision," Laats says. According to Laats, an employee might think "I'm going to go for the hope and give up the reality of ongoing vesting of money." But every single one of them is leaving money on the table when they leave.

The Process of Getting Serious

Having the ability to check on the company's stock price every single day is not the only difference between a private and a public company. As the president of publicly traded Microtouch, Davis is "much more cognizant of financial exposure and the threat of litigation" than he was when he was the president of a private company. "At a public company, you have to be more careful about what you say and what information you put out," Davis says. "When you talk about the prospects for the company, you start hedging more than you normally would if you were talking publicly, and you just generally have a lot more sensitivity to litigation issues."

The reason for this increased fear of litigation is that a public company is financially beholden to scores of shareholders, each of whom, Davis tells me, is vaguely aware of the "large number of law firms out there that love to sue.

"In a public company, if you are out talking about the prospects of the company and somebody claims that they made an investment based on what you said about the prospects and it turns out that you are totally wrong, you're much more vulnerable to a lawsuit."

The situation is different in a private company, Davis says, because the managers of a private company are much more insulated. "In a private company maybe you have five or six investors from different investment firms, and by the time you go through the process of raising equity, you've gotten them to sign all kinds of agreements that say, 'Whatever I've said is false and misleading and you won't sue me about it.'" Thus, when a group of private investors finally make the decision to invest, "it's not based on what you've told them verbally, so you just don't have that financial-performance-litigation exposure."

There is also another significant difference between remaining a privately held corporation and selling one's shares on the public market. Private equity investors might be located far from the company, but there are usually only a handful of them, and they are generally willing to travel to the company to attend board meetings. When the head of a public company wants to keep its individual shareholders apprised of the company's prospects, he has to arrange a variety of public presentations. And when a company wants to interact with its institutional investors, it has to assume the risk of revealing valuable secret information to industry analysts. "You have to constantly be out there," Davis says. "There are six-thousand companies on the NASDAQ, and you have to make sure that XYZ fund is buying your stock and holding it, so you're constantly selling the company."

At a private company the situation is very different, since the process of raising money from VCs occurs at discrete times and under highly controlled conditions. "You go through a very intense process when you're trying to raise funds, but you don't necessarily have to keep doing that between the financings," Davis says. "It's done, it's over, you got the money, you can move on." In contrast, at a public company, "everything you do is influenced by the fact that you have three-thousand or five-thousand shareholders out there saying, 'You may think you're doing well, sales may have doubled, but the stock isn't going up. What are you going to do?'"

A Really Interesting Day

No matter how difficult it is to run a public company, there are still many, many people who would love to try it. One of the people who actually did have the opportunity to watch his company transition from a privately held company to a publicly traded corporation was Akamai's Jonathan Seelig.

Akamai's initial public offering was more exhilarating than most because the amount of money that was raised vastly exceeded everyone's expectations. The investment bankers who helped take Akamai public told the company's managers to sell their shares for $26 apiece. But on the first day of trading there was so much demand for these shares that by the time the first share hit the market, the price had more than quadrupled.

Watching the stock jump from an expected price of $26 per share to an actual price of $110 per share made for a "really exciting day," co-founder Jonathan Seelig recalls. "We had a conference room set up where the bankers brought in screens that showed you what was going on and the markets as they were starting to trade. The bankers explained that this is what the bid-and-ask means, and this is what it means when there's a spread, and this is when your stock is going to start trading. They thought our stock would start trading at one o'clock in the afternoon, so at about twelve-thirty we had a little party, with champagne and cake. We had the whole company, all three hundred of us at the time, squeezing into a room and watching this thing start to trade.

"There was this buildup, and they start trading in fifteen-minute intervals. So, at one o'clock it doesn't happen because they haven't made a market yet, and at one-fifteen it doesn't happen because they haven't made a market yet, and it kind of looks like it might happen at one-thirty. At one-thirty it starts trading, and you see that first number flash up on the screen."

Expecting to see $26 and seeing instead $110 and watching it trade up to $145 was electrifying for Seelig and his colleagues. "You get everybody in a room watching a tangible number on a screen that says, 'The market says you guys have built a really cool company that is going to do really valuable and really interesting things today and in the future,'" Seelig recalls.

But the party didn't last long: Half an hour after the screen first registered $110, "the room was empty, and everybody was back at work," Seelig recalls. "Because everybody kind of looked at this and said, 'We have a huge market opportunity that the market has just validated, and we need to make sure that we execute on that.'"

Speaking about the phenomenal IPO, Seelig says, "It puts a lot of pressure on the company to really execute. You know they're not valuing you on what you're doing today; they're valuing you on the potential of what your company can be. And you say, 'Gee, people really believe in the things that we dreamt up.' So the idea you had very early on in your corporate history of 'Oh, we can kind of try things and play around and do what we feel like—and if it works that's great, and if it doesn't that's okay, we'll go back to being students'—that's gone.

"Now you have a big, big market saying that they want you to do good things, and you had better do them."

Is the World Any Different Because You Were Here?

Clearly, watching your company's stock shoot up to a sky-high level or arranging an extremely lucrative acquisition by a larger competitor gives an entrepreneur a sense of accomplishment. But many entrepreneurs measure their personal success or failure not by how much money they were able to make but on whether or not they were able to change the world.

For example, entrepreneur Barry Star judges his own success not by how many companies he has started or how much his most recent company is worth but by whether OneCore has achieved its objective of making the world a better place for small-business owners. "I got a call the other day from a reporter," Star remembers, "who said, 'ABC Company is getting into this marketplace and is going to compete with you. What is your response?'

"My response was 'That's terrific.' One of the reasons why I wanted to start this business was because small businesses were not being paid attention to. If OneCore has been instrumental in getting people to realize that the small-business marketplace is not a marketplace to be ignored, then we've achieved one of our objectives."

Entrepreneur Andy Sack shares Star's belief that there are many different ways to figure out whether a person is successful. "The amount of salary in our society, which is a measure of one's success and ultimately one's happiness, is totally incongruous with what happiness is about," Sack says. "Doing what you want to do and loving what you do has a real dollar value, and people don't talk about that.

"I did have an economic goal, but early on, when you start a company, you have no idea how much money you're going to make or if you're going to make any. And anyone who tells you otherwise is lying. I did have a financial goal, but it was low on my priority list. I was just loving what I was doing. Absolutely loved it."

When Pehr Anderson wants to gauge how successful he was with NBX, he types "NBX 100" into an Internet search engine and sees how many hits come up. This makes him feel good for a while because it shows that people are talking about—and using—his telephone system.

But then he starts to wonder if maybe making the NBX 100 was the greatest thing he was ever going to do. What if it was a fluke that he was able to build a good telephone system? What if it was an accident? What if he wasn't really so smart, after all, but was just in the right place at the right time?

What if it was all just luck?

When Anderson starts thinking like this, he talks about trying to do it all over again. But Anderson says he is also aware of how foolish it is for an entrepreneur to think that "just because you did something before, you'll be able to do something again." The second time around the bar is much lower because everyone who has heard about the first success—friends, headhunters, VCs, and fellow programmers—assumes that a person who has been successful before is likely to be successful again. Therefore, an entrepreneur needs to be certain to apply the same amount of scrutiny to his postsuccess corporate ideas as he did to the idea that made him successful in the first place.

There is such a thing as second-start-up syndrome, where a person who has been successful before becomes convinced that he can do anything else he wants to as well and goes on to invest all of his money in a foolish enterprise. The entrepreneur may not have the stamina required to take the idea to fruition the second time around, or the second idea may not be as good as the first. In either case, the person has wagered all his wealth on the belief that anything he touches turns to gold.

Of course, some entrepreneurs are able to start successful companies time and time again. VC Pat Latterell tells me about a number of entrepreneurs he knows who have started companies as many as ten times. "One of our favorite people has gotten so good that he will literally start and sell a company in less than a year," Latterell says.

"He does that repeatedly. He does telecom-related start-ups, and he has a very good pulse of the market. He looks out there, and he's acutely aware of the problems that people have with bandwidth and how to send packets of information, and he figures out how to get to the next step. Then, while he's doing that, he figures out the next generation, and the next generation, so he just repeatedly comes up with a better product."

Starting and selling high-tech companies year after year, decade after decade, requires a level of motivation that is almost otherworldly. In fact, a surprising number of the more visionary entrepreneurs *are* driven by a desire to set up a home base in the heavens.

For Jason Solinsky, being successful means having the resources to launch a sustainable space colonization, "which I think is somewhere around $100 or $500 billion current U.S. dollars," Solinsky says. To get there, the entrepreneur envisions starting a string of start-up companies until he has amassed that much cash, or at least one-tenth that much cash, "at which point I will have to be more creative."

It would be easier to dismiss Jason Solinsky as being completely eccentric and totally out there if it were not for the fact that his idea is currently being pursued by a number of different people. For example, the Russian government went to the trouble of building the semisustainable space station Mir, which orbited the Earth for fifteen years. And although the Russian government ultimately fell on hard times, an entrepreneur named Walter Anderson picked up the torch and made a sincere effort to uphold the Mir mission.

An article in the *New York Times Magazine* stated that Anderson put up $21 million in seed money toward a lease that would eventually cost $200 million a year. "It will give MirCorp the rights to Mir for the remainder of its lifetime, the use of two or three manned Soyuz rockets and two or three unmanned Progress rockets annually, exclusive control over Mir's visitors and technologies, forty days of active operation and the privilege of fixing Mir up," the *New York Times Magazine* reported.

The article gave the impression that Walter Anderson's entrepreneurial space-station efforts were driven by a frustration with the slowness of the U.S. space program and an entrepreneurial desire to take matters into his own hands. Because the forty-six-year-old Anderson was already worth almost a billion dollars, he could operate as an independent angel investor, unhindered by the demands of conservative VC partners and unworried about pleasing the U.S. taxpayer. To put it another way, Anderson's wealth gave him the freedom to act quickly, taking the Mir project away from the conservative and bureaucratic Russian government and using it however he wanted.

Sadly, around the time the U.S. stock market began to lose momentum, the Russian government began to doubt whether Anderson's company, MirCorp, would be able to raise enough money to support the ailing space station. Ultimately, the Russian government decided to back out of the deal with MirCorp, allowing the space station to crash-land in a remote part of the Pacific Ocean.

Why Can't We All Get Along?

Like many entrepreneurs, Walter Anderson appears to believe that things will move faster and more efficiently if they are driven by passionate individuals rather than large bureaucratic institutions. But at least one space-loving, cashed-out entrepreneur prefers to use his new financial freedom to work within the system.

After leaving NBX, cofounder Chris Gadda went to work for Lockheed Martin as a product-integrity engineer, helping to improve the quality of NASA-funded missions to Mars. And although Gadda admits that working at a big company can sometimes be frustrating, he says he enjoys having a chance to make a real impact on mankind's explorations of deep space. "Sometimes you feel like you're just a tiny little speck and you don't necessarily make a huge difference," Gadda tells me. "But the end objective is to make something that goes to other planets and finds out if there were ever life-forms there."

While Jason Solinsky and Walter Anderson's entrepreneurial space-colonization ventures seem driven by the belief that Earth will one day become uninhabitable, Chris Gadda's activities are driven by a perceived real-estate crunch. "We're kind of heading toward outgrowing this planet," Gadda explains. Once human beings have outgrown Earth, Gadda believes that the next logical step is to pursue colonies on other planets. "It's worthwhile to explore our solar system and see if it's useful," Gadda says, noting that "it was worthwhile to cross the ocean six hundred years ago." Speaking of what the deep-space explorations may actually yield, Gadda says, "Maybe we'll discover that it's really a great place, and that a whole lot of people really like living there. At any rate, we're doing the engineering legwork for more scientific exploration."

Chapter Fourteen

EPILOGUE

I am sitting in a Thai restaurant on Mass Avenue, talking with professional card counter (and occasional attorney-at-law), Andy Bloch. Bloch is telling me why he considers casino blackjack safer than high-tech entrepreneurship.

"There is a certain kind of security in blackjack that you don't have in other risky ventures," Bloch explains. "With blackjack, you know you are going to make a certain amount of money. You don't know if it's true in poker, and you don't know it's true when you're starting a new company."

Bloch enjoys walking into a casino, playing his game well, and walking out of the casino with a pile of cash. But he worries about the way that his actions may affect the people around him. "Sometimes when I'm betting a lot of money, the count might be really high, and I'm making some strange plays," Bloch says. "People are sitting there watching me, and they'll think that that's the right way to play." The people who watch Bloch put down a thousand dollars a hand don't realize that Bloch is counting cards and that he is varying his behavior based on the information he has collected.

"When I'm counting cards and getting 'lucky,' it just looks too easy,"

Bloch says. "It looks like 'Oh, anyone could go and make money.' And *anyone can*. Except you need a certain amount of practice. And you can't get that kind of practice inside a casino because you are going to be losing too much money in the process. You won't even know whether you are making mistakes, and you will make mistakes."

Bloch believes that the best way to learn how to beat the odds at blackjack is to spend time with people who have already mastered the art of card counting. This means going to practices held by the MIT Blackjack Team and learning the ropes from the more senior players.

The same thing is true with high-tech entrepreneurship: Before a person can succeed as a high-tech entrepreneur, they need to spend time with some people who already know what they are doing.

"If you are not with the right lawyer, with the right business, or with the right VC and you don't have this network, you will not be able to build a company or sell a good product or go to the market," says Dr. Xavier L. Comtesse, counselor for science and technology and head honcho at the new Swiss Digital Consulate in Cambridge, Massachusetts.

"One very important thing that the Sloan business school is doing and that the Harvard Business School is doing is supporting networking," Comtesse tells me. By supporting networking, Comtesse says, the schools "create the conditions so that businesses can succeed later on."

If an entrepreneur is able to meet the right VC, Comtesse says, "then everything is smooth, everything is great. But if you don't have this partner right from the beginning, you have a tough time."

Comtesse watched huge numbers of VCs enter the marketplace during the latter half of the 1990s, but he did not believe that most of the newcomers were going to be successful. "It was really a lose-lose situation," he says. "Too much money, not enough new product, too many people."

The Blackjack Ball

One reason why entrepreneurial networking events are so important is because they give people a sense of their own identity. "That's one problem with being a card counter," Bloch says. "I never really felt like I was anyone.

"You make a lot of money, but you are always trying to hide yourself from casinos. And then you're always a little bit reluctant to talk about it, at least in Las Vegas."

When card counters get together at the annual Blackjack Ball, "you feel like you're part of an underground society," Bloch says. "You meet people who have written books about blackjack and who are legends in the blackjack field."

The centerpiece of the Blackjack Ball is a contest to see who the best player is. "But it's mostly a lighthearted event," Bloch says. "What goes on behind the scenes is that you have a lot of people from the blackjack circles meeting each other and talking about the places they play." At the Blackjack Ball, Bloch says, professional card counters "talk about which casinos are best to play at, which casino hosts are the most friendly, which counting strategies work well, and things like that. Sometimes people will have conversations about how you split up the profits: How much goes to the players and how much to investors."

All in all, Bloch says, "it's probably the major networking event for the highest level of professional card counting."

A Number of Smaller Events

The world of high-tech entrepreneurship is much too large to have all of the interested parties coming together at a single event that's held only once a year. For this reason, most high-tech networking events occur in small, easy-to-get-to locations, often within a stone's throw of a major research institution.

Joost Bonsen's networking events, which take place at the Muddy Charles Pub, are the perfect example.

When students come to a place like MIT, Bonsen says, "a substantial percentage of the value they end up deriving from their participation in the school ends up being all of this intangible, extracurricular, social-connection stuff. But it's scandalous how few of those people end up connecting with one another."

Still, Bonsen says, "We know from historical evidence how many start-ups are founded by people who knew each other while in school." For example, Bonsen says, "consider the fellows from NetGenesis: fraternity brothers at Delta Upsilon. Consider the Art Technology Group: Alpha Delta

Phi. Analog devices: two guys who lived at Baker House, an MIT dorm. MicroStrategy, a couple of Theta Delta Chis. It goes on and on and on.

"People end up doing serious activities, founding and building organizations of whatever kind, with people who they know and trust. How do you know and trust people? By having worked with them, having lived with them, by having seen people at their worst and at their best."

The Ideal Venue

"A venture café or a Muddy Charles Pub or any of the venues that people like to gather in are sources of personal inspiration," Bonsen tells me. "They're places where people can successfully connect with those that they don't already know but really ought to."

The reason why a person would go to a beer-and-pizza bash at the Muddy Charles Pub is to find people "who can help you think out of the box and to think about stuff that you hadn't previously thought of," Bonsen says. "These are extremely intangible things. Nevertheless, all of that exchange occurs in tangible places. There are physical people involved, and they have to be somewhere. And you need a venue for that kind of thing to occur."

It doesn't really matter where people gather or what they're drinking. What matters is how they feel while they are there.

"The venture café is an ideal," Bonsen says. It is a venue for adventurous thinking or a cauldron of creative ferment. Who the hell knows what will pop up from it? In fact, nothing is likely to. But you never know. When it does happen, it does have powerful consequences.

"Now, a person like me? What do I add to that mix? A venue alone isn't sufficient. You also need some kind of catalyst—some kind of connection machine. An engine of introduction. A tangible mechanism by which two people who ought to connect do.

"Why? Because most people don't make connections spontaneously. People don't like to get to know those that they don't already know. Most people, especially technologists, end up being pretty closed-minded about meeting beyond their narrow circles.

"I've certainly seen people who are unable or unwilling to say hello to people they don't already know. And yet, after an introduction, everything changes. Especially if the person doing the introduction is known by both parties and can provide enough mutual introductory glue to get people past the fear barrier.

"I think the biggest problem is that when you are faced with a room of anonymous and unknown people, it's daunting. You have no idea who to talk to. It looks like a lot of work. It is a lot of work. So, when there is a friendly face in the crowd, you tend to migrate to them.

"That's why people at cocktail parties end up talking to those who they already know."

Bonsen believes that the reason why people are so wary of beginning conversations with people they don't already know is because "to a lot of people, schmoozing is hard work. You end up spending a lot of time telling your story to somebody you didn't really want to talk to. Or worse, somebody who doesn't understand what the hell you're talking about. Then you feel like: 'How can I get out of this conversation *now,* without being rude?'

"You have that happen often enough in a shitty environment, where the people who you're talking to are idiots, you feel like: 'Screw this! This is a waste of my time. I've got stuff to do. I've got things to build.'

"On the flip side, if you can create a special-event venue where the people who are invited are interesting, then the odds of you running into somebody who is worth talking to are really high."

A large part of "being interesting," and "being worth talking to" is "sharing a common interest." Therefore, before Bonsen will put a new person on his invitation list, he ascertains that the person really does have a sincere interest in a subject related to high-tech entrepreneurship.

"The venture café is an ethos, more than anything," Bonsen says. "It's an attitude that says, 'I want to make sure I know the most adventurous and interesting people around, either because of a direct thing that I need tomorrow—new hires, new investors, new ideas—or because I like to hang out with people who spark my imagination and allow me to vent about my latest idea.

"It sounds very formal, but all it really is is a crew of people who will give you an objective opinion about your idea. That is something that will be of value regardless of economic boom or bust times and regardless of the success or failure of any given business."

Appendix A

The following term sheet was provided by attorney Gordon R. Penman of the law firm Brown, Rudnick, Freed & Gesmer as part of a one-day workshop entitled "Legal Issues for Entrepreneurs." It is reprinted here with Mr. Penman's permission.

[NAME OF ISSUER]

Term Sheet

These terms do not constitute any form of binding contract, but only are for the purpose of outlining the principal terms pursuant to which a definitive agreement may ultimately be negotiated.

Type of Security:	Series A Convertible Preferred Stock (the "Preferred")
Orig. Issue Price:	$[NUMBER] per share
Percentage Equity:	The Preferred is convertible into Common Stock representing [PERCENT] of the outstanding securities of the Company on a fully diluted basis.
Valuation:	$[NUMBER] pre-financing $[NUMBER] post-financing

TERMS OF THE PREFERRED STOCK:

Rights, Preferences, Privileges and Restrictions of Preferred Stock:	(1) <u>Dividend Provisions</u>: [OPTION A, NO RETURN: at the same rate as the Company's Common Stock when and as declared, based on the number of whole shares of Common Stock into which convertible.]

[OPTION B, FIXED RETURN: On a cumulative basis at the rate of [___] per annum. [OPTION: Cumulative dividends shall be payable only in the event of a liquidation, dissolution or winding up of the Company or upon redemption. [OTHER ALTERNATIVES — REDEMPTION ONLY OR LIQUIDATION ONLY, NOT BOTH.]

(2) Liquidation Preference: In the event of any liquidation, dissolution or winding up of the Company, the holders of the Preferred will be entitled to receive in preference to the holders of the Common Stock an amount equal to the Original Purchase Price, plus all accrued but unpaid dividends (the "Liquidation Amount"). Thereafter Common Stock received all residual amounts. [OPTION, IF PRIOR ROUND: The Series <◆> Preferred will share, pari passu based on aggregate invested dollars, with the holders of the Series A Preferred Stock in all assets available for distribution upon any liquidation, dissolution or winding up prior to payments made to the holders of the Common Stock.]

Issues for Investor:
Investor wants right to choose to receive return of investment as if he converted to Common Stock or return of dollars invested, whichever is more

[OPTION A: (3) Cash-Out Election: At the election of the holders of a majority of the Preferred, a consolidation or merger of the Company or sale of all or substantially all of its assets or stock will be regarded as a liquidation, dissolution or winding up for purposes of the liquidation preferences (i.e., receives return of investment plus accrued, cumulative dividends).

Investor wants return of investment plus ability to share in upside

[OPTION: Fully Participating Preferred: After payment of the Liquidation Amount to the preferred, Preferred and Common Stock share in remaining proceeds available for distribution on an "as if converted" basis.]

Issue for Investor:

*Investor wants to get out of investment at some point

(4) <u>Mandatory Redemption</u>: The Company will redeem the Preferred [in three equal annual installments] commencing [5–7] years from the date of purchase by paying the cash a total amount equal to the Liquidation Amount [including accrued but unpaid dividends].

<u>Put</u>: In the event control of the Company is transferred to someone other than the existing shareholder group, the Investors shall have the right to put to the Company any or all of the Preferred at cost [plus dividends] or at a value mutually agreeable to the Investors and the Company, or in the absence of an agreement, at the average of the fair market value determinations of three professional appraisers selected by each of the Investors and the Company. Costs of appraisal will be borne by Company.

Issue for Company:

*conversion only if certain % of Preferred shares agree to convert on a "cash out" election

(5) Optional Conversion: The Preferred is Convertible at any time, at the option of the [holder/holders of a majority of the Preferred], into shares of Common at an initial conversion price equal to the Original Purchase Price. Initially, each share of Preferred is convertible into [one] share of Common Stock. The conversion price will be subject to adjustment as provided in paragraph (7) below.

Issue for Investor:
*Investor wants the certainty of
some guaranteed return, a sizable
offering, and the stability of a solid
float in the aftermarket*

(6) Mandatory Conversion: The Preferred will be automatically converted into Common, at the then applicable conversion price, in the event of a "firm commitment" underwritten public offering of shares of Common at a price per share that is not less than [2X–4X TIMES THE ORIGINAL PURCHASE PRICE] in a public offering resulting in [gross/net] proceeds to the Company of not less than $ [AMOUNT] (a "Qualified Public Offering").

Issue for Company:
*Company wants ability to clean
out small residual position*

[OPTION: The Preferred is also automatically converted into Common Stock in the event that fewer than [10%–30%] of the shares of Preferred originally issued remain outstanding.]

Issue for Investor:
*Investor wants protection against
"price dilution" if Company sells
shares below issue price to investor*

(7) Antidilution Provisions: The conversion price of the Preferred will be subject to adjustment to prevent dilution in the event that the Company issues additional shares of convertible debt or equity securities (other than the Reserved Employee Shares described under "Reserved Employee Shares" below) at a purchase price less than the Original Purchase Price. The conversion price will be subject to adjustment on a [weighted-average/full ratchet] which takes into account dilutive issuances of additional shares at prices below the Investor's conversion price. [Weighted-average formula price adjustment is calculated by the following:

Issue for Company:
*Company should vigorously resist
"full ratchet"*

$$CP_\square = \frac{(CS/O \times CP) + CR}{CS/O + CA/I}$$

CA/O = number of shares of Common Stock outstanding immediately prior to the dilutive transaction (and assuming conversion of all classes of Preferred and all presently exercisable options or warrants to determine shares of Common Stock outstanding).

CP = Old Conversion Price for each class or series of Preferred outstanding

CP□ = New Conversion Price

CR = total Consideration Received by the Company for the specific dilutive transaction

CS/I = number of shares of Common or Common Equivalents actually issued or sold in the specific dilutive transaction]

(8) <u>Voting Rights</u>: The holders of Preferred will have the right to vote that number of votes equal to the number of shares of Common Stock issuable upon conversion of the Preferred on the record date for the vote. Except with respect to matters which adversely affect the Preferred or as required by law, the Preferred and the Common Stock shall vote together as a single class.

Issues for Investor:
Investor wants to control liquidity events like a merger or an acquisition

(9) Protective Provision: Consent of the holders of at least [majority vs. two-thirds] of the Preferred shares will be required for:

* any sale by the Company of a substantial portion of its assets or stock, or any consolidation or merger of the Company with another entity

*Investor wants prior approval of
events which impair his liquidity*

* the certain of any <u>senior</u> or <u>pari passu</u>
  equity security control (excluding debt)

* transaction in which control of the Company is transferred

* repurchase or redemption of equity securities, or payment of dividends or other distribution on equity securities (other than
  the Preferred)

* sales, transfers or encumbrances of technology other than licenses granted in the
  ordinary course of business

* liquidation, dissolution, recapitalization or
  reorganization

THE STOCK PURCHASE AGREEMENTS:

Information Rights:

The Company will timely furnish the Investors with annual audited and monthly and
quarterly unaudited financial statements, an
annual budget and business plan, and
monthly and quarterly comparisons to the
annual budget. [OPTION: The obligation of
the Company to furnish monthly financial
statements and other non-public information
will terminate upon a public offering.]

Observer Rights:

Representatives of the Investors will have the
right to receive notice of and attend all meetings of the Board of Directors and any com-
mittees, to visit with management of the
Company, and to inspect the books and
records of the Company.

Registration Rights:

Issues for Company:
limit number of registrations

insist on minimum market value for a registration so Company does not waste dollars on a small registration

(1) Demand Rights: If on any [two-four] occasions (but not within [180] days of the effective date of any Company registration) Investors holding at least [30–60%] of the Preferred (or Common Stock issued upon conversion of the Preferred) request that the Company file a registration statement covering the Common Stock issuable upon conversion of the Preferred, the Company will use its best efforts to cause such shares to be registered as quickly as possible, so long as the anticipated aggregate offering price, net of underwriting discounts and commissions, would exceed [NUMBER: $2–5 million].

Try to get investors to advance expenses for a demand registration

The Company will not be obligated to effect more than [two-four] registrations (other than short-form registrations on Form S-3) under these demand registration right provisions.

(2) Short Form Registrations on Form S-3: Holders of the Preferred (or Common Stock issued upon conversion of the Preferred) will have the right to require the Company to file [an unlimited number] [NUMBER: 2–4] of short-form registration statements on Form S-3 [but no more than one for every (9–12)-month period and provided each registration on Form S-3 has a minimum market value of $500,000–$1,000,000).]

Issues for Company:
*limit number of registrations
*registration rights terminate after
4–5 years after initial public offering
*directors & officers can participate
in piggyback registrations

(3) Piggy-Back Registrations: The Investors will be entitled to [unlimited] [three–five] "piggy-back" registration rights on all registrations of the Company, subject to the right of the Company and its underwriters to reduce the number of shares of the Investors proposed to be registered in view of market conditions. [OPTION: Piggy-back registration rights expire [four–five] years after initial public offering.]

Issues for Company:
*expense of interim audit or special
reviews borne by Investors
*expenses of any registration
abandoned or withdrawn by
Investors are paid by Investors
*try to get Investors to pay for their
own counsel fees
*Investors lose registration rights
when stock can be sold under Rule 144

(4) Registration Expenses: All registration expenses (exclusive of underwriting discounts and commissions, fees of more than one counsel for the selling shareholders, and the fees and expenses of any special or interim audit for any registration initiated by the Investors) shall be borne by the Company. All other expenses of registered offerings shall be borne by the selling shareholders.

(5) Other Registration Provisions: Other provisions with respect to registration rights as are reasonable, including cross-indemnification provisions, [the Company's ability to delay the filing of the demand registration for a period of not more than [120–180] days], a "lockup" or "market standoff" agreement by holders of the Preferred (if requested by the underwriter in a public offering) not to sell any unregistered Common they hold for a period of [120–180] days following the effective date of the registration statement covering such offering, and the period of time in which the registration statement will be kept effective [90–180 days].

Board Representation:

Issue for Both Sides:

*Board control often a sensitive
issue*

The Board will consist of [5–7] members.
[Two] directors will be representatives of the
Investors; [two] directors will be representatives of management; at least [one] director
will be an outside director. Directors will be
elected annually. The Board will meet at least
once every [six weeks or two months].

Right of First Refusal to Purchase
New Securities:

Issue for Company:

*Better to have only preemptive
right to participate for pro rata
share of Company equity vs. this
right to take entire financing*

If the Company proposes to offer additional
shares (other than Reserved Employee Shares
or shares issued in the acquisition of another
company), the Company will first offer all
such shares to the Investors and the holders
of Series A Preferred Stock of the Company.
This right of first refusal will terminate upon
an underwritten public offering of shares of
the company of a sale of all or substantially
all of the capital stock or assets of the Company.

Events of Default:

Issue for Company:

*Board takeover rights for material
breaches of the Stock Purchase
Agreement, failure of redemption or
liquidation preference*

An Event of Default shall exist if any of the
following occurs and is continuing:

*   Failure to pay the Preferred Stock dividend
    when due or the failure to make any liqui-
    dation or redemption payment which the
    Company is obligated to make.

*   Failure to perform or observe any covenant
    contained in the stock purchase agreement

*   False or misleading warranties, representa-
    tions, or other statements made by or on
    behalf of the Company in any material re-
    spect.

*   [Failure to make payment due on any in-
    debtedness or other security and/or if the

Company is in default under any other financing agreements.]

* Voluntary or involuntary bankruptcy, receivership, assignment for the benefit of creditors, liquidation, acceleration of third party obligations, unsatisfied judgement in excess of $50,000.

Default Remedies:

If an Event of Default exists, the Investors holding a majority of interest of the Preferred may at their option:

* Declare immediate redemption on the Preferred Stock and/or

* Elect a majority of the Board of Directors

Reserved Employee Shares:

Issue for Company:
*Need a "basket" of shares to provide equity incentives to management and employees

The Company may reserve up to such number of shares of Common equal to [10%–15%] of outstanding capitalization, calculated on a fully-diluted basis, for issuance to employees, directors, officers and consultants of the Company, (the "Reserved Employee Shares"). The Reserved Employee Shares will be exempt from the antidilution formula protection. The Reserved Employee Shares will be issued from time to time under such incentive stock option or non-qualified stock option agreements or plans, stock restriction agreements or other option, arrangements, contracts or plans as are recommended by management and approved by a majority of the then present members of the Board [OPTION: which approval shall include at least <◆> of the <◆> directors designated by holders of the Preferred].

Stock Restriction and
Stockholders Agreements:

Issue for Company:

*whether management has to give
back shares already earned*

All present holders of Common Stock of the
Company who are officers, employees or consultants of the Company will execute a Stock
Restriction Agreement with the Company
pursuant to which the Company will have an
option to buy back at cost a portion of the
shares of Common Stock held by such person in the event that such shareholder's employment with the Company is terminated
prior to the expiration of [48] months from
the date of employment. Each year, [25%] of
the shares will be released from the repurchase option based upon continued employment by the Company. In addition, the
Company and the Investors will have a right
of first refusal with respect to any such shares
proposed to be resold, or, alternatively, the
right to participate in the sale of any such
shares to a third party, which rights will terminate upon a public offering.

Noncompetition Nondisclosure
and Assignment of Inventions
Agreements:

Each officer and key employee of the Company will enter into a Noncompetition,
Nondisclosure and Assignment of Inventions
Agreement in a form reasonably acceptable to
the Company and the Investors. Noncompetition period for officers and key employees
will be [1 year–18 months] following termi-
nation of employment.

Key Man Insurance:

The Company will provide "Key Man" insurance on the life of [CEO, VP - Technology],
each in the amount of $ [NUMBER: 1–2 mil-
lion], the proceeds of which shall be payable
to [the Company/Investors].

Co-Sale Rights:	Investors can participate <u>pro rata</u> in any transfer or sale by officers, founders or any (3%–5%) shareholder of any portion of their stock.
The Stock Purchase Agreement:	The purchase of the Preferred will be made pursuant to a Stock Purchase Agreement drafted by counsel to the Investors, which agreement shall contain, among other things, customary and appropriate representations and warranties of the Company, customary and appropriate affirmative and negative covenants to the Company, and appropriate conditions of closing, including an opinion of counsel to the Company reasonably satisfactory to the Investors.
Expenses:	The Company will bear the reasonable legal fees and other expenses of the Investors with respect to the consummation of the transaction. If the transaction is <u>not</u> consummated, each party will bear its own legal fees and expenses.
Standstill:	From and after [90–120 days] from the date hereof or until the earlier mutual agreement between the Company and the Investors to terminate the understanding reflected by this term sheet, the Company shall not directly or indirectly solicit discussions or engage in negotiations with any potential Investors other than the Investors concerning the possible acquisition of an interest in the Company (whether by way of merger, purchase of capital stock or purchase of assets).
Memorandum of Terms Only:	Except for the Standstill section immediately above, this Memorandum of Terms does not

reflect any binding commitment on either the Investors' or the Company's behalf to participate in a financing of the Company. Unless and until the Closing pursuant to a Stock Purchase Agreement duly executed by the parties, no party shall have any liability or obligation to the other with respect to the subject matter hereof.

By:_____   By: _____

Title: _____   Title: _____

Appendix B

The following confidential disclosure agreement was provided by attorney Mark A. Hofer, of the law firm Brown, Rudnick, Freed & Gesmer. It is reprinted here with Mr. Hofer's permission.

Dear <>:

RE: CONFIDENTIAL DISCLOSURE AGREEMENT

In recent conversations between yourself and representatives of [CLIENT] (hereafter "[CLIENT]"), it has been proposed that we disclose certain confidential information including business, economic and scientific information to you with regard to _____ (collectively, "INFORMATION") for purposes of evaluating a potential relationship between the parties. [CLIENT] considers such INFORMATION to be confidential and proprietary and is willing to disclose the INFORMATION under the following terms and conditions:

1. You will take precautions, utilizing the same degree of care you would use with your own information of like importance, to prevent disclosure, directly or indirectly, of all or any of the INFORMATION received by you from [CLIENT] to any third party except with the prior written consent of [CLIENT], and you will not use any INFORMATION received from [CLIENT] except as may be necessary for purposes of this Agreement. INFORMATION given to you shall not be provided to any persons who have not undertaken an obligation of confidentiality substantially similar to that contained herein and then only when such disclosure is necessary for purposes of this Agreement. All originals, copies, and samples of INFORMATION provided to you shall be returned following the evaluation except for one copy to be retained by counsel solely for purposes of enabling compliance hereunder.

2. Your obligations of non-disclosure and non-use hereunder shall continue, with respect to INFORMATION disclosed to you by [CLIENT], for a period of five (5) years from the date hereof.

3. Your obligations, under paragraphs 1 and 2 hereof, shall not apply to any INFORMATION: (i) known to you prior to disclosure of such INFORMATION

which you can prove by your prior written records; or (ii) lawfully obtained after the date of this Agreement by you from sources, other than [CLIENT], having no obligation of confidentiality to [CLIENT]; or (iii) which is or becomes generally available to the public through no fault of yours.

4. This agreement contains our entire understanding with respect to matters contained herein. This does not constitute a license or research agreement and you shall have no further obligation to [CLIENT] other than your obligations of non-disclosure and non-use.

ACCEPTED AND AGREED   [CLIENT]

By:_____   By: _____

TITLE:_____   TITLE:_____

DATE:_____   DATE:_____

Acknowledgments

I am greatly indebted to those individuals who helped me create this book.

My agent, Charlotte Raymond, read numerous drafts of my proposal and persuaded me to avoid sending it out until everything was "absolutely perfect." My editor at Warner Business Books, Dan Ambrosio, gave me a contract, pointed out passages that could be improved, and shepherded the finished manuscript through the publication process.

Richard Shyduroff introduced me to various members of the entrepreneurial community, provided me with numerous opportunities to practice my presentation skills, and created the kind of trust environment that allows entrepreneurs to feel comfortable sharing difficult stories. Joost Bonsen served as an enthusiastic cheerleader and performed a great deal of public-relations work on my behalf. Matt Utterback gave me the job of "official note taker" for Ken Morse's E-Lab entrepreneurship class, thereby providing me with an opportunity to meet (and interview) many of the class's distinguished guests.

Hillary Hudis took me on a guided tour of ArsDigita's Cambridge office, told me about the company's unusual hiring practices, and introduced me to several individuals who were hired through these unconventional means. Ben Williams introduced me to many of the "boutique" venture capitalists whose offices abut Boston's "financial freedom trail." Charles Harris threw two exceptional parties in private dining rooms on the third floor of Boston's Locke-Ober Café and provided me with an opportunity to meet (and interview) many of the movers and shakers who founded NBX Corporation.

My copyeditor, Abigail Vargus, read countless drafts of both the proposal and the manuscript and pointed out areas that could be improved. Readers Christopher Johnson, Margaret Sanford, Rob Zehner, Becky Moran, Brian Hone, Ginger Lazarus, Cat Brenn-Bear, Sharon Wachsler, and Heather Wasserlein provided constructive criticism on all or part of the manuscript.

This book could not have been written without the assistance of those entrepreneurs, venture capitalists, corporate lawyers, and others who told me about their experiences. Thanks to each and every one of you.

Bibliography

Abramson, Albert. "Pioneers of Television—Philo Taylor Farnsworth." *Journal of the Society of Motion Picture and Television Engineers* 101, no. 11 (November 1992). Presented at the 133rd SMPTE Technical Conference in Los Angeles (paper no. 133–107) on October 29, 1991.

"ArsDigita closing its Open Source door." *GEEK.com.* 12:31 am EST Fri Apr 06 2001.

ArsDigita. "Corporate Culture." Web site: *http://www.arsdigita.com/pages/mission/index. adp.* Viewed October 2, 2000.

Birchard, Bill. "Intangible Assets + Hard Numbers = Soft Finance." *Fast Company.* October 1999. pp. 316–36.

Bounds, Wendy, and Rachel Emma Silverman. "Young Dot-Commers Hit Really Early Midlife Crisis." *Wall Street Journal.* November 15, 2000.

Bronson, P. "Is Anyone in Silicon Valley Still Making Things?" *Wall Steet Journal.* August 16, 1999.

Cha, Ariana Eunjung. "Collapse of Dot-Coms Stifles Tech Innovators." *Washington Post.* April 29, 2001.

Cohen, Scott. *Zap: The Rise and Fall of Atari.* New York: McGraw-Hill, 1984.

Collins, Jim. "Built to Flip." *Fast Company.* March 2000. pp. 131–40.

Creswell, Julie. "Economic Slowdown: The View From Ground Zero Isn't So Bad." *Fortune.* November 13, 2000. pp. 50–52.

Daly, James, and Jeffrey Davis, eds. "Do Profits Matter?" Bloomberg, Mike, writer. *Business 2.0,* April 2000.

Didion, Joan. *Slouching Towards Bethlehem.* New York: Farrar, Straus and Giroux, 1999.

Everson, George. *The Story of Television: The Life of Philo T. Farnsworth.* New York: W.W. Norton, 1949. p. 128.

Farhi, Paul. "The Dotcom Brain Drain: Print journalists are heeding the siren song of the Internet." *American Journalism Review.* March 2000.

Farnsworth, Elma G. *Distant Vision: Romance & Discovery on an Invisible Frontier.* Salt Lake City, Utah: Pemberly Kent Publishers, Inc., 1989.

Fineman, Mark. "The Rise and Fall of Africa.com." *eCompanyNow.* December 2000. pp. 135–42.

Fost, Dan. "Awash in Red Ink, Online Magazine Salon.com Lays off 20% of Staff:

Belt-tightening comes as site garners awards, enjoys record traffic." *San Francisco Chronicle*. December 21, 2000.

————. "Journalists Like Security of Old Media After Being Burned at Dot-Coms: Laid Off Editors, Writers Enjoy Web Experience But Won't Do It Again." *San Francisco Chronicle*. Thursday, November 9, 2000.

————. "TheStreet.com's Slippery Slope: Once high-flying financial news site fights for survival." *San Francisco Chronicle*. November 2, 2000.

————. "Top Writers at Business Magazines Commanding Six Figures: Salaries soaring as eCompany joins Bay Area tech mags." *San Francisco Chronicle*. February 24, 2000.

Greenspun, Philip. "Ars Digita: From Start-Up to Bust-Up." *http://philip.greenspun.com/arsdigita/litigation-story*

————. "Berlin and Prague: Nazis, Jews, Stamp Collectors, and Beautiful Women." *http://www.photo.net/bp/*

————. *Philip and Alex's Guide to Web Publishing*. San Francisco: Morgan Kaufmann, 1999.

Gupta, Udayan, editor. *Done Deals: Venture Capitalists Tell Their Stories*. Harvard Business School Press. 2000 by President and Fellows of Harvard College.

Hansell, Saul, and Matt Richtel. "VC Forsaking the Internet." *New York Times on the Web*. November 6, 2000.

Hedegaard, Erik. "The Genius of Change." *Worth*. November 2000. pp. 124–31, 166.

Hellweg, Eric. "New Power Centers." *Business 2.0*. January 2000. pp. 136–47.

Herman, Edward S., and Noam Chomsky. *Manufacturing Consent: The Political Economy of the Mass Media*. New York: Pantheon, 1988.

Heyboer, Kelly. "On the Upswing: Thanks to a strong economy, a tight labor market and competition from dotcoms, journalists' salaries are moving upward. But the profession still lags behind other fields." *American Journalism Review*. September 2000.

Holding, Reynolds, and William Carlsen. "Hollow Words: Federal Prosecutors Say White-Collar Crime Is a Priority, But They Have Filed Only a Few Charges Against Silicon Valley Executives." *San Francisco Chronicle*. November 16, 1999.

————. "Phantom Riches: Beneath the Glitter of Booming Silicon Valley, Executives Have Been Accused of Lying About Their Products and Doctoring Their Books, Leaving Devastated Investors in their Wake." *San Francisco Chronicle*. November 15, 1999.

Horton, Brian. *Associated Press Guide to Photojournalism.* New York: McGraw-Hill Professional Publishing, 2000.

Hua, Vanessa. "Ideas For Sale or Rent: What Happens to the Intellectual Property When a Company Closes." *San Francisco Chronicle.* May 29, 2001.

Huffstetter, P. J. "Dot-Com Feast Turns: Laid-off workers face a lean holiday." *San Francisco Chronicle.* December 25, 2000.

Kaplan, David A. *The Silicon Boys and Their Valley of Dreams.* William Morrow. 1999.

Kelly, Kevin. "The Roaring Zeros." *Wired.* September 1999. pp. 148–54.

King, Ralph. "Do You Believe in Jim Clark?" *eCompany Now.* December 2000. pp. 123–30.

———. "My Hunt for America's Dumbest VC." *eCompany Now.* January/February 2001. pp. 107–12.

Kleppner, Daniel, and Robert J. Kolenkow. *An Introduction to Mechanics.* New York: McGraw-Hill, 1973. p. 197.

Kruger, Justin, and David Dunning. "Unskilled and Unaware of It: How Difficulties in Recognizing One's Own Incompetence Lead to Inflated Self-Assessments." *Journal of Personality and Social Psychology,* December 1999. vol. 77, no. 6, 1121–1134.

LeDuff, Charlie. "What a Long, Strange Trip: Pseudo.Com to Dot.Nowhere." *The New York Times on the Web.* October 27, 2000.

Lewis, Michael. *Liar's Poker: Rising Through the Wreckage on Wall Street.* New York: W. W. Norton, 1989.

"Living in Freefall." *Economist.* November 18–24, 2000.

Lloyd, Carol. "Sex for Rent: The Erotics of Bay Area Real Estate." *San Francisco Chronicle.* Tuesday, November 21, 2000.

Loomis, Carol J. "Inside Jay Walker's House of Cards." *Fortune.* November 13, 2000. pp. 127–38.

Mornell, Dr. Pierre. *Hiring Smart: How to Predict Winners & Losers in the Incredibly Expensive People-Reading Game.* Berkeley, Calif.: Ten Speed Press, 1998. pp. 105, 124.

Munk, Nina. "Finished at Forty." *Fortune.* February 1, 1999.

Mura, Jessika Bella. "Riding out the tech-wreck: Gone is the laugh-it-off spirit that made earlier spates of dot-com failures a community-wide bonding experience. These days, it's getting downright grim. But will our pessimism end up making our greatest fears come true?" *Boston.com's Digital Mass.com.* December 1, 2000.

Narayan, Sanjoy. "There's Something about Waves." *Business Today.* http://www.india-today.com/btoday/exclusives/sanjoy2711.html

Pence, Angelica. "Bay Area Backlash on High-Tech Boom: Dot-coms viewed as threat to lifestyle." *San Francisco Chronicle.* October 23, 2000.

Pratt, Stanley E., ed. *Pratt's Guide to Venture Capital Sources 2000.* Venture Economics, April 2000.

Pressman, David. *Patent It Yourself.* Berkeley, Calif.: Nolo Press, 1999.

Ramo, Joshua Cooper. "Person of the Year." *Time.* December 27, 1999. p. 50.

Richtel, Matt. "E-Commerce Dream Proves the Undoing of a Solid Business." *The New York Times on the Web.* November 24, 2000.

Rosenberg, Ronald. "Internet speeds money." *The Boston Globe*'s boston.com. May 16, 1999.

Ryan, James. "Stop the Presses: Journalism will never be the same, as the fourth estate hurries to remain relevant in the online world." *Business 2.0.* December 1999.

Said, Carolyn. "Dot-Com Disasters Have Opened Door a Crack for Unions: Stock price crash makes employee ownership less real." *San Francisco Chronicle.* December 3, 2000.

———. "In the Doghouse: Pets.com to close after e-tailer fails to find a new owner." *San Francisco Chronicle,* November 8, 2000.

Saracevic, Alan T., Carolyn Said, and Carrie Kirby. "Economy Comes Down with Dot-Com Flu: Ripple effect from Internet failures felt far and wide." *San Francisco Chronicle.* December 10, 2000.

Schonfeld, Erick. "Naveen Jain is the Absolutely, No-Doubt-About-It, Einstein-Was-a-Chump, Look-Ma-No-Calculator, One-Zillion-on-the-SAT Greatest High-Tech Entrepreneur of All Human History {And if you don't believe it, just ask him.}" *eCompanyNow.* December 2000. pp. 113–18.

Schwartz, Evan I. "Who Really Invented Television?" *Technology Review.* September/October 2000: 96–106.

Schwartz, Peter. "Long Live the Long Boom." *Wired.* September 1999. pp. 161, 164.

Sellers, Patricia. "Executive Searches: Geezer Chic." *Fortune.* November 13, 2000. pp. 45–50.

Shankland, Stephen. "Open-source firm reverses strategy." *c|net's News.com.* April 5, 2001.

———. "ChiliSoft founder plans to give away most of windfall." *CNET News.Com.* 23 March 2000: 5:45 P.M. PT.

Sinton, Peter. "Startups Losing Allure: CEOs want more from VC financiers." *San Francisco Chronicle.* November 7, 2000.

Slaton, Joyce. "Dotcom Yuppies Gone Home: Slightly-Reduced Apartments for Rent." *San Francisco Chronicle.* December 28, 2000.

Squatriglia, Chuck. "Sacramento Report Fired for Plagiarism, Phony Sources." *San Francisco Chronicle.* Wednesday, November 22, 2000.

Stoughton, Stephanie. "N.Y. Times cutting 69 Internet unit jobs." *Boston.com's digitalMass.com.* January 8, 2001.

Strasburg, Jenny. "Dot-Com Fallout: E-tailers' failures bit into ad agency revenues." *San Francisco Chronicle.* November 26, 2000.

Stross, Randall E. *eBoys: The True Story of the Six Tall Men Who Backed eBay, WebVan, and Other Billion-Dollar Start-Ups.* New York: Crown, 2000.

Wallace, David Foster. *A Supposedly Fun Thing I'll Never Do Again.* Boston: Little, Brown, 1998.

Webber, Alan M. "New Math for a New Economy." *Fast Company.* January/February, 2000. pp. 214–24.

Weil, Elizabeth. "American Megamillionaire Gets Russki Space Heap! Sells Joy Rides to Fellow Tycoons! NASA Fumes!" *New York Times Magazine.* 23 July 2000: 36–41.

"When the Bubble Bursts." *The Economist.* January 30–February 5, 1999. pp. 23 25.

Winans, Foster. *Trading Secrets: Seduction and Scandal at the Wall Street Journal.* New York: St Martin's Press, 1986.

Wolff, Michael. *Burn Rate: How I Survived the Gold Rush Years on the Internet.* New York: Simon & Schuster, copyright 1998.

Index

About the Author

Teresa Esser lives with her husband in Cambridge, Massachusetts. The couple owns stock in two of the companies mentioned in this book: 3Com and E Ink Corporation.

The author operates a Web site: www.theventurecafe.com.